PERSON-CENTRED THERAPY AND CBT

Siblings not Rivals

Roger Casemore and Jeremy Tudway

SAGE

Los Angeles | London | New Delhi
Singapore | Washington DC

Los Angeles | London | New Delhi
Singapore | Washington DC

SAGE Publications Ltd
1 Oliver's Yard
55 City Road
London EC1Y 1SP

SAGE Publications Inc.
2455 Teller Road
Thousand Oaks, California 91320

SAGE Publications India Pvt Ltd
B 1/I 1 Mohan Cooperative Industrial Area
Mathura Road
New Delhi 110 044

SAGE Publications Asia-Pacific Pte Ltd
3 Church Street
#10-04 Samsung Hub
Singapore 049483

© Roger Casemore and Jeremy Tudway 2012

First published 2012

Library of Congress Control Number: 2011943777

British Library Cataloguing in Publication data

A catalogue record for this book is available from the British Library

Editor: Alice Oven
Editorial assistant: Kate Wharton
Production editor: Rachel Burrows
Marketing manager: Tamara Navaratnam
Cover design: Lisa Harper
Typeset by: C&M Digitals (P) Ltd
Printed in India at Replika Press Pvt Ltd

ISBN 978-0-85702-391-9
ISBN 978-0-85702-392-6 (pbk)

PERSON-CENTRED THERAPY AND CBT

SAGE has been part of the global academic community since 1965, supporting high quality research and learning that transforms society and our understanding of individuals, groups and cultures. SAGE is the independent, innovative, natural home for authors, editors and societies who share our commitment and passion for the social sciences.

Find out more at: **www.sagepublications.com**

To: Ruth and all those past students and colleagues who have walked
along this path with me over the past seventeen years

RC

To: Julia, Rufus and Isabella

JT

CONTENTS

ABOUT THE AUTHORS

 **Roger** retired recently after 17 years as Senior Teaching Fellow and Director of Counselling and Psychotherapy Courses at the University of Warwick. He is now an Associate Fellow in the Centre for Lifelong Learning. He has practised privately as a therapist for over 44 years, and as a supervisor and trainer of counsellors for the past 30 years. He is a Chartered Fellow of the Chartered Institute of Personnel and Development and a Fellow of the British Association for Counselling and Psychotherapy. He is a past Deputy Chair, Chair and Governor of the British Association for Counselling, was President of Counselling in Education for 15 years, Chair of the BACP Complaints Committee and a member of the Professional Ethics and Practice Committee for more than six years.

 **Jeremy** completed his first degree in psychology in 1989 and has worked in a dual academic and clinical role with clients presenting with very complex needs and difficulties, including developmental and intellectual disabilities and severe mental health problems. Much of his clinical work was in highly specialised forensic mental health services. Jeremy's Doctoral research investigated the relationship between negative social comparison, affiliation motive and emotion from a CBT perspective and it was during this time that he became influenced by the work of Albert Ellis and REBT. Jeremy has continued to engage in applied psychology research and he was research-liaison tutor in Clinical Psychology for the joint University of Coventry/Warwick University Doctoral programme in Clinical Psychology and has served as an external examiner in Clinical and Forensic Psychology to universities around the UK.

Jeremy became involved in providing teaching input to the counselling courses run by Roger at the University of Warwick in 2002 and has continued to provide teaching on the CBTs and psychopathology.

In 2005 he established Phoenix Psychological Services with his colleague Dr Liz Gillett, and Jeremy continues to see clients privately and provides expert witness assessments relating to psychological and therapeutic issues to the Courts.

INTRODUCTION AND RATIONALE

In this book, we are setting out to develop a reflective exploration comparing and contrasting the differences and similarities in the underlying philosophies, theories and practices of Cognitive Behavioural Therapy and Person-centred Therapy. We intend to examine our perception of the range of dissonance and harmony between the two approaches.

Understanding CBT and the Person-centred approach to counselling can only really come about through connecting the theory to counselling practice, in order to bring it to life. Throughout this book we will be using a number of examples from our client work to try to show how each of us works as a therapist. These casework examples will be composites from our work with a variety of clients, with the individuals' details changed in order to protect confidentiality. None of the examples used will portray any particular individual.

We are presenting both a structured academic text and a personal dialogue of our views and opinions as two very experienced practitioners and counselling and psychotherapy educators. We anticipate that this will make a consistently authoritative yet personal contribution to an important debate. Our aim is to make this book accessible to those who want a simple, informed read as well as to those who are seeking an in-depth critique and comment.

The aim of the book

For many years there has appeared to be a 'War of the Tribes', between the different therapeutic modalities and also to some extent within the modalities. While there can be some positive advantages to the tribal structure, often these conflicts have been based on misunderstanding, narrow definitions, even intolerance, with therapists being highly disrespectful to therapists from modalities other than the one in which they trained. The authors wish to challenge that conflict and encourage therapists to become more knowledgeable about and respectful of other approaches and identify ways in which they may draw on another approach.

It is very clearly our intention to challenge the conflict between CBT and the Person-centred approach. We really do want to produce a book which enables the reader to understand the important similarities, the essential harmony and the critical differences in philosophy, theory and practice. It is not possible to understand either practice effectively without a good understanding of the philosophy and the theory. We would want the text to be as readable as possible, which will involve describing aspects of practice and how these examples are rooted in relevant theory and philosophy. Rather than setting out to 'educate' Person-centred and Integrative therapists, our intention is to enable CBT, Person-centred and Integrative therapists, and those in training, to understand why it is they do what they do.

This book draws on the experiences of the authors in running an Advanced Diploma in Cognitive Behavioural Methods for Person-centred Therapists at the University of Warwick and will also draw on the authors' extensive experience as therapists from those two approaches, over a significant period of years. We hope it will enable readers to gain a better understanding of both approaches in order to challenge 'dislike of' and 'disrespect for' other approaches, based in ignorance. It will also set out to encourage readers to question either their ungoverned adherence to the rigidity of their original training or their unconsidered flight into other ways of working and to question as to who ultimately benefits from sticking rigidly to a 'purist' approach or becoming too naïvely pluralistic.

We will begin by describing the core theoretical and philosophical principles of the two approaches and use this to examine any complementarity and dissonance between the two approaches and the impact this may have on practice. The authors are firmly committed to a belief that therapists need to be secure in their own core modality in order to draw on aspects of other approaches in a theoretically coherent manner, rather than attempting to develop a naïve integrative approach.

CHAPTER 1
EXPERIENCES OF MISUNDERSTANDINGS, CONFLICTS, PREJUDICES AND DISRESPECT ABOUT AND BETWEEN THE TWO APPROACHES

This chapter comprises a dialogue between the authors, clearly describing the conflict we have experienced between the two approaches which we represent and the ways in which we have experienced misunderstanding, even prejudice and disrespect, towards those approaches. This will include some reflection on our perception of the political landscape in the world of therapy, leading to a challenge to the reader to suspend disbelief and be mindful of the question, 'Whose purpose is being served by the conflicts?'

The chapter will also consider our opposition to the concept of 'doing a bit' of either person-centred or cognitive behavioural approaches and our commitment to the need for therapists to feel secure in their own chosen modality. This will include some exploration of what appear to be misunderstandings of both approaches, demonstrated through examples of therapists who either stick too rigidly to the purist principles of their original training or (mis)understandings of that, as well as therapists who draw on methods from other approaches without the required theoretical rigour or coherence.

For the purposes of this book, we use the collective terms 'PCA' and 'CBTs' to reference the core generic models and, where necessary, will make explicit any reference to one or another of the specific sub-types when a particular element is not apparently central to the model.

So, where do we begin, why are we writing this book?

We set out to write this book because the perceived conflict between our modalities has long been acknowledged but never openly addressed and explored. Instead of expressing this in attitudes of disrespect towards each other's modalities, we wished to open up the issues to challenge and dispute the prejudices and assumptions that have built up around both CBT and PCA. This book aims to dispel ignorance about the fundamental differences and similarities in the therapeutic approaches in an open, balanced and non-defensive way.

We both recognise and accept that in the past we have been guilty of having what amounts to missionary zeal to convert others to believe that our particular approach is actually the 'Holy Grail' and no other approach is worthy.

Jeremy recalls that when Roger first invited him to come and do some teaching on the Diploma in Person-centred Counselling at Warwick, his reaction was to immediately think of 'spreading the light about CBT' and converting the students to his beliefs and practice! Jeremy quickly discovered the need to dispute his own irrationality when he discovered how undefended and non-defensive the person-centred tutors and students were in response to his challenges about their approach.

We wondered if we might begin by surfacing some of the range of stereotypes that we have experienced being attached to us and to our approaches.

Stereotypes of the person-centred approach

- Woolly
- Nice
- Soft and fluffy
- Superficial
- Easy
- Theory thin
- Excessively warm
- Completely non-directive
- Amateurish
- A religion
- Not challenging
- No scientific basis
- Just listen, nod and say, 'Uh, huh'
- Mirroring and simple repetition
- Just repeating what the client says
- Useful for middle-class neurotics with no real problems
- Can't work with abuse victims
- No good for clients with mental health problems
- No good for short-term therapy
- Tea and sympathy
- It's all about the core conditions

Person-centred counsellors are usually either:

- Men with beards and Jesus Boots who nod a lot
- Women with flowing skirts and lots of hair and beads and candles who hug a lot
- Soft and fluffy
- Determined to be nice
- Not very intellectual

Stereotypes in the cognitive behavioural approach

- Cold
- Not interested in feelings
- Abusive
- Very directive aggressive
- Very medical
- Disrespectful to clients
- Aloof
- Not interested in the client's story
- Only working to the counsellor's agenda
- Homework is the only technique that is used
- It's all about the ABC model
- Technique, technique, technique and no process
- The therapeutic relationship doesn't matter
- Reductionist
- All about solutions and quick fix
- Simplistic
- Couldn't work with abuse victims
- No good for mental health problems
- Can't work with people with learning difficulties

Cognitive behavioural therapists usually are either:

- Always male, with PhDs in psychology
- Young
- Snappily dressed and carrying clip boards
- Very intellectual

One thing we both know about stereotypes is that they always contain some truth and they are not THE truth. It is the truths that these stereotypes carry that we want to dispute in this book because we hold the view that these stereotypes are at the root of a really unhelpful and unprofessional set of prejudices by one school of therapists towards another. We are choosing to do this in particular in relation to the two approaches which we represent. We hope that, as a result, colleagues from other approaches will begin to reflect on what they might need to choose to do in order to be properly respectful of colleagues from other modalities. We would like to challenge the reader to be aware of their own prejudices, even to write them down, with an aspiration to recognise them for what they really are and dispense with them. We want to encourage you to take in their place a position of evenly suspended judgement, towards the philosophical, theoretical and practice belief systems, held by other colleagues from different modalities.

By working together over a number of years and developing a much deeper understanding of the theory, philosophy and practice of others' approaches, we have been able to develop a significant respect for each other as practitioners and for each other's belief systems. This respect holds within it a deeply held willingness to agree to differ and to be accepting of different points of view as a paradox to be held, rather than as a polemic which must forever be argued. This respect transcends mere liking and sycophancy and has enabled us to discover the important similarities and parallels in what we do as therapists and the reasons why we do them. This has been alongside the process of getting a real understanding of the different beliefs we have and the different ways of practising and the theoretical reasons for these. For both of us, this has not resulted in a change in our practice or in either of us becoming 'integrative'. It has, though, brought a richness of understanding of how our approaches work for us. For Roger as an 'Orthodox' client-centred therapist and for Jeremy as a very rational Rational-Emotive Behavioural therapist, we have both become more clearly attuned and committed to our respective core modalities while at the same time developing a very challenging accepting of the other's modality. Through the process of our developmental journey, we have learned to stop anthropomorphising our respective models by recourse to recalling personal attributes and idiosyncrasies of bad examples of practitioners from the other's modality. We would like to invite and encourage the reader to take a stroll along a similar path in this book.

We are both firm proponents of the need for therapists to have a core modality and are rather suspicious of the concept of 'integrative'. We both have difficulty in understanding how very different philosophies can be integrated when they are so diametrically opposed. In the same manner, we are both opposed to the notion of, in Roger's case, 'doing a bit of person-centred' or, in Jeremy's case, 'using a bit of CBT'. This is anathema to both of us!

With the development of the so-called Layard model of therapy, the CBTs have increasingly been perceived as being associated with a medicalised model. Much of this assumes that such a process of medicalisation enables the CBTs to achieve kudos *per se* (Tudor, 2010); that the predominance of the CBTs through the aegis of Improved Access to Psychological Therapies (IAPT) has led to the marginalising of other approaches (Cooper & McLeod, 2010); and that the model is simplistic and reduces client choice (Tudor, 2008).

It is evident that some of these criticisms relate to fundamental differences in language and philosophy, although it is also probable that this is indicative of a considerable degree of rhetorical semantics. It is also likely that the proliferation of the CBTs following the Layard model has done little to address these differences. The assumptions underpinning the Layard model have been explored by some authors (e.g. Tudor, 2010), particularly the political and philosophical 'utilitarian flavour' and 'the UK government's obsession with promoting brief (time-limited) cognitive-behaviour therapy (CBT) to the greatest number for what it thinks is the greatest good' (Tudor, 2008: 118–136).

The political landscape in the world of therapy is such that therapists of whatever persuasion cannot escape or ignore the developments which are taking place at a national level. It is very clear that the government and the army of civil servants and health service managers are not the least bit interested in the differences between the therapeutic models. They are caustically critical of what they see as tribal bickering inside the profession and have no patience with it. In a very real sense, this plays right into the hands of those who are totally focused on reducing expenditure and resources for psychological approaches to mental health.

We would like to offer now two examples from our experience of therapists 'trashing' the other modality.

● ● ● *Example 1* ● ● ●

The first example is about a proposal from a young psychiatrist to a Team Leader of a small team of therapists working in a National Health Service setting. All the counsellors in the team had qualified with a University Certificate and Diploma in Person-centred Counselling and Psychotherapy. They had all been practising for several years and had continued to undertake regular continuing professional development courses to enhance their practice. The psychiatrist recommended that the counsellors in the team should only be working with clients who had been given a diagnosis, either by himself or by a GP, of a mental health condition. The psychiatrist and the Team Leader then jointly proposed that all the counsellors in the team should undertake a full course of training in CBT in order to be competent to work with clients with mental health issues.

When challenged by the team, they were told that they needed to do the training because it was politically expedient to do so. They were then told that they could do the training, but that when they closed the door of the counselling room, they could choose to continue to work as they had always done! In addition to suggesting they should do something which seems highly unethical, this also implies a high degree of professional disrespect towards the counsellors concerned and a substantial level of ignorance about the approach they have been trained in.

● ● ● *Example 2* ● ● ●

The second example involves an experienced counsellor who was working within a multi-professional team dealing with clients who posed a risk owing to dangerous behaviours. At a team discussion regarding a client, the counsellor presented her conclusions and a tentative formulation and included a description that the client had disclosed severe childhood abuse and that this was to be the focus for their work during the coming sessions.

Members of the team expressed concern that, given the nature of the risk associated with the client combined with their history of sexual offending, it was both appropriate and necessary for the team to share information about their contact with the client, and particularly when very difficult and sensitive information was being considered. However, as she had external supervision arrangements, the counsellor believed that these issues would be discussed and dealt with in that context alone.

The counsellor reacted very strongly to the team's concern to share information, stipulating that she considered that it would be 'unethical' for her to disclose the content of sessions as this would 'breach confidentiality' and could undermine the therapeutic relationship between her and the client. Despite the arguments posed by the team, the counsellor stated that, as the professional in the team who had the therapeutic relationship, she was best placed to understand and empathise with the client. Furthermore, it would be through her acceptance of the client that change could occur; other members in the team would not be placed to understand the process or how this might relate to the client and their behaviour. In addition, according to the client, the incidents that resulted in the convictions had occurred historically and he had not been in a position to defend himself, whereas now it would have been unlikely to have resulted in a conviction.

The counsellor simply refused to discuss the matter and indicated that, in the event that she considered that there was a risk posed by the client, she would detail a general concern to the team but would not provide specific detail. In response to a member of the team whose orientation was cognitive-behavioural, the counsellor suggested that this was a 'simplified model that ignored the emotional impact of these events in his life' and that therefore this colleague would inevitably have a 'simplified view of the client'.

The counsellor was obviously acting in an unethical manner and chose a very rigid interpretation of the nature of confidentiality, and her use of the supervision relationship reflected her generally defensive reaction. Given the risks involved in the case, it was both necessary and appropriate to share critical information with colleagues and also to have respect for their own professional boundaries. Similarly, the rather offensive dismissal of a CBT colleague as being 'simplistic' and ignoring the emotional context appears to have served purely to bolster her justification and defensive position. It appears evident that this overlooks the very central issue of different 'truths', all of which have value.

These examples suggest a significant issue for both approaches, in relating to practitioners in each approach being prepared to fully value the other approach. This parallels a shared fundamental philosophical position that human beings are intrinsically of value and that no one human being is more valuable than another. It is tempting and easy to suggest that in the two examples above these are inappropriate practitioners. However, their attitudes may also be evidence of an un-reflected attitude in both approaches, that their approach is of more value than the other. And yet, above, we have identified at a philosophical belief level that both approaches believe the same thing about human beings.

A link to the next chapter

In the next chapter we intend to briefly compare the main philosophical tenets which are the basis of each of the approaches, clarifying the similarities and the differences. This will include sections on: humanism, phenomenology and existentialism as philosophical principles. It will also make reference to elements of theory and practice in both approaches and how these are rooted in and are expressions of philosophical principles.

Recommended reading

Casemore, R. (2011) *Person-centred Counselling in a Nutshell* (revised edn). London: Sage.

Neenan, M. & Dryden, W. (2011a) *Cognitive Therapy in a Nutshell* (revised edn). London: Sage.

Neenan, M. & Dryden, W. (2011b) *Rational Emotive Behaviour Therapy in a Nutshell* (revised edn). London: Sage.

CHAPTER 2
THE BASIC PHILOSOPHIES OF THE TWO APPROACHES

It is not the intention of this book to engage in a process of rewriting the history of the development of either the PCA or the CBTs, although we will offer some basic historical facts. In this chapter we intend to provide an outline of the main philosophical tenets which are the basis of each of the approaches, clarifying the similarities and the differences. This will include sections on: humanism, phenomenology and existentialism as philosophical principles. It will also make reference to elements of theory and practice in both approaches and how these are rooted in and are expressions of philosophical principles.

Our primary objective will be to show the need to be cognisant of and respectful towards both approaches. We will also introduce an alternative way of understanding various 'techniques' as integrating the therapeutic approach into the person of the therapist. For instance, 'inference chaining and disputation' need to be fully integrated aspects of the therapist's way of being rather than being applied as mechanistic tools, in much the same way as the three central core conditions of empathy, unconditional acceptance and authenticity need to be integrated aspects of the PCA therapist's personality. At the end of this chapter we will list some recommended reading which will take those interested to more detailed accounts.

We are using our views of the following very brief summary of the principal philosophical bases of both approaches.

Humanism

Humanism relates to a wide range of belief that centres on the philosophical system or mode of action that promotes the interests, values and dignity of humanity and the promotion of human welfare. As such, it relates to a theory of human ethics that is based on reason and empirical enquiry. Thus, humanism rejects supernatural explanations or reference, relying on the essence of being human as the basis for ethical judgement, self-realisation and action.

'Humanistic psychology' is often defined as being a theory in which humans are considered to hold the basic elements of self-determination, and therefore it is a constructive and hopeful position. When defined in this manner, however, it contains a somewhat contradictory value-judgement. The notion of self-determination and hope do not necessarily rest together. Indeed, following this inherent contradiction to a logical conclusion could lead to the philosophically nihilistic conclusion that an individual acting upon this self-determination could decide to become the 'baddest of the bad', and this is hardly a constructive or hopeful position. Such naïve notions of humanity miss the rather difficult, yet for us, central notion of humanism that our capacity for self-determination *does not have an inherent value*. Rather, we are inextricably yoked to our construction of reality and, consequently, we have an inherent human tendency to assume that our perception of, and therefore responses to, reality not only reflect this but are also correct. In essence, a defining component of humanity is a tendency to misconstrue, misperceive, misrepresent and therefore inevitably generate our own disturbance. However, this does not preclude our capacity to react to this by an active and ongoing process.

Phenomenology

Phenomenology is a branch of philosophy that is concerned with the attribution of meaning to experience, and particularly how this is achieved. Notable thinkers associated with this tradition include Edmund Husserl, Søren Kierkegaard and Friedrich Nietzsche.

In his conceptualisation of phenomenology, Husserl (1912) sought to establish a study of consciousness via 'intentionality'. Husserl's work suggests that the meaningfulness of the experience of things, as 'some-things', depends both upon the individual being directly open to the world *and* that intentionality is not a property of the individual mind but the categorical framework in which both the mind and world are meaningful. Therefore, the phenomenology of consciousness is neither concerned with metaphysical aspects of being nor the causal origin of things, but rather how they are given meaning.

Existentialism

Existentialism is a philosophical school that has often been summarised as being concerned with the notion that existence precedes essence. It is most famously associated with the French scholar and writer Jean-Paul Sartre. The existential focus on 'existence' becomes particularly refined into a system by which it attempts to understand what being a human being is; and that it is not possible to arrive at such knowledge by recourse purely to the 'truths' of reductionist science or the morality of theology. As such, it introduces the concept of *authenticity*, as a necessary way of being, as the means to conceptualise human existence.

Although Sartre is most commonly associated with this school of thought, the roots of his thinking were heavily influenced by Martin Heidegger. It was Heidegger who initially considered the tension between the individual and the 'public' and the grounded nature of human thought and reason and 'authenticity' as the norm of self-identity. This is linked to the belief in the importance of self-definition through freedom, choice and commitment. There is also a clear link between Kant's thinking, the phenomenological method of Husserl and Sartre's existential system.

Earlier existentialist philosophers such as Kierkegaard (1844 [1985]) and Nietzsche (1973) were concerned with the self at a point of conflict between ethics and faith (sometimes referred to as 'the anguish of Abraham'). In other words, when we make very significant decisions about ethical issues we are alone and cannot authentically rely upon rules bestowed by religious morality or other sources of authority. From the perspectives of both approaches, there are no unilateral rules which govern the ways in which human beings should behave or feel and think.

Existentialism concerns itself with the emotion of anxiety as a necessary consequence of freedom (the dizziness of freedom) that can be assuaged by the self-conscious exercise of responsibility and choice, and therefore the challenge of existential philosophy is, bluntly, that thinking about existence requires new frames of reference. A final central theme of existentialist thought relates to the notion of alienation of self from the world and the self, which Heidegger identifies as the sense that the world is a place in which I have no sense of belonging.

Existential philosophy is also concerned with the state of being, and consequently the reflection of non-being, and therefore the necessity of becoming aware of mortality in order to live fully – 'As soon as man comes to life, he is at once old enough to die' (Heidegger, 1962: 289) – which is linked to Heidegger's concept of nothingness and is referred to as death anxiety, a pre-eminent condition of human nature.

The person-centred approach – the philosophical roots

The two basic assumptions of the Person-centred approach

In order to better understand the theory and practice of the person-centred approach (PCA), it is important to begin with Carl Rogers' fundamental beliefs held about the nature of the universe and the nature of human beings. It was out of these beliefs that Rogers developed his theory of personality and behaviour and the concept of the six necessary and sufficient conditions for therapeutic growth. Rogers strongly challenged the almost universally held paradigm that there was only one tendency in the universe and all things within it. That tendency was seen as a tendency towards 'entropy', where everything in the universe was in a process of decay and disintegration. Rogers firmly challenged this view, drawing on the law of physics which states that for every force there must be an equal and opposite force. There could not just be one force or tendency at work in the universe; there had to be an equal and opposite force, which he named the 'formative tendency'.

Rogers suggested that the formative tendency was one in which the universe could be seen to be constantly expanding, developing and becoming more complex (Rogers, 1980). Rogers suggested that this universal formative tendency might be better described, in human beings, as the 'actualising tendency'. He took the view that the basic driving force in all human beings is a positive drive to achieve their potential, to self-actualise and to become a fully functioning person. He believed also that this actualising tendency should be trusted and that even in the worst conditions human beings will strive to be as healthy and successful as they can be. He believed that the self-actualising drive is the one central source of energy for human beings, perhaps even that it is present in our DNA.

The philosophy from a Person-centred perspective

The philosophy of the person-centred approach developed by Carl Rogers is very much rooted in philosophical belief systems, humanism, existentialism and phenomenology, which we have outlined above.

From a person-centred perspective, humanism is based, first, on a fundamental attitude that emphasises the dignity and worth of each individual human being, along with the belief that people are rational beings with the capacity for truth and goodness. This is clearly present in Rogers' view of the person as based on a model of growth, in which the person is seen as always striving to create, achieve or become better in some way. He held a fundamental presumption that people are basically good and that, given the right conditions, they will always strive to self-actualise. For Rogers, from a humanistic point of view, fulfilment and growth are achieved through the search for meaning in life and not through supernatural claims. His humanistic view of the person as actively and continually seeking meaning and fulfilment puts a strong focus on the concept of process. Self-actualisation or fulfilment is a continual challenge or journey to be experienced, not an end-state to be attained.

Drawing on its existential roots, which emphasise the uniqueness and isolation of the individual's experiencing of life in a hostile or indifferent universe, PCA regards human existence as unexplainable, and stresses freedom of choice and responsibility for the consequences of one's acts. It offers the view that it is our experiencing of life which is important and that the only important meaning that can be attached to an individual's life is that which they attach to it themselves. Only we can determine our own vocation.

Within PCA, and clearly evidenced in Rogers' writings and practice, a strong focus is placed on the careful examination of phenomena, as they are experienced, avoiding any inferences or assumptions based on past experience and seeking simply to describe what is being experienced as neutrally and as clearly as possible.

Rogers believed strongly in these principles and developed his approach which suggested that the individual is the only expert in their own internal world. He suggested that the therapist should offer the client an opportunity to experience the core conditions of acceptance or unconditional positive regard, accurate empathy, and the authenticity of the counsellor in the counselling relationship. If the client experiences those conditions to some degree, they will 'heal themselves'. Rogers believed that these core conditions alone were necessary and sufficient for therapeutic growth to take place.

The core of the person-centred approach is that it is the relationship between the client and the counsellor which is therapeutic in itself. Rogers also placed great importance on enabling clients to develop an internal, centralised locus of evaluation of the self. This leads to less dependence on the goodwill of others and an enhanced ability to cope with others; there is a reduction in an individual's dependence on others' views of them, which result from conditions of worth, introjected into the child by parents, society and significant others.

The most important and singularly most different aspect of the person-centred approach is the belief that this is about a way of life, not about a set of tools to be 'switched on' in therapy. The necessary and sufficient conditions for therapeutic growth need to be lived in order that they become an integrated part of the expression of the self, rather than a set of techniques which may be turned on in the therapeutic encounter. Rogers also believed this process would lead to a quiet revolution.

The basic assumptions of Cognitive Behavioural Therapy

Similarly to PCA, in order to understand the basis of the CBTs it is necessary to understand the philosophical tenets upon which they have grown. It is not the intention of this book to rewrite the history of the development of the CBT tradition. If readers are interested in more detailed accounts, we would direct them to the following texts for accessible yet scholarly summaries (Dryden, 1995a; Robertson, 2010; Wills and Sanders, 1997).

Within the broad cannon of the CBTs, we take the view that Ellis's Rational Therapy, the forerunner of Rational-Emotive Behaviour Therapy (REBT), was the first published work to integrate the developments in psychology, psychotherapy and the application of humanistic principles to therapeutic change in humans. Always a prodigious writer, Ellis had been publishing work relating to psychological therapy, and particularly sex therapy and work with sexual offenders, since 1945. A number of more key publications then emerged in the later 1940s, and in 1948 Ellis wrote a critique of the theoretical contributions of nondirective therapy (Ellis, 1948). By the early 1950s he was beginning to publish his reformulations of 'scientific psychoanalysis' and introducing new techniques (Ellis, 1950, 1955, 1956), and finally the term 'Rational Psychotherapy' was first coined in 1957 (Ellis, 1957, 1958, 1959a, 1959b). It was not until 1961 that Ellis and Harper published their seminal *Guide to Rational Living* (Ellis & Harper, 1961).

It was Ellis who provided a framework by which the pioneering works that applied the advances in theoretical individual, behavioural and cognitive psychology to a therapeutic approach. This moved far beyond the more esoteric aspects of what has latterly become contained, and we would argue wrongly, within the broad description of the 'existential therapies'. Ellis was later, and in our view, wrongly criticised by Padesky and Beck (2003). It is ironic that the very central theme of their critique is more appropriately applied to other therapies and they fail to acknowledge the centrality of REBT philosophy to CBT and its various evolutionary pathways.

Similar to Rogers, Ellis too argues that human beings have two inherent capacities which distinguish them as 'human'. Unlike Rogers, Ellis defines these capacities as the capacity to be rational and irrational. The terminology is not one of value, i.e. to be 'rational' is of greater relative value than to be 'irrational'. Although not directly comparable on all levels, the terminology 'cognitive distortion', 'dysfunctional belief' or 'thinking error' has a similar use, and is not a value-judgement but is a defined intra-psychic phenomenological process rather similar to Rogers' description of 'introjected beliefs', which he saw as leading to distortions in the self concept. The irrational capacity (or distortion, dysfunctional belief, etc.) directs the individual to become distressed and non-fully functioning whereas the rational capacity (or functional belief, healthy cognition, etc.) directs the individual to become non-distressed and fully functioning.

The core philosophical principles of the CBTs

It is of interest that Ellis notes that he and other CBT theorists (e.g. Beck and Michenbaum) were clearly influenced by the notions of phenomenology and existentialism. Although it is Sartre's existentialism that can be detected more readily than that of Heidegger, a central difference between Heidegger and Sartre was Sartre's conceptualisation of nothingness, not as a complete state but as one that co-exists with being; and that the individual becomes aware of it. The source material can be notoriously complex and a humorous summary enables greater clarity. Heath (1967: 254) noted this difference as follows: 'It is not nothing that has been worrying them [existentialist philosophers], but they who have been worrying it.' Consequently, the interplay of awareness and loss of awareness appears to have a clear parallel with the conceptualisation within the CBTs. Another example of how existential concepts are manifestly correspondent with cognitive concepts would be Sartre's concept of 'bad faith'. This relates to self-deception, or a situation in which the individual 'lies' to 'the self' and effectively 'forgets' that this has taken place. It is in many ways analogous to the process of cognitive dissonance. In cognitive dissonance, the anxiety experienced by holding two incompatible beliefs about something is reduced by systematic endorsement of biases towards one belief over the other – basically convincing oneself. Sartre illustrates this phenomenon in *Being and Nothingness* (1992), in his story of the abstinent gambler who becomes anguished by the realisation that his resolve not to gamble only has power while he is anxious that he may gamble again. More importantly, that he cannot simply re-establish his resolve without reconstructing himself and engaging in self-deception.

Existential (or death) anxiety is thus conceptualised as being integrated with beliefs about the self and mortality. However, empirical research relating to death anxiety suggests that this is increased relative to the extent to which individuals have actualised life goals (Robinson & Wood, 1984). Therefore, within the CBTs death anxiety is conceptualised more as an irrational belief relating to health and well-being, and consequently is an exaggeration of 'normal' experience, which is similar to any other type of anxiety, as opposed to a pre-eminent condition of human nature.

A significant issue with contemporary models within some of the CBTs, despite some authors falling into the trap of using diagnostic constructs and writing 'specific treatments for…' particular disorders, is the tendency to operate from the position that the fundamental model of pathology is both central and correct. In other words, treatment must fit diagnosis. It is our contention that this is antithetical to the entire notion of psychological therapy and to the underlying principles of the CBTs and also of the PCAs. Empirical study may provide broad categorical similarities between presentations (e.g. anxiety associated with failure to perform ineffectual behaviours); however, to consider that only treatment along a closely prescribed set of rules will be effective is not only illogical but runs worryingly close to an evangelism for the truth of diagnosis.

Similar to PCA, the CBTs hold the position that human beings have core worth, and it is of interest to note that it was only in his later writing on self-esteem that Ellis really drew together the vast strands that had formed his thinking into a single work. Furthermore, despite the atheism of the two approaches, it is worthy that Ellis states his view that he and Rogers were likely to have both been influenced by the thinking of the theologian Paul Tillich, and particularly his concept of unconditional self-acceptance as a notion that all humans have worth.

A central theme of the REBT philosophical position is drawn from Albert Korzybski, especially his concept that behaviour, whether good or bad, represents merely a part of the individual but certainly not the whole of us as human beings. In CBT, it is often unspoken, yet nevertheless essential, that individuals attain a point of unconditional self-acceptance. Ellis went further to develop this into unconditional other acceptance and unconditional life acceptance and it remains unclear as to why, and indeed where, the other CBTs diverged from this principle given that it is inherently central to the basis of the model.

The core defining component of humanity for the CBTs is the tendency to misconstrue, misperceive and misrepresent 'reality', and therefore inevitably generate the seeds of our own disturbance. Ziegler (1999) suggests that empirical research strongly supports Ellis' REBT position regarding the fundamental nature and biological basis of irrationality. Human beings are flawed and imperfect, and consequently our thinking and perceiving is also flawed and imperfect. Given that our emotions are intimately linked to our thinking and perceiving, then our distress is, to a significant extent, maintained by our irrationality as we have the capacity to be irrational and to use this to cause our disturbance.

Although this can be construed as an ultimately nihilistic point of view, the essence of our experience and core sense of being does not preclude a further human capacity to react to this tendency by an active and ongoing process of disputation and re-construing. Indeed, an inherent part of the theory is that human beings also have the capacity to be rational as well as irrational.

The phenomenological position of the CBTs is very clear and Ellis particularly referenced this alongside the work of Sartre. As such, it is the recognition of our fallibility and tendency to disturb ourselves that drives our difficulties and, in order to change this, it is necessary to become aware of this and dispute these tyrannical 'shoulds'.

A reflection on the similarities and differences in the relative philosophical positions of the two approaches

It may be seen as a somewhat contentious idea that PCA and the CBTs are both rooted in the same philosophical traditions, yet we believe this to be so. For us, both are rooted in humanism, existentialism and phenomenology. At the same time, we also recognise that there are some differences in how these philosophies are understood and expressed.

For both PCA and CBTs the concept of *authenticity* as a necessary way of being and the means to conceptualise human existence is of great importance. The difference in emphasis lies in the extent to which this is emphasised as central to the process of change and becoming *the self*.

This humanistic view of the person as actively and continually seeking meaning and fulfilment puts a strong focus on the concept of process. Self-actualisation or fulfilment is a continual challenge or journey to be experienced, not an end-state to be attained. Only we can determine our own vocation. (You can choose 'Who ever' and 'How ever' you want to be.) In other words, both approaches in this respect are constructivist and postmodern.

The most important and singularly most different aspect of the person-centred approach is the belief that this is about a way of life, a way of being that is in itself therapeutic and not about a set of tools to be 'switched on' in therapy.

A link to the next chapter

In the next chapter we intend to develop a brief outline of the historical development of the two approaches from their beginnings to the current day. This will include a description of the different 'Tribes' which have emerged in the two approaches, particularly in recent years. It will also include a brief description of each of the models.

Recommended reading

Casemore, R. (2011) *Person-centred Counselling in a Nutshell* (2nd edn). London: Sage.

Cooper, M., O'Hara, M., Schmid, P.F., & Wyatt, G. (2007) *The Handbook of Person-centred Psychotherapy and Counselling*. Basingstoke: Palgrave.

Robertson, D. (2010) *The Philosophy of Cognitive-Behavioural Therapy (CBT): Stoic Philosophy as Rational and Cognitive Psychotherapy*. London: Karnac.

Sartre, J.-P. (1946) *Existentialism and Humanism*. Edited by P. Mairet (1974). London: Methuen.

Wills, F. and Sanders, D. (1997) *Cognitive Therapy: Transforming the Image*. London: Sage.

CHAPTER 3

THE HISTORY AND DEVELOPMENT OF THE APPROACHES

In this chapter we will set out to provide a brief outline of the historical development of the two approaches from their beginnings to the current day. This will include some brief description of the different 'Tribes' which have emerged in the two approaches, particularly in recent years. It will also include a brief description of each of the models of the PCA and the CBTs.

A brief biographical history: Carl Rogers (1902–1987)

Carl Rogers was born in 1902 in Oak Park near Chicago. In 1919 he enrolled at the University of Wisconsin, majoring in scientific agriculture, from where he graduated in 1924, and he then enrolled at Union Theological Seminary. In 1940 he began teaching at the University of Ohio and was elected president of the American Psychological Association (APA) in 1946.

In 1926 Rogers began his training as a clinical psychologist at Columbia University and finally completed his PhD in 1931. Rogers' first professional role as a psychologist was at the Child Study Department of the Rochester Society for the Prevention of Cruelty to Children, in New York. In this work he was influenced by the ideas of Otto Rank's school of thinking, and in particular by the work and thinking of social workers Jessie Taft and Frederick Allan, who were attached to Rank's clinic. Their influence enabled him to move away from a psychoanalytic approach that focused on interpreting the client's past, to one that was more focused on the relationship between client and therapist, and the client's own tendency towards growth. Based on his clinical experience, he became more and more convinced of the centrality of the clients' understanding of themselves and their self-direction as opposite to interpretation, traditional diagnosis or modification techniques. He came to the conclusion that the client is the only expert in their own internal world.

As a consequence of his experience of what he saw as a very controlling and directive approach to therapy, Rogers began to develop his concept of what he at first called 'non-directive therapy' (Rogers, 1942). Rogers described his approach as 'non-directive' (Rogers, 1942) in order to stress the self-directive movement of the 'client' (a term that he introduced to replace 'patient', which he saw as rooted in the traditional medical model for psychotherapy).

In 1951 Rogers renamed his approach 'Client-centred' in order to emphasise that the focus of psychotherapy should be on the inner world of experience of the client. He also wanted to refute the misunderstanding which had developed that therapy should be completely non-directive and merely a process of mirroring or reflecting back what the client had said.

Carl Rogers died on 4 February 1987, the same year in which he was nominated for a Nobel Peace Prize.

The development of the approach

In 1959 Rogers was invited to publish a paper on his 'Theory of Therapy, Personality, and Interpersonal Relationships, as Developed in the Client-Centred Framework' in *Psychology: A Study of Science. Volume 3: Formulations of the Person and the Social Context*. In this paper, published earlier as Chapter 11 in *Client Centred Therapy* (Rogers, 1951), Carl Rogers sets out the basic principles on which his person-centred approach rests (pp. 483–524). Although Rogers terms this base theoretical (p. 482), it is also partly philosophical, for in it he lays out the humanistic, phenomenological and existential credentials of the approach. Rogers describes 19 propositions which are based both on his own clinical observations over many years of therapeutic work, and also rest on the work of many other writers, researchers and clinicians. Having spent much of his early career holding views opposed to these propositions, Rogers arrived at these conclusions because the evidence before him demonstrated to him the inadequacies of the approach with which he had been working and also, importantly, his experience of therapy as a client.

These propositions are a little difficult to read and attempting to translate them into more readable contemporary language does not appear to make them more accessible. They are therefore presented here as they were originally written because they are useful to understand when comparing and contrasting this approach with the CBT approach.

i Every individual exists in a continually changing world of experience of which he is the centre.

ii The organism reacts to the field as it is experienced and perceived. This perceptual field is, for the individual, 'reality'.

iii The organism reacts as an organized whole to this phenomenal field.

iv The organism has one basic tendency and striving to actualize, maintain, and enhance the experiencing organism.

v   Behaviour is basically the goal-directed attempt of the organism to satisfy its needs as experienced, in the field as perceived.

vi   Emotion accompanies and in general facilitates such goal-directed behaviour, the kind of emotion being related to the seeking versus the consummatory aspects of the behaviour, and the intensity of the emotion being related to the perceived significance of the behaviour for the maintenance and enhancement of the organism.

vii   The best vantage point for understanding behaviour is from the internal frame of reference of the individual himself.

viii   A portion of the total perceptual field gradually becomes differentiated as the self.

ix   As a result of interaction with the environment, and particularly as a result of evaluative interaction with others, the structure of self is formed – an organized, fluid, but consistent conceptual pattern of perceptions of characteristics and relationships of the I or the me, together with values attached to these concepts.

x   The values attached to experiences, and the values which are a part of the self structure, in some instances are values experienced directly by the organism, and in some instances are values introjected or taken over from others, but perceived in distorted fashion, as if they had been experienced directly.

xi   As experiences occur in the life of the individual, they are either, (a) symbolized, perceived, and organized into some relationship to the self, (b) ignored because there is no perceived relationship to the self-structure, (c) denied symbolization or given a distorted symbolization because the experience is inconsistent with the structure of the self.

xii   Most of the ways of behaving which are adopted by the organism are those which are consistent with the concept of self.

xiii   Behaviour may, in some instances, be brought about by organic experiences and needs which have not been symbolized. Such behaviour may be inconsistent with the structure of the self, but in such instances the behaviour is not owned by the individual.

xiv   Psychological maladjustment exists when the organism denies to awareness significant sensory and visceral experiences, which consequently are not symbolized and organized into the gestalt of the self-structure. When this situation exists, there is a basic or potential psychological tension.

xv   Psychological adjustment exists when the concept of the self is such that all the sensory and visceral experiences of the organism are, or may be, assimilated on a symbolic level into a consistent relationship with the concept of self.

xvi   Any experience which is inconsistent with the organization or structure of self may be perceived as a threat, and the more of these perceptions there are, the more rigidly the self-structure is organized to maintain itself.

xvii Under certain conditions, involving primarily complete absence of any threat to the self-structure, experiences which are inconsistent with it may be perceived, and examined, and the structure of self revised to assimilate and include such experiences.

xviii When the individual perceives and accepts into one consistent and integrated system all his sensory and visceral experiences, then he is necessarily more understanding of others and is more accepting of others as separate individuals.

xix As the individual perceives and accepts into his self-structure more of his organic experiences, he finds that he is replacing his present value system based so largely upon introjections which have been distortedly symbolized with a continuing organismic valuing process.

In 1957 he published his well-known paper 'The Necessary and Sufficient Conditions of Therapeutic Personality Change' in the *Journal of Consulting Psychology* (Rogers, 1957). In this paper, Rogers made a major statement about his theory of psychotherapy. He began by posing the problem of whether it was possible to identify the psychological conditions which are both necessary and sufficient to bring about constructive personality or psychotherapeutic change? By that he meant change in the personality structure of the individual that would lead to the individual being more integrated, with less internal conflict, having greater energy leading to more effective living; accompanied by a change in behaviours away from behaviours generally regarded as immature and towards behaviours regarded as mature.

The six conditions for therapeutic change

Rogers hypothesised that for constructive personality change to occur the following six conditions needed to exist and to continue over a period of time in the relationship between the therapist and the client and to be experienced by the client.

1 Two persons are in psychological contact.

2 The first, whom we shall term the client, is in a state of incongruence, being vulnerable or anxious.

3 The second person, whom we shall term the therapist, is congruent or integrated in the relationship.

4 The therapist experiences unconditional positive regard for the client.

5 The therapist experiences an empathic understanding of the client's internal frame of reference and endeavours to communicate this experience to the client.

6 The communication to the client of the therapist's empathic understanding and unconditional positive regard is to a minimal degree achieved.

In expanding on his first condition, Rogers stated that it was essential for a minimal relationship that a psychological contact must exist. He suggested that significant positive personality change does not occur except in a relationship. Rogers suggested that this apparently simple condition should be considered as a 'pre-condition', without which the other conditions would have no meaning. In other words, without psychological contact, therapy would not occur.

Rogers further stated that for therapeutic change to occur, no other conditions are necessary. If these six conditions exist, and continue over a period of time, this is sufficient. The process of constructive personality change will follow.

The seven stages of the process of becoming fully functioning

A common criticism of the PCA is that it lacks structure. In *On Becoming a Person* (1961), Rogers described seven stages in the process of growth in the therapeutic process which he developed based on empirical research, to conceptualise the changes that take place in the behaviour and experiencing of a client through the process of psychotherapy. Through his research Rogers was able to identify the characteristics of a continuum of seven stages in the process of personality change in and through psychotherapy.

Rogers (1961: 132–158) suggested that progress through these seven stages of psychological development is characterised by:

- movement from internal rigidity (fixity) towards increased internal fluidity (flowingness);

- a deepening sense of self and one's internal life, and internal fluency; a progressive awareness of, acknowledgement of, and acceptance of one's own feelings; and

- a widening realisation that far from being simple and clear-cut, the world, other people, and oneself involve complexity and ambiguity.

The first stage

Clients can often seem very defensive and quite resistant to change. In this first stage, clients seem unable talk much about themselves and their feelings. Instead they tend to talk mainly about their problems, difficulties, the things or other people that are problematic in their life.

The second stage

As the client begins to experience being accepted, then the ways in which they have tended to express themselves in the earlier stages of therapy seem to change, often almost imperceptibly at first. The client will start to talk about things other than the details of their story or the things that happen to them or that are problematic. It is as though there is a slight easing of how the client is being in the relationship with the counsellor.

The third stage

Rogers suggests that in the third stage of the process, the client will talk about themselves, but almost as though they are an object. They will often avoid discussion of present events. This seems to lead the client to begin to identify and challenge some of the strongly held constructs or personal beliefs they hold about how they should be and will begin to recognise that they have some choice in their responses to these introjections.

The fourth stage

The client begins to talk about deep feelings and develops a relationship with the therapist. Rogers suggested that this is when the client will allow their feelings to flow much more freely and will begin to experience them much more in the counselling room rather than just talking about them. It is likely that this will still be a rather frightening thing for them and they may wish to resist it. They may be quite fearful and distrustful of this process and may experience counselling as being a very painful thing to be involved in.

The fifth stage

The client can express present emotions and is beginning to rely more on their own decision-making abilities and increasingly accept more responsibility for their actions. In the fifth stage, clients begin to more readily own their current emotions and begin to accept more responsibility for their actions and for being as they are. Clients then begin to recognise that what is happening to them is no longer somebody else's fault and that they have some agency in dealing with their feelings.

The sixth stage

The client shows rapid growth towards congruence, and begins to develop unconditional positive regard for others. This stage signals the end for the need for formal therapy. Rogers suggests that at this crucial stage the client becomes really free to directly experience their feelings in the here and now of the counselling room. They lose their fear of being in touch with their feelings and to recognise that they need to accept and value their feelings in the way that the therapist does.

The seventh stage

The client is a more fully functioning individual who is empathic and shows unconditional positive regard for others. This individual can relate their previous therapy to present-day real-life situations. Rogers suggests that the evidence of progression to this stage can be seen outside the therapeutic relationship as well as within it. The client begins to show that they are taking their newly learned ways of being in the therapeutic relationship and developing them in their life and relationships outside therapy.

It is important to remember that Rogers saw these seven stages as fluid points on a continuum along which clients would ebb and flow backwards and forwards as they moved towards becoming more fully functioning.

A living, growing theory and practice

Carl Rogers never intended that the person-centred approach should become a set of inflexible rules or that his theory should be seen as some form of dogma. He always presented his theories as a hypothesis of what might be true, based on the experience of his own research. He was committed to the principle that his ideas should be the starting point for new ideas and further development, tested out through rigorous research. He was strongly opposed to the Person-centred approach standing still and strongly supported its continuing growth as a living, developing theory and practice. Some developments took place during his life time and others after his death. Prominent among these are those which Sanders calls 'the schools of therapy related to the Person-centred approach' (Sanders, 2004) and others have referred to as the 'Tribes' of the Person-centred approach.

Sanders suggested the following 'Tribes':

Classical Client-centred Therapy

This is the 'original' approach, the starting point of it all, as described in Carl Rogers' early writings.

Focusing

Springing from the work of Eugene Gendlin, Carl Rogers' close colleague.

Experiential Therapy

Developments which embrace ideas from both Rogers and Gendlin, infused with cognitive psychology and Gestalt Therapy.

Existential therapies

Based on the work of European existential philosophers, existential psychotherapy is a powerful approach which takes the human condition seriously. It is an approach that embraces human potential, at the same time recognising human limitations and fallibility. Based within the tradition of the insight-orientated psychotherapies, existential therapy has much in common with psychodynamic, humanistic, experiential and relational approaches to psychotherapy.

Integrative Person-centred Therapy

Presented here as a way of approaching therapy from a person-centred base of values, philosophy and theory.

Schmid (2002) has described a range of developments of the approach which have taken place. He outlines those which might be described as phenomenological-existential orientations and lists 'Clinical and Process-orientated' (Binder & Binder, 1991, 1994; Swildens, 1988), Constructivistic (Frenzel et al., 2001; O'Hara, 1998; Fehringer, 2002), 'Hermeneutic' (Finke, 1994), 'Spiritual' (Thorne, 1998) and 'Personal-dialogical' (Schmid, 1991, 1994, 1998a, 1998b, 1999) as the most significant of these.

Schmid describes a second range as more behaviouristic and cognitive-psychological orientations which developed in the 1960s and 1970s (Martin, 1972; Tausch & Tausch, 1960), empirical-descriptive and developmental-psychological ones (Biermann-Ratjen et al., 1997). Schmid then identifies that a separate person-centred modality was developed by Eugene Gendlin (1996), with his Experiential or Focusing-orientated Psychotherapy.

Further developments from this are 'process-experiential' or 'process-directive' therapy (Greenberg et al., 1993, 1997), 'goal' and 'intervention-oriented' procedures by Sachse (1992, 1999).

The history and development of the CBTs

In order to consider the development of the CBTs it is necessary to consider the advances made in academic and theoretical psychology in the early to mid-twentieth century, particularly the emergence of behaviourism. It is important to make reference to behaviourist psychology and its application to psychological distress as this is a clear, direct application of empirically derived psychology theory.

Behaviourism refers to an empiricist philosophical school in which the focus of interest is purely based on the 'observable', and therefore the study of the relationship between actions and stimuli are a central concern. As psychology developed into an academic discipline, behaviourism emerged as the dominant theoretical model. It is a common misconception that behavioural psychology is unitary; nothing could be further from the truth, and Miles (1966) identified three basic forms of the model. Indeed, more recent developments have seen the reconceptualisation of behavioural theory as a 'level of explanation' through which a whole range of psychological elements can be understood.

Development and important principles

Ivan Pavlov (1927) was the true founding father of modern behaviourism as he made the link between physical responses and the environment. Pavlov's research is probably best known for the dog salivation experiments, in which he demonstrated that a biologically predetermined reflex (salivation prior to eating) could be changed to occur in the presence of a non-biological trigger (the ringing of a bell). His research changed for ever our thinking about evolution, human behaviour and approaches to social problems. Pavlov's work described conditioned and unconditioned reinforcers. These discoveries and his theoretical framework are commonly known as 'classical conditioning' or 'stimulus–response psychology'. In summary, it predicts that any behaviour can become associated with any stimulus and the presentation of the stimulus will produce the desired behaviour.

Following on from this, behavioural psychology became the dominant method for investigating behaviour and interaction, and this form of thinking identified a number of governing principles. Many famous researchers are associated with this period in psychology, not least of whom is Thorndike, who was interested in goal-directed behaviour, principally those behaviours that are designed to achieve an effect. He defined the 'law of effect' (Thorndike, 1905) which was an attempt to explain why animals apparently engage in goal-directed learning.

Thorndike's law of effect

Behaviour that produces pleasurable (or desired) effects tends to occur more often. For example, smiling at people we find attractive usually results in a return smile (which we find pleasurable) and therefore increases the likelihood that we will smile at people we find attractive when we meet people we find attractive in the future.

Possibly the greatest and most widely known (although most widely misunderstood) of the behaviourists is Skinner, who coined the term 'operant' (Skinner, 1938) and who exhaustively researched the subject. Classical conditioning is dependent on the timing and predictability of the stimulus, whereas 'operant conditioning' is dependent upon the characteristics of the reinforcer. Both produce a strong response, although operant conditioning is considerably stronger than classical conditioning.

Following on from the law of effect, operant elements can become powerful influencing factors, together with the frequency and predictability reinforcement, which are referred to as schedules of reinforcement and relate to maintenance. These can be broadly grouped into fixed ratios, in which reinforcement occurs after a fixed number of responses, and variable ratios, in which reinforcement occurs after a variable number of responses or adjustment of the timing of reinforcement. The manipulation of the reinforcement schedule has demonstrable and significant effects on behaviour.

Behaviour theory identifies different types of reinforcer and punisher that influence behaviour in other subtle, yet important ways. Reinforcers always increase behaviour frequency whereas punishers involve aversive consequences and reduce behaviour frequency (see Figure 3.1).

Therefore, it is possible to influence behaviour in many ways and the most influential of these is positive reinforcement as this can lead to very strong learning that does not suffer from some of the pitfalls and ethical dilemmas of the other forms.

Three basic forms of behavioural model/philosophy (Miles, 1966)

Metaphysical behaviourism

The mind and thoughts do not exist. The person is simply the sum of their behaviours.

Methodological behaviourism

The mind and thoughts may exist, but they cannot be studied scientifically. Therefore, it is not necessary to postulate 'internal events' (thoughts, emotions). They are simply constructs that allow us to predict behaviour through equations.

Radical or analytical behaviourism

It is necessary, but not sufficient, to postulate 'internal events'. Full understanding of human action depends on understanding external behaviours, internal behaviours and the interaction of the two.

While the three forms differ primarily over their positions on 'private events' (e.g. thoughts and cognitions, etc.), at the core of all behavioural models is the assumption that animals (and other organisms) act in ways that are predictable at a phenomenological level (e.g. x is likely to be associated with y but not with z).

	Presented	Omitted
Type of reinforcer		
Positive	↑˙ Positive reinforcement	↓˙ Frustrative non-reward
Negative	↓˙ Punishment	↑˙ Negative reinforcement

˙ Denotes the frequency of behaviour

FIGURE 3.1   *Reinforcement and punishment*

Such predictability depends upon knowledge of the contingencies, or schedules, under which the behaviour occurs. The patterns of association are summarised in a number of principles (e.g. operant conditioning, classical conditioning). Therefore, an understanding of these basic principles allows us to predict behaviours and to predict responses to changes (e.g. through behavioural psychotherapies). As a result, it is the overt behaviours that can be observed and consequently analysed. While internal events may, or may not, occur, the province of scientific statements relates to those phenomena that are amenable to recording and observation. It is possible to summarise the main misunderstandings of behaviourism as follows:

Determinism: genetic versus environmental influence

There are widely different points of view on where behaviour originates. For example, Watson and Rayner (1920) viewed genetic contributions as minimal, whereas Skinner (1971) considered that evolution would effect and influence through the selection of particular behavioural patterns 'best fitted' to their environment and therefore of greatest evolutionary use. In essence, this debate is irrelevant to the theory of behaviourism and its practical application in that, as long as there is a degree of environmental determination (whether absolute or partial), it is possible to produce change through direct intervention.

Cognition

No behavioural model or philosophy denies the existence of mental events. Rather, the analysis of these is considered as less central to psychological understanding, given that the reduction in the reliability of secondary sources of information necessarily means that these are vulnerable to considerable extraneous variance.

Ethics

Behaviourism itself, and particularly applied behaviourism, has been, unfairly in many cases, slated as unethical. The most basic of these arguments is that behaviourism reduces human beings to little more than mechanical systems that can be adjusted. As such, behaviour therapy led to situations in which it was assumed that control of the appropriate contingencies would lead to an increase in desired along with a decrease in undesired behaviours. At times this was applied inappropriately (for example, 'treating' homosexuality by the use of aversive counter-conditioning). However, it seems more realistic to conceptualise that these misapplications reflected more significant misconceptions about, and pathologisation of, the diversity of human behaviour as opposed to problems inherent to behaviour therapy *per se*.

Despite the many criticisms of behaviour therapy, it is ironic that many ethical guidelines relating to intervening to address human difficulty contain significant reference to the need for interventions to be rooted in clear theoretical models which behaviour therapy clearly had in abundance. Furthermore, it is necessary to demonstrate empirical evidence of clinical efficacy, and again behaviour therapy had such empirical evidence.

Limitations on techniques and application

Quite simply this is not supported by empirical evidence, and behaviour theory and behaviour therapy developed a vast range of interventions and techniques (e.g. Baldwin & Baldwin, 1998; Bellack & Hersen, 1987), many of which have been integrated into other therapies, particularly the CBTs. Indeed, it is reasonable to suggest that the development of the CBTs owes much of their evidence base and success to behaviour therapy and behavioural theory. It is useful to consider the development of some of the fundamental elements of behaviour theory that were applied to behaviour therapy and have been integrated in wider therapy via the CBTs.

Formulation of cases

Behavioural theory is one of several constructs that can easily be used to explain the links between antecedents, behaviours and consequences. Functional analysis uses a concept of functionality (Goldiamond, 1974) and this is central to the psychological assessment of problem behaviour. Functional analysis is a core part of the formulation that is present across a wide variety of modalities and this is directly derived from the behavioural therapies. Finally, there is a wealth of experimental evidence to support the 'effectiveness' of behavioural interventions in reducing problem behaviours. Consequently, to suggest that there is little or no evidence of efficacy is, frankly, nonsense.

Despite strong theoretical criticisms of behaviourism, behaviour therapy suffered from the effects of misapplication seen in the era of aversive counter-conditioning for '*sexual deviance*' (i.e. homosexuality). However, any therapeutic model can be abused and ethical conduct is a function of the therapist and not the theory.

The development of the CBTs follows a rather more complicated route, with a number of 'founding fathers'. The CBTs originate with the work of Albert Ellis and his distinguished publishing record, which started with his study of, and challenge to, the prevailing dynamic psychotherapy that was traditionally on offer to clients at that time in the United States. Ellis was born in Pittsburgh in September 1913. He received his first degree in business from the City University of New York and was briefly employed as a writer of fiction. Ironically, his talent lay in the writing of non-fiction and he began writing about human sexuality and became a sought-after lay counsellor in the field. He then commenced his studies for an MA in Clinical Psychology at Columbia University in 1942 and stayed on to study for his PhD. Always a prolific writer, and before receiving his Doctorate, Ellis began publishing papers on a range of topics, including the validity of psychometric tests!

As with many practitioners in the United States at that time, Ellis commenced post-doctoral training in psychoanalysis at the Karen Horney Institute. Increasingly, Ellis began to question both the efficacy and scientific foundation of psychoanalysis, resulting in his 1950 monograph, which represents his significant shift away from the more open-ended, interpretative phenomenology of the individualistic psychotherapies based on the theories of Adler and Horney towards the development of his key theories regarding irrationality and the link between this and intense dysfunctional emotions.

Ellis's breakthrough moment was his identification that virtually all people labelled as neurotics had in common the tendency to invoke irrational and rigid thinking. Ellis took the view that people will act in ways which seem self-defeating and foolish and that people can be fully aware of irrational beliefs but tend to tenaciously maintain them despite their leading to continual despair.

By early 1953 Ellis started to refer to himself as a 'Rational Therapist' and openly advocated his active-directive psychotherapy, which he titled Rational Therapy (RT) in 1955. In 1954, Ellis began teaching his new techniques to other therapists, and by 1957 he introduced the behavioural component to RT, suggesting that change not only required cognitive and emotional change but also behavioural change too.

In 1959 Ellis founded the Institute for Rational Living, a non-profit organisation and in 1968 the Institute was granted a charter by the State of New York as a training institute and psychological clinic.

The central component to Ellis' theory was the operationalisation of both the principles of Sartre's existentialism and the principles of the stoic philosophers into responsible hedonism which is clearly linked to the concept of 'apathea', or the absence of ruling passions. Ellis combined Karen Horney's notion of the 'tyranical shoulds and musts' with the concepts drawn from the philosophies of Korzybski and Tillich regarding human value. Indeed, Ellis continued to write extensively about his philosophical position with regard to human value throughout his life and, at times, took direct issue with his interpretation of Carl Rogers' position in this respect. Ellis' pioneering work was widely published and clearly developed as a formal structure and a clear alternative within a cognitive framework in the early 1950s. Albert Ellis died on 24 July 2007, leaving a significant heritage of written work. He published in excess of 900 articles and books and his legacy was, despite their theoretical differences, honoured by Aaron T. Beck in his obituary.

Aaron T. Beck was born in Rhode Island in 1921 and graduated from Brown University in 1942 and then Yale Medical School in 1946. As with Ellis and Rogers, Beck's primary therapeutic training was in psychoanalysis. While working as a psychiatrist at the University of Pennsylvania, and quite independently of any knowledge of Ellis' work, Beck began to conduct a number of empirical studies to test psychoanalytic concepts of depression. Beck observed that the clients he worked with reported spontaneous streams of negative thoughts which he termed 'automatic thoughts' and observed that these fell into three broad categories: negative ideas about the self, the world and the future. Beck found that by helping clients to challenge these thoughts, by comparison with empirical reality, their depression lifted and they were able to function as they had previously done.

As with both Rogers and Ellis, Beck became increasingly disillusioned with traditional models of psychodynamic psychotherapy and began to apply his model to the treatment of depression with clear research evidence of effectiveness. It is, perhaps, a critical issue that Beck maintained an essentially medico-diagnostic model of depression, which consequently influenced both his thinking and research, and this aspect of the model has been maintained. Nevertheless, he drew a significant body of research evidence into his work on the tripartite theory of depression that formed the basis of his Cognitive Therapy. Although similar to Rational Therapy, at that time Cognitive Therapy did not differentiate between evaluative and influential thought. For Beck, the issue was associated with dysfunctional thought, which formed a core set of difficulties, and that the validity of these could be challenged through collaborative empiricism as opposed to the more stoical and fundamental challenge that Ellis posed with regard to the failure of individuals to acknowledge their irrational, evaluative beliefs and dogmatic insistence upon imposing artificial conditions to their value as a human being. It was this initial difference between Rational-Emotive Therapy and Cognitive Therapy that gave rise to the less-than-helpful terms 'elegant' and 'inelegant' Cognitive Therapy. Similarly to Ellis, Beck founded the Beck Institute for Cognitive Therapy and Research in Philadelphia in 1994, assisted by his daughter Judith Beck.

By the 1970s Donald Meichenbaum began synthesising his own work as a radical behavioural therapist with Cognitive Therapy into an emergent model. He integrated the advances and theoretical principles from cognitive psychology with the sizeable body of behaviourist psychology. This provided a coherent model for the interrelationship between cognitive appraisal, affective response and behavioural maintenance, usually by avoidance or anticipatory behaviours, into a formal structure and unified theory. This is succinctly summarised in his *Cognitive Behavior Modification: An Integrative Approach* (1977) and then in his 1985 *Stress Inoculation Training*, which presents one of the first Cognitive-Behavioural approaches to anger-based difficulty. From this point, both Cognitive-Behavioural Therapy and Rational-Emotive Therapy developed and acknowledged the impact of this synthesis. It is notable that Ellis included the term 'behavioural' in latter reconceptualisations of Rational-Emotive Therapy into Rational-Emotive Behaviour Therapy. Similarly, within the broad cannon, Cognitive-Behavioural theorists have included a conceptualisation of the evaluative belief into core beliefs, more latterly in the work of Jeffrey Young's Schema Therapy as core schema (Young, 1990). A careful consideration of these concepts reveals striking complementarity between the notion of introjected value, core schema, core beliefs and evaluative beliefs in as much as these are often implicit in nature, highly dogmatic and rigid, and undoubtedly undermine goal attainment for the individual. Furthermore, these are associated with very strong negative emotions.

The main theoretical components of the CBTs

Influence and change

Behaviour therapy predicts that problem behaviours are operant (functional activities that are under the control of aberrant reinforcement schedules) and this affords the psychological-level explanation to remain essentially a non-disease concept. Thus, it is the nature of contingencies that remains the central key to theories of clinical behavioural applications. Later behavioural researchers, such as Eysenck, Rachman, Wolpe (Eysenck & Rachman, 1965; Wolpe & Rachman, 1960; Wolpe, 1981) and Bandura (1997), worked on therapeutic aspects of applying behavioural theories to psychological and psychiatric problems. The pioneering work of Wolpe, while greatly improving the range and potential for change in mental health, rapidly demonstrated theoretical shortfalls and it was Rachman (1977, 1981, 1990) who described the inadequacies of simple conditioning theories for phobias and fear itself.

Bandura's Social Learning Theory provides an early insight into the very significant role played by the observation of behaviour. Stated simply, this suggests that the social environment influences behaviour and that modelling is a very strong and indirect method for influencing behavioural change and, consequently, social context is a strong influence upon behaviour. Another significant contribution from Social Learning Theory is self-efficacy, that is, beliefs regarding individual ability to successfully master an activity, which are more predictive of positive affect and behaviour than direct measures of self-concept or self-esteem (Parjares & Miller, 1994). The theory has also emphasised the cognitive component and tended to minimise behavioural level theories. However, this has been criticised by some theorists as a shift in terminology as opposed to a paradigm shift.

Alongside applications to individual distress, behavioural methodologies were applied to groups and institutional settings, collectively referred to as the 'token economies', although growing dissatisfaction at the dehumanising aspects of behavioural methods, together with clear evidence that behaviour change was not maintained when the environment changed, weakened the appeal of the model (Fullerton et al., 1978; Léduc et al., 1990). In an attempt to address this, Social Behaviourism was developed.

Behavioural models of phobic acquisition and maintenance

Early behavioural models of phobias centred on classical conditioned aversive response to a neutral stimulus. This effect generalises to other stimuli that differ from the original along one or more dimensions and can involve more complex effects, such as higher order conditioning, sensory preconditioning, counter-conditioning and habituation. Watson and Rayner (1920) provide a paradigm with the case of 'Little Albert' in which a young boy has his pet rat presented to him at the same time as a loud noise is made. After a number of trials, the presentation of the animal alone, without the noise, is sufficient to generate the conditioned startle and fear response which he then generalises to other small furry objects. Despite the clear ethical problems with this demonstration, the account is vague and incomplete and subsequent studies have reported poor replicability (Harris, 1979; Valentine, 1930).

The two factor theory of phobic acquisition was proposed by Mowrer (1951). Here, phobic acquisition comprises two elements. An initial acquisition phase in which an aversive stimulus is associated with a neutral object and the phobic behaviour is maintained by an operant avoidance schedule through negative reinforcement. The responding (escape and avoidance) is reinforced by temporary relaxation and a transient sense of well-being. Again, this does not coherently account for variation across stimuli type and many apparently traumatic events do not necessarily seem to condition the phobic neuroses that the conditioning model predicts (Rachman, 1977). Similarly, many people with phobias do not report ever having experienced the required conditioning episode in which the phobic stimuli were paired with some other frightening event (Murray & Foote, 1979).

A more critical problem for behavioural models of psychopathology is that the pattern of phobias is non-random and most are social or small animal phobias whereas the conditioning model predicts that stimuli likely to be paired with pain and fear (e.g. hot objects, knives) should form the most likely objects of phobias. In fact, kettle and knife phobias, for example, are rare (Seligman, 1970, 1971). Seligman proposed a theory of 'biologically prepared learning' to account for these, characterised by easy acquisition, wide generalisability, irrationality and resistance to the influence of information or instructions. These are also selective and resistant to extinction.

Seligman also proposed that human neurotic anxiety could be explained as the result of prepared fear conditioning. He predicted that it would have the characteristics listed above.

More recent developments from behavioural psychology have been combined into Acceptance and Commitment Therapy (ACT) by Hayes and his colleagues (Biglan & Hayes, 1996; Hayes, 1993). In ACT, the cognitive components of acceptance and mindfulness are taught as strategies alongside encouraging clients to make an explicit commitment to behaviour change and increasing psychological flexibility. As opposed to the CBTs, ACT does not attempt to teach people better control of their thoughts, feelings, sensations, memories and other private events, but focuses on what they can control more directly (arms, legs and mouth) and emphasises the capacity to *'just notice'*, accept and embrace their private events, especially previously unwanted ones.

A new incarnation of behaviourist philosophy is called 'functional contextualism'. This utilises empirically-based concepts and rules to predict and influence events. As such, theories that do not contribute to the achievement of practical goals are ignored or rejected.

Within the cannon of the CBTs behavioural elements abound and it is no surprise that the acronym CBT contains the letter B! It is of note that Wolpe's systematic desensitisation for anxiety involves the use of emotive imagery.

For the CBTs, behaviour is constructed largely as a consequential element. However, there is evidence that behaviours cue emotional reactions and can determine that certain situations will evoke strong emotional and cognitive processes (e.g. the discriminative stimulus).

The CBT models adopted the behaviourist concept of breaking down complex sequences into smaller and conceptually more digestible units which unfortunately used a similar structural notation of 'ABC'. In strict behavioural terms, this refers to the Antecedent, Behaviour and Consequence, whereas in the CBTs, these broadly refer to an Activating Event, Beliefs and Consequences, which can be emotional, behavioural or cognitive. This is a somewhat confusing array of terminology. However, these are linked to the different 'brands of CBT' which are in many ways not dissimilar to the 'Tribes' of PCA.

The CBTs all work from the position that humans have limited capacity to accurately understand causal relationships and the nature of probability. Indeed, this has been a consistent finding in contemporary cognitive and social psychology (Wason, 1966; Kahneman and Tversky, 1979). As such, the model adopts a 'short-hand' to describe discrete emotional episodes into component elements in order to enable clients to consider the proximal relationship between the elements and begin the process of comprehending their disturbance from a less egocentric position. The most basic form of the model is represented by the ABC formulation. In this form, the A represents the activating event or temporally proximal event assumed to 'cause' the emotional, behavioural and cognitive consequences that are experienced as the disturbed state. The B represents the beliefs or cognitive components that are functionally linked (and consequently causative) to the C, which represents the consequences, which can be emotional, behavioural and cognitive.

Ellis first described these components in his early work and he further defined the beliefs into two general forms, the inference and the evaluation. This distinction is a very elegant one as this discriminates between interpretation and assumption in as much as the inference implies a meaning to perceived reality. The evaluation assumes or confers a value or worth to the inferred interpretation. This distinction enables both therapist and client to identify, and predict, the nature of the disturbance and the root cause.

The ABC model is strongly rooted in the existential proposition that the individual perceiving 'reality' applies their own belief system and consequently is responsible for their disturbance. For example, it is not the individual who has behaved in a particular manner towards me that CAUSED me to become angry; rather it is my damning of that individual as someone who has transgressed my personal behavioural standards. For Ellis, the first and possibly most critical task of therapy is to educate the client so that it is their thinking and belief system which is the 'cause' of their disturbance and not the apparent adversity of the activating event. Therefore establishing a coherent understanding of the B–C link as opposed to the A–C link is critical to the outcome of therapy, and progress for the client.

Ellis introduces an important distinction between different forms of knowledge (epistemology) at this stage to discriminate between more or less functional ways of interpreting the client's experiences.

Narcissistic (essentially, because I say it is or should be so!) epistemologies are inevitably self-serving but self-evidently non-applicable to a relational or social experience.

Authoritarian (essentially, because it says here...) epistemologies are useful to those for whom they appeal, although they are very restrictive and undermining to others. Again, an authoritarian epistemology is easily vulnerable to disputation on the basis that the designation of the authoritative source is usually not open to empirical or objective scrutiny.

Empirical (essentially, objective and experiential knowledge based upon observation) epistemologies represent the most flexible, adaptive and therefore rational knowledge systems as they are open to refutation and can be flexible in response to new or contradictory information.

Ellis then developed the basic ABC model to include the D, the disputation of the irrational belief, which is followed by E, the effective new philosophy.

The characteristic feature of an irrational belief (irB) for Ellis is that it is logically inconsistent, inconsistent with empirical reality, absolutist, dogmatic. Often learned and rehearsed since childhood, irBs are frequently based on narcissistic or grandiose demands placed on the self, others or the universe (Ellis, 1979) and he identified several types of irB:

Demands

These are always unrealistic and absolute and usually they are associated with the use of must, should, ought, have to, need.

Awfulising

These exaggerate the real and potential negative consequences of adversities.

Low frustration tolerance

These often have the form that such-and-such *must not* happen and are, in essence, demands for ease and comfort.

Global evaluations of human worth

These are over-generalised statements about the value of others and take the form that so-and-so is an utterly valueless individual and therefore worthy of utter contempt.

Beck identified and described a number of characteristic thinking errors that lead directly to disturbed emotions and described these as:

Selective abstraction

This is the erroneous process by which a conclusion is derived from either isolated detail or by ignoring contradictory evidence.

Over-generalisation

This is the error of extracting a general rule on the basis of a single instant or event and subsequently applying this to other, dissimilar instances or occasions.

Magnification

This is an error associated with over-estimating the significance of particularly undesirable consequent events.

Dichotomous (all-or-nothing thinking)

Thinking in extreme and absolute ways.

Personification (self-reference)

This relates to egocentric interpretations of events that have no personal significant or the over-interpretation of events that marginally relate to the self.

Superstitious thinking

This is based on the error of concluding cause–effect relationships between factors that are non-contingent.

Emotional thinking

This is based on the assumption that strong negative emotions represent completely accurate reflections of the state of reality.

Self-actualisation and the CBTs

Self-actualisation reflects a clear complementarity within the CBTs and PCA, although it is more associated with REBT. Ellis records that actualisation represents an active process by which the client achieves, and does not merely endorse, a fully functioning sense of self. Although not necessarily defined as such, this clearly assumes that endorsement or intellectual acknowledgement is insufficient for effective change. This insight bridges the psychodynamic notion of 'intellectualising' as a defence process and also acknowledges the need for behavioural rehearsal as an operant. Ellis defines the actualisation process as one in which the client actively chooses self-actualisation and engages in disputing their absolutist shoulds and musts that block the achievement of actualising. Hence his often quoted concept that therapeutic change requires a significant and fundamental change in self-philosophy in which greater flexibility is adopted. Thus problem-solutions are preferred and not required, and problems become effectively cognitively reframed as something to be redesigned or reconceptualised. Therefore these become circumstances that can either be solved or not solved. In the instance of those problems that cannot be solved, disputing the basis of the absolute and dichotomous demands that this should-not-be-the-case effectively enhances life experience.

The process of actualisation within the CBTs actively promotes tolerance of both self and others. At a behavioural level, this is achieved by active strategies to overcome procrastination and low frustration tolerance by engagement with circumstances that have previously been avoided.

Again, it is Ellis who explicitly identifies and emphasises the need for a change in the client's philosophical position so that they move from either/ors towards and/ors and introduces ambiguity, paradox, inconsistency, confusion, etc. before moving towards an integrated wholeness of these new ways of interpreting and experiencing the self and world.

Primarily by identifying and reinforcing the phenomenological aspects of human perception and reasoning, this highlights the ultimate and unavoidable conclusion that alternative and, at times, contrary conclusions are available and therefore, fundamentally, clients prime themselves to be distressed.

Unlike his fellow CBT theorists, Ellis developed his theory to include 12 sub-goals aligned to his philosophy of 'responsible hedonism' (Ellis & Bernard, 1986) as an operationalised ethical system that, if adopted, would lead to less disturbance. The principles can be stated as follows:

Acceptance of uncertainty

In general, absolute certainties do not exist; one can strive for a degree of order, but not demand complete predictability.

Contentment

Most people tend to be happier when vitally absorbed in something outside themselves. At least one strong creative interest and some significant interpersonal involvement seem to provide structure for a happy daily existence.

Self-acceptance

Freely deciding to accept oneself unconditionally, rather than measure, rate, or try to prove yourself.

Risk-taking

Being prepared to take risks and have a spirit of adventurousness in trying to do what you want to do, without being foolhardy.

Realistic expectations

Accepting that it is unlikely we will get everything we want or will avoid everything we find painful and therefore not wasting time striving for the unattainable or for unrealistic perfection.

Self-acceptance

Freely deciding to accept oneself conditionally (i.e. I am human, I have faults and that is OK), rather than to measure, rate or try to prove oneself.

High frustration tolerance

Recognising that there are two sorts of problems that are likely to be encountered: those with, and those without, solutions. The goal is to modify the conditions that can be changed and learn to tolerate those that cannot.

Self-responsibility

Accepting responsibility for your own thoughts, feelings and behaviours rather than blaming others, the world or fate for distress.

Irrational beliefs, dysfunctional assumptions, inferences and evaluations

Common to all the CBTs to differing degrees is the model that, in one form or another, it is the belief or thinking that maintains or 'causes' distress. To some extent there is a considerable degree of blending within the CBT literature with regard to the various elements identified and considerable terminology representing cognitive phenomena. Beck (1976) detailed 'negative automatic thoughts' and 'dysfunctional assumptions', and described negative automatic thoughts as the stream of consciousness. These are situation-specific cognitive events which emerge into conscious awareness when they experience emotional distress. Ellis differentiates between assumptions that are inferred as if they are facts, which he describes as inferences and evaluations, and statements relating to the worth or value of things. In Ellis' framework, it is the evaluations that give rise to disturbance and these are often implicit whereas the inferences activate the linkage between events and the disturbed consequences.

A central element to all CBTs, therefore, is the mechanism by which both the therapist and, more importantly, the client can access the cognitive events and processes which underlie their disturbed emotions.

The ABCs of CBT and the DEs of REBT

As previously acknowledged, the CBTs all use the essential ABC-type framework to deconstruct the cognitive, affective and behavioural sequence of events in order to provide a structure by which clients can begin to conceptualise their distress in a more manageable format. Broadly speaking, the ABC model involves three basic elements: A refers to either antecedent or activating event, the proximal trigger to the distressed state; this is followed by B, the beliefs/appraisal in which the A is interpreted and then either the self, world or others is evaluated in some form; and this is followed by the C, or Consequence. The

C represents the emotional, behavioural and cognitive reactions to the A as it is interpreted via the B. At a psychological level, it is the perception of the setting event/s and the meaning or significance of particular aspects of this that gives rise to the emotional C and the cognitive and behavioural Cs are sometimes referred to as 'action tendencies'. These Cs can therefore, in turn, become new As linked to deeper or more implicit Bs with their own resultant Cs.

● ● ● *An example* ● ● ●

A client experiences sudden and significant anxiety in response to a situation in which a parking space into which she was reversing is suddenly and recklessly taken by another driver who then gesticulates rudely as he walks away from his parked vehicle. The client is with friends who are supportive and indicate their annoyance at the recalcitrant driver. The client, however, reports intense feelings of anxiety and shame and that she dropped her friends off and then went home and had a miserable evening.

The initial A (setting events)

I was legitimately reversing into a parking space and the other driver forced his way into the space, causing me to have to stop and find another space. Furthermore, he shows contempt for what he has done by gesticulating at me.

The initial B (beliefs)

This is both dangerous and irresponsible driving. How dare you cause me to have to brake suddenly, endangering both me and my passengers, and then cause me to have to find another parking space you…..!

The initial C (consequences)

Emotional: Initial intense arousal and anger.
Behavioural: A desire to remonstrate with the other driver or even call the police.
Cognitive: 'I really ought to. I was in the right. If I had any moral fibre, I would.' In this example, however, these Cs become a new A to a subsequent B.

The subsequent B

'I don't have any moral fibre. In fact I'm scared and won't say or do anything… I'm weak and pathetic! Now everyone will see how poorly I cope with this situation!'

The subsequent C

Emotional: Distress and shame.
Behavioural: A desire to escape from the situation and the immediate distress.
Cognitive: 'I'm useless. Who'd want to know me?'
And so on…

It is within this general framework that the CBTs can then begin to identify 'typical' ways of interpreting and responding to challenges and adversities in order to elucidate the thinking that characterises such episodes.

Ellis includes within his REBT framework two further elements in the ABC model, the D and E. The D represents the 'dispute' or methods for attacking the irrational beliefs that stifle goal attainment for the individual by disputing or challenging the thought identified in B. In his work, along with other authors such as Windy Dryden, examples of how clients can be taught effective ways of disputing their own beliefs are provided in the canon. After the D, REBT in particular argues that it is necessary to encourage clients to consider the difference between unhealthy negative emotions and healthy negative emotions, and subsequently to note, rehearse and experience the effects of these disputes. The E therefore refers to the 'effect'.

Socratic questioning

Socratic questioning is a method or model which underpins all the therapeutic approaches in which answers are drawn from individuals regarding their own theories. As this relates to CBT, this is a process in which therapists ask questions to 'draw' answers from their clients about their thinking and, consequently, their disturbance. It is recorded that Socrates identified six types of question to challenge the accuracy of thinking to enable people to achieve their goals.

Probing

This effectively tests the logical conclusions and implications of a particular way of thinking and enables the questioning of whether the 'predictions' actually make sense. For example, *Then what would happen? What would be the consequences of that? What makes most sense?*

Probing presuppositions

Probing presuppositions and unquestioned beliefs on which assumptions are based exposes the basis of thinking. For example, *If this is the case, what else could we assume? You seem to be assuming... ?*

Probing rationale and method

By using probing questions related to the thinking method, it is possible to enable clients to expose the irrationality of the rationale, i.e. the reasons and evidence behind their position. For example, *How do you know this? Show me... ? What evidence is there to support what you are saying? Where is it written...?*

Clarification

Conceptual clarification questions are intended to encourage clients to 'prove' the concepts behind their thinking and effectively think about their thinking. For example, *Why are you saying ...? What exactly does ... mean?*

Questioning underlying assumption/s

By questioning the basic perspective of the underlying assumption, and therefore the argument, it is possible to demonstrate that there are alternative and equally valid assumptions and conclusions. For example, *Another way of looking at this is... Does this seem reasonable? Why is it necessary?* Or the more pragmatic emphasis, *Who benefits from this? Why is it better than...? How are you likely to feel if you assume this?*

Questioning questions

When clients disturb themselves by raising questions (for example, the infamous 'Why me?' question), the therapist raising a question about questions introduces reflection, effectively using the argument against itself. For example, *What was the point of asking that? What does that mean? What else might I ask?*

The use of Socratic technique is central in the CBTs and this has been developed in various ways. It was Burns (1980) who described his 'Downward-Arrow' technique in which each automatic negative thought or inference is linked to the same disturbed emotion in order to elicit irrational ideas or dysfunctional thoughts. One possible difficulty with this method is that it can inadvertently lead to therapists challenging the accuracy of assumptions which may, ironically, be accurate. For example, that close friends or lovers do not respect or love us.

Inference chaining

The notion of inference chaining is defined by Moore (1983) as a therapist-initiated inquiry based on 'Then what?' and 'Why?' questions. Clearly this owes a significant debt to the Socratic method, However, Moore adopts this within Ellis' model to enable the therapist and client to identify the most relevant inference and how these might 'chain' together.

This model is developed further by Neenan and Dryden (1996), who introduce the notion of the 'critical A'. This is the activating event that leads directly to the emotional consequence, or C. Inference chaining is therefore the process by which therapists uses the Socratic probing-type method to enable clients to identify personally significant inferences about an event which are linked to establish the critical A (or adversity) that activates irrational beliefs which then directly leads to the emotional consequence.

Client: (crying) I don't know why I'm so upset but I just hate it when mum starts...

Therapist: What did your mum say that leads to you being so upset?

Client: (crying) I know it's silly to get so upset even in here...

Therapist: And what happens when mum starts?

Client: Well she gets angry that I've not done the housework, then she shouts and if I try to show that I have done stuff she says I'm just trying to vie for attention with my brother.

Therapist: We've discussed that your mum can be very declarative in her anger before. Do you think it's possible that she tends to say things in the heat of the moment that she doesn't actually believe in reality?

Client: (crying more) Well, she says it, and I'm frightened that she probably means it.

Therapist: And...

Client: (crying) That's horrible, for my mum to think things like that about me!

Therapist: Again, does the fact that she says something, no matter how horrid, mean that this is actually what she thinks of you? Or is it possible that she might actually be saying something as the result of her own stress, at work for example?

Client: Well, yes....

Therapist: I'm just noticing that you also mentioned something very important about this. Let's think about how you feel about your mum seeing you as vying for her attention?

Client: I feel hurt because I try so hard and he does virtually nothing but, more importantly, I feel rotten because that's my mother saying that.

Therapist: And...

Client: No one's mother should say that about them.

Inference chaining, like any other therapeutic technique or process, is a skill and consequently is liable to mistakes, which Neenan and Dryden (1996) helpfully describe. These include inadvertently strengthening the association between the adversity and consequence (reinforcing A–C thinking), therapists engaging in the disputation of inferences as opposed to correctly identifying the irrational beliefs to emerge and consequently confusing the client. Other errors include shifting the focus of the session between one emotion and another before the first has been effectively worked through and terminating the process of inference chaining too early.

The CBTs advocate a range of methods to assist clients to retrieve 'hot' cognitions about the A and thereby move closer to the adversity or the critical A, for example, Rational Emotive Imagery (REI). So there you are in the pub, with all of your friends, and your husband calls you 'stupid'. Now what's anger-producing in your mind about that?

One clear difference within the CBT cannon is the potential for therapists to dispute the inferences ('What evidence do you have?') as opposed to following along the inference to enable the client to ascertain the critical point and, consequently, the belief that is most associated with the disturbance.

Consider a client who reports feeling distressed in response to a situation in which her husband behaves in an insensitive and devaluing manner towards her.

Therapist: What provokes anger in you about your husband speaking to you in this way in front of your friends?

Client: He shouldn't do that!

Therapist: And if he does, which you suggest is a fairly regular occurrence, what would be the element that results in most anger for you?

Client: Other people will also think I am stupid.

Therapist: Can I just clarify why they might think you're stupid?

Client: For allowing myself to be treated like that by him … and that I am just stupid anyway.

Therapist: For argument's sake, let's assume that your friends do think you're stupid. Why would you make yourself angry about that?

Client: Well, I suppose I'd feel hurt, upset.

Therapist: And what would you be hurt about?

Client: I don't want my friends to think I'm stupid. I want them to understand my point of view. That it's not right for my husband to speak to me like that.

Therapist: (*being provocative*) How would you feel if they don't understand your position?

Client: I'd feel horrible… stupid … ashamed.

Therapist: What would you be ashamed about?

Client: That I'd shown myself up as weak, incompetent ….no good. I guess that is what upsets me most.

Therapist: I suggest that we tackle this first then.

Homework and the CBTs

A common theme in the CBTs is the explicit use of between-session structured activities, often rather unfortunately labelled 'homework'. Typical to the CBTs, clients undertake these tasks in anticipation of the next appointment and then use the activities (e.g. thought diaries) to inform the content of the following session. In addition, this forms a basis upon which clients can begin the process of behavioural experimentation or rehearsal *in vivo* of new ways of responding to potentially challenging situations.

Contrary to the common misconception, this is not an extension of the 'teacher–pupil' model of CBT. Rather, it is a reflection of somewhat clumsy terminology. No effective CBT therapist would 'set' or impose homework on a client but would work with the client to agree that some work between the sessions would be useful.

Homework from a person-centred perspective

A person-centred therapist would never 'set' homework, but might actively encourage a client to think about how they might choose to continue to work on their issues between sessions. An example might be something like the following:

The client begins the session by recounting the story of all the things that have happened to him since the previous session....

Counsellor:	I'm getting a sense that every week you come here and just tell me what has happened for and to you since we last met. I don't get any sense of you reflecting on or thinking about the things that came up last time we met.
Client:	Well, yes, I suppose I don't think about it much. I don't seem to have the time to do that.
Counsellor:	That feels to me like life just keeps getting in the way and you don't feel that it is important to carry on working on things till you see me next time. Is that how it is for you?
Client:	Well... yes... that's just about how it is.
Counsellor:	And you really want things to change?
Client:	Yes, I do.
Counsellor:	Well, I feel a bit concerned about that. It feels like you think that just by coming to see everything will change. It feels like you're expecting me to wave a magic wand?
Client:	Mmmm.....
Counsellor:	I really understand how pressurised you are by all the things that go on in your life and I guess it might feel pretty scary to just stop and think about what went on in our last session... like you really just want things to change.
Client:	Yes, that's just about it, I suppose....

Counsellor: Well, I don't know if you realise that there are 168 hours in a week and you are spending just one of those hours working with me and not doing any work on yourself in the other 167 hours. (*Pauses*)....

I guess you can choose to carry on doing that and I suspect that if you do, nothing much is going to change. Or you could choose to begin to do some work on yourself during some of those hours, even if you only reflect on how the last session was and what came up for you in it. I wonder how you feel about choosing to do something like that?

Client: Instead of just sitting back and waiting for it to happen, you mean?

Counsellor: I'm not telling you to do it, just wondering if you might find it helpful.

Client: Well, I could give it a go ...

It seems unlikely that a person-centred therapist would ever call this homework, but would be more likely to describe this as finding a way to get the client to engage and take responsibility for themselves and stop being dependent on the counsellor to make change happen. In reality, it also sounds like enabling the client to choose to do some homework! In this case it seems to us that there is enough evidence of a non-directive attitude in the therapist.

A link to the next chapter

In the next chapter we will explore the underpinning theories and consider points of dissonance and complementarity.

Recommended reading

Ellis, A. (2001) *New Directions for Rational-Emotive Behaviour Therapy: Overcoming Destructive Beliefs, Feelings, and Behaviours*. New York: Prometheus.

Kirschenbaum, H. (2007) *The Life and Work of Carl Rogers*. Ross-on-Wye: PCCS Books.

Robertson, D. (2010) *The Philosophy of Cognitive Behavioural Therapy (CBT): Stoic Philosophy as Rational and Cognitive Psychotherapy*. London: Karnac.

Rogers, C.R. (1961) *On Becoming a Person: A Therapist's View of Psychotherapy*. London: Constable (especially, pp. 132–155).

Yankura, J. & Dryden, W. (1994) *Albert Ellis: Key Figures in Counselling and Psychotherapy*. London: Sage.

CHAPTER 4

THE UNDERPINNING THEORIES: DISSONANCE AND COMPLEMENTARITY

In this chapter we will set out to provide a description of some of the underpinning theories of the two approaches, focusing on the authors' perspectives on the main areas of dissonance and complementarity. These will include, among others, rationality versus irrationality, unconditional positive regard versus unconditional self-acceptance, actualisation versus the self-actualising process, directiveness versus a non-directive attitude, necessary and sufficient versus necessary and not sufficient, introjected values versus core beliefs, techniques versus integrated conditions, teaching versus enabling learning, and challenge versus disputation. We will also include some brief examples from our practice as therapists to illuminate our understanding of similarities and differences.

We began our thinking process about the content of this chapter with a phenomenological noticing that we had used the word 'versus' in our desire to identify dissonance and complementarity between the two approaches. We recognised that this could imply a hidden attitude of assumed polemic that motivates a search for what is unique about 'my' approach and 'his' approach, and therefore what makes mine better! Being aware of this, we chose to write this chapter as a dialogue between us, and in this way we seek to describe our individual perceptions of the differences in certain features of the two approaches and avoid making any value judgements.

Fundamental irrationality – exquisite rationality

Hjelle and Ziegler (1992) developed a continuous bipolar dimensional model of nine basic assumptions concerning human nature (see Figure 4.1).

Ziegler applied this to REBT and has subsequently further developed his analysis (Ziegler, 2000, 2002, 2003), suggesting that the differences between the practice of REBT, psychoanalysis and PCA is based on three basic differences in the conceptualisation of 'client personality'. In his 2002 paper, he argues that this relates to a nature versus nurture construction of personality. From the therapist's perspective, the extent to which clients respond is a function of their

Freedom–Determinism	How much internal freedom do people have and how much are they determined by external and internal (e.g. biological) factors?
Rationality–Irrationality	To what extent are people primarily rational, directing themselves through reason, or to what extent are they guided by irrational factors?
Holism–Elementalism	To what extent are people best comprehended as a whole or to what extent by being broken down into their constituent parts?
Constitutionalism–Environmentalism	To what extent are people the result of constitutional factors and to what extent are they products of environmental influences?
Changeability–Unchangeablity	To what extent are people capable of fundamental change over time?
Subjectivity–Objectivity	To what extent are people influenced by subjective factors and to what extent by external, objective factors?
Proactivity–Reactivity	To what extent do people generate their behaviour internally (proactivity) and to what extent do they respond to external stimuli (reactivity)?
Homeostasis–Heterostasis	To what extent are humans motivated primarily to reduce tensions and maintain an inner homeostasis and to what extent are they motivated to actualise themselves?
Knowability–Unknowability	To what extent is human nature fully knowable?

FIGURE 4.1   *Assumptions about human nature*

Source: Dryden, W. (2009) *Skills in Rational Emotive Behaviour Counselling & Psychotherapy*. London: Sage.

unique constitutional makeup or the result of environmental forces which represent a significant theoretical and practical issue. Ziegler (2002: 76–91) argues that psychodynamic and PCA theories are 'moderately constitutionalist' regarding personality in terms of biology and that environment only makes an influence in very early formative experiences. He argues that Rogers 'also appears moderately committed to constitutionalism' and cites his use of the term 'human nature', 'man's inner nature', 'man's true self' and 'man's innate potential' as indicative of a biological base of human personality and development. Ziegler makes his final point that it is in the concept of the actualising tendency where Rogers' constitutionalism is most obvious, and again he suggests that within PCA the environment is considered as early experience and internalising of the reference of others. With regard to REBT, Ziegler suggests that this is strongly constitutionalist and the constructs of 'rational' versus 'irrational' thinking, which are conceptualised as largely biologically based and therefore the related 'real' causes of human disturbance, are largely innate. It is of note that Ellis (2000) also suggests a philosophical problem with conceptualisations of early environmental impact in as much as this actually provides further evidence, in his view, of the biological nature of this: 'only a special, innately predisposed kind of person would be so prone to be environmentally determined' (Ellis, 2000: 205).

The second crucial aspect Ziegler suggests is the ways in which the different theories conceptualise the potency of reason in human behaviour. Ziegler makes a tantalising comparison between Psychodynamic, PCA and REBT with regard to the constitutional position of each, suggesting that the Psychodynamic position is negative while the PCA is essentially positive, whereas he considers the REBT position to be a balance of the positive and negative with a tendency to 'reindoctrinate themselves' by irrationality. From this point, and initially somewhat surprisingly, he argues that REBT places humans at a mid-point with regard to irrationality, referencing Ellis' assertion that humans are 'uniquely rational, as well as a uniquely irrational' (Ellis, 1962: 36). He then argued that humans possess a 'duality of rationality and irrationality'. Zeigler suggests that this provides REBT with a distinct theoretical advantage over the more extreme positions of psychodynamic thinking, which construct the individual as strongly irrational and at the mercy of the unconscious (and manifestly irrational) forces, whereas the PCA considers humans to be strongly rational and 'eminently capable of directing their behavior through reason' (Ziegler, 2002: 82). Indeed, Rogers referred to rationality and the actualising tendency as 'inextricably interwoven'. Finally, in regard to the possibility of fundamental personality change, Zeigler asserts that both PCA and REBT present a very optimistic conceptualisation of the possibility and capacity for change whereas psychodynamic theory does not.

Within the CBTs there is an *a priori* assumption, whether stated or otherwise, that human perception of 'self' and 'the world' (other people, events, etc.) is prone to idiosyncratic distortions or irrational beliefs. Indeed, the body of psychological literature has repeatedly demonstrated the fallibility of human perception and judgement, a condition which is both marvellous (in regard to our capacity to conclude based on very limited or degraded information) and seriously undermining (in regard to our capacity to arrive at erroneous conclusions based on limited, flawed or no evidence whatsoever).

In attempting to achieve a reasonable definition of irrationality from the perspective of the CBTs, we have tried to identify the essence of this concept. Given the previous insight regarding the flawed nature of human perception, irrationality is, therefore, a fundamental human tendency that exists without recognition of the capacity for choice that humans have in *how* we exist. Although not clearly stated by all of the CBTs, this is supported by both the vast background of psychological research unconnected to psychological therapy or psychopathology and that operating from necessarily flawed assumptions that relate to the value of the self, others or the world which will result in the experience of distress. Furthermore, methods to avoid or negate circumstances that might expose these assumptions to challenge or dispute are likely to be avoided as the distress associated with this is likely to be feared as being too great to bear.

For the CBTs there is another dimension which is, ironically, the logically necessary converse to this. Counter to this irrational tendency towards disturbance, there is a fundamental capacity for rationality in all humans. All of the CBTs work from the assumptions that human beings have an innate tendency towards perceiving the world and relationships in ways that reflect their thinking, regardless of whether or not their thinking is positive. Inevitably this reasoning does not reflect 'the truth' or 'reality' and leads to the belief that human beings are basically irrational. There are some subtle differences in the expression of this philosophical position between different theoreticians within the CBTs. For instance, Meichenbaum (1977) applied the behavioural and cognitive models to a therapeutic approach that relied upon the monitoring of 'inner speech' and Young (1990) identified early maladaptive schemas that lead to the use of maladaptive coping strategies. These are challenged in therapy in order that clients are encouraged to experience the use of the emotional responses that subvert their capacity to change. Both Meichenbaum and Young are clinical psychologists, as was Ellis, and are strongly reliant upon behavioural and cognitive experimental psychology, whereas Beck (1967, 1972, 1975), a psychiatrist by training, worked from a pathology model yet integrated empirical research into his framework *a posteriori*. Ironically, neither Meichenbaum, Young nor Beck declared that philosophical foundation, although it is nonetheless present as an underpinning assumption within their thinking.

The ABC model initially developed by Ellis has been, in large part, adopted or applied by almost all of the CBTs, albeit in different guises. Again, it was Ellis who succinctly identified and classified the important milestones of therapeutic change that follow from a client comprehending the model. Indeed, Ellis (2003) proposed what he referred to as the three major insights of REBT. First, that the acknowledgement and acceptance of the reality that emotional disturbances at point C only partially stem from the events or adversities at point A. Therefore, while the A contributes to the C, the more direct causal source of extreme emotional disturbances at C remain the irrational beliefs at B. Secondly, that it does not matter how or when these irrational beliefs are acquired. If people are currently disturbed, they have a tendency to maintain these beliefs and therefore perpetuate their disturbance by this process. The maintenance of disturbance has little to do with the historic development of the irrational belief. Rather, that people continue to hold these irrational beliefs in the present, although often implicitly and often not attended to, and therefore continue to reaffirm them by behaving and emoting as if these beliefs are valid and true. Thirdly, that insight into the irrational nature of these beliefs, no matter how elegant or convincing, will rarely enable people to counteract their disturbed emotional responses. Therefore it is essential to maintain awareness and engage in creative, robust disputation of these irrational beliefs, challenging unhealthy extreme emotional reactions and firmly addressing fear and avoidance.

It is only by the adoption of a persistent, combined cognitive, emotive and behavioural approach to addressing emotional problems that the client can move from their disturbed position, unable to contemplate or achieve change, to a point where change can begin to occur. Although not explicitly clear within many of the basic books on the CBTs, basic irrationality is rarely defined. However, there are some glimpses and Ellis (2002: 81) wrote that human beings 'have innate and learned self-defeating tendencies that interfere with their constructive abilities'.

It may be that an implicit complementary aspect of the canon of the CBTs, similar to that of the PCA, is that there is a balance of forces between energy (valuing tendency, rational, functional, healthy) and decline (entropy, irrationality, dysfunctional, unhealthy).

Rogers' approach to the study of persons is phenomenological and idiographic, his view of human behaviour is that it is 'exquisitely rational' (Rogers, 1961: 194). Furthermore, in his opinion: 'the core of man's nature is essentially positive' (1961: 73), and he is a 'trustworthy organism' (1977: 7). These beliefs are reflected in his theory of personality, outlined in the 19 propositions presented in Chapter 2.

● ● ● *Examples from our practice* ● ● ●

From Roger:

Tina, a young woman in her late twenties, was struggling with the pressures of coping with a new baby (Jake) and getting anxiety attacks which were quite debilitating. She didn't want to go on any medication, so her GP had referred her to see if counselling would help. For several weeks I worked hard with her, focusing strongly on getting an accurate understanding of how she experienced her anxiety and enabling her to feel heard and understood. During the next session she began to talk about having a severe anxiety attack the evening before, which she said had been caused by her mother during a telephone call with her.

Tina: I was telling Mum that I had decided I was going to start bottle feeding Jake because I was getting fed up with all the breast feeding nonsense. Mum shouted that I was a silly girl, that it was a stupid idea, that it would harm Jake and I shouldn't be so selfish. I should go on breast feeding him as long as I could. I was furious with her, treating me like a little girl, telling me what to do. He's my baby and I'll decide what is best for him. How dare she tell me it would be harmful to him? I slammed the phone down on her and right away started to have a really bad panic attack and it was all her fault!

Roger: I can really hear how angry and upset you are about how your Mum treated you. It sounds like you felt like she was treating you just like a little girl and not giving you any respect as a mother yourself. I'm wondering if you felt really criticised and especially about being accused of doing something that would harm Jake? .... I guess I can really understand you feeling that way, especially as Jake means so much to you. Was it like she was invading your territory as a mum?

Tina: (*very forcefully*) Yes, that's it exactly. He's my baby and it's not her place to tell me what to do and make me have a panic attack!

Roger: (*responding quietly with a quizzical look on my face*) So – you're saying that your Mum *made* you have a panic attack? (*with an emphasis on the 'made'*)

Tina: (*after a brief silence, sitting back in her chair*) That's silly, isn't it? She can't possibly 'make' me have a panic attack.

Roger sits waiting silently as she reflects on what she has just said.......

Tina: You know, it wasn't until I heard you say what I had said, that I realised how irrational it was…….. I am angry with her though!

Roger: (*responding quietly and tentatively*) Still really angry with her for treating you like she did – and realising that she didn't 'make' you have the panic attack?

Tina: Mmmm, I suppose she didn't make me angry either, I just did that to myself.

This, for me, is an example of acceptingly restating what the client has said, enabling her to discover her own exquisite irrationality for herself. This approach is much more effective for me, I think, than pointing out her irrationality to her!

From Jeremy:

Jenni experienced significant difficulties with anxiety and jealous feelings about her former partner which eventually led to the end of the marriage. She then commenced a new relationship and subsequently married. The decision to attend therapy followed an increase in angry feelings about the potential for her husband to leave her. From her description, this resulted in interrogative behaviour, angry outbursts and this has increased her concern that this marriage might also end. At this point Jenni is suggesting that her husband causes her anger.

Jeremy: It seems to me that the issue is, then, not how your husband behaves, or indeed doesn't behave. It makes little difference as these assumptions are part of your thinking.

Jenni: Well, yes I suppose.

Jeremy: I've explained to you before that this kind of therapy acknowledges that what we assume is driven by our beliefs, and that it is these that give rise to strong distressing emotions.

Jenni: Like my anger and hurt you mean?

Jeremy: Yes, considering the last example. When I asked you to slightly shift the inference you drew from the available information, your conclusion was different and you predicted that you might feel very different.

Jenni: Well, yes... but I don't believe it though!

Jeremy: I understand that. However, this way of thinking about your thinking is new to you. Also, I guess that the really important thing is not whether your husband has noticed an attractive woman, though. If that didn't matter to you, then you might notice that he was looking at another woman and maybe think he found her attractive.

Jenni: But he's married to me... he shouldn't be looking elsewhere. I should be enough for him!

Jeremy: And if you hold that belief, then how are you likely to feel if you believe that he has been looking at another woman?

Jenni: Bloody furious!... What a bastard!

Jeremy: I wonder how you would feel if you believed that, **ideally** he shouldn't look at other women, but if he did it wouldn't be a hanging offence? Would you still think he was a bastard?

Jenni: (*laughing*) Well... I'd probably still feel irritated but I guess not; and no, he's not really a bastard...which is why I end up feeling so bad.

Jeremy: Remember when I suggested about the way you interpret what happens when you see an attractive woman? You assume that your husband has seen her, is attracted to her and then attempts to conceal his attraction from you ....because he's going to have an affair.

Jenni: Yes, suppose it sounds a bit silly when you put it like that...

Jeremy: Well, perhaps we could use a less judgemental word... like irrational? A striking feature of humans is that they have a great capacity for thinking, particularly for identifying links between things.

Jenni: Like that... I'm not very good at it then!

Jeremy: And neither are humans in general... Research tells us that humans are not good at understanding cause and effect. Often we assume one event has caused a reaction. In this case you assume that your husband claiming that he has not noticed an attractive woman has caused you to be angry whereas it seems that it is what you assume that he is thinking. Something that you have decided he simply **should not do** which gives rise to your anger.

In this segment I encourage Jenni to integrate key aspects of the model and experience the potential impact of changing her thinking on her experiencing and emotions in the safety of the therapy session. Furthermore, her inferences about her husband's potential infidelity are linked to an implicit theory she holds about herself and that it is this which amplifies the potency of her inferences as opposed to the events she perceives.

Actualisation and self-actualising

Although the concept of actualisation is most often attributed to Maslow, it is actually derived from Kurt Goldstein, a Jewish-German psychiatrist who first developed the term (Goldstein, 1939). Rogers and Maslow were both influenced by Goldstein. Maslow, in particular, studied what he considered to be exemplary people and was critical of generalising from studies of abnormal functioning which suggested that 'the study of crippled, stunted, immature, and unhealthy specimens can yield only a cripple psychology and a cripple philosophy' (Maslow, 1954: 236).

Maslow defined actualisation as the process through which 'a man can be what he must be'. It is about the realisation of the individual's potential or the desire to become everything that one is capable of becoming. As conceptualised within this framework, actualisation is a process, leading to a state which can be achieved, with which the CBTs would concur. However, Maslow and his works are not without their critics, not least by those who consider his ideas to be strongly ethnographic in nature.

Rogers' view of actualisation was slightly different from Maslow's. As Casemore (2011: 19) states, 'Rogers referred instead to the "actualising tendency", which he believed was the principle basic tendency in all human beings, the tendency to want to become the self that one truly is, rather than the self that others want us to be.'

Maslow and Rogers both drew close parallels between Maslow's self-actualising person, whose most basic drive was the desire to become all that one is capable of becoming, and Rogers' fully-functioning person, whose basic drive was to become the person that one truly is.

Rogers believed that the actualising tendency could be inhibited but could never be destroyed, except by death, and that it was directed only towards positive objectives, to enable the individual to function to the best of their ability in whatever conditions they might find themselves. He suggested that the actualising tendency in human beings was the drive towards becoming more fully functioning. Another significant difference between Maslow and Rogers was that Maslow believed that self-actualisation was a state that could actually be achieved whereas Rogers believed that self-actualisation was a process with a continuing potential for further growth that could only be terminated by death.

Potentially, a naïve and rudimentary application of the concept of self-actualisation can be Pollyanna-ish, whereas the CBTs enact a more active-pragmatic approach and require practice and effort in order to maintain change. Indeed, Ellis (2002: 82) wrote, 'A major goal of REBT and CBT, therefore, is to have clients solidly achieve a basic philosophy of effort.' As such, self-actualisation follows from a process that is dynamic and requires a philosophical and behavioural change as insight alone will do little to achieve this. To a certain extent and purpose, actualisation becomes more likely after a profound change in belief that is followed by a change in emotion and behaviour.

Ellis considered that self-actualisation represented achieving, and *not merely endorsing*, a fully functioning sense of self that participates in an active actualisation process. He referred to this as a 'philosophy of effort' which requires active disputation of absolutist *shoulds* and *musts*, changing *requiring* beliefs and statements to *preferring* ones (sometimes referred to as *should* musts versus *want* musts). As such, it is necessary to develop a tolerance both for the self and others and also life conditions in general. Ellis argued that shifts in these basic beliefs would then enable the individual to overcome the tendency to engage in procrastination and by increasing a tolerance to frustration in which demands are not met.

Rogers would maintain that this is about the client having the right to choose or not choose to be different. The therapist's function was to enable the client to identify the choices open to them and not to be in any way directive about how the client should be.

For the CBTs, it is therefore necessary to reframe some problems as things that can be either solved or not solved and moving from dichotomy to a point where ambiguity, paradox, inconsistency, confusion are accepted as simply being part of the world. These are contained in Ellis' principles of responsible hedonism and were described in Chapter 3.

● ● ● *Examples from practice* ● ● ●

From Jeremy:

I often provide hand-outs to summarise the content of sessions with clients to give them an *aide-mémoire* of the theory but also to assist them in developing and integrating the theory into their own lives, so that it can become integrated into their language and therefore they can become more adept at using the theory. Dave and I had worked together for about eight sessions and I had given him my summary 'responsible hedonism' and a copy of Richard Wessler's irrational diagonal (see Figure 4.2) which he reported was useful. Dave was concerned about the direction that his life was going in. He had suffered from a lack of confidence for many years and believed that this had undermined his capacity to achieve a sufficiently high status in life. Dave attributed his lack of a relationship and general life dissatisfaction to this.

Jeremy: Remember when we talked about linking feeling good about yourself with either success or someone else providing you with positive feedback?

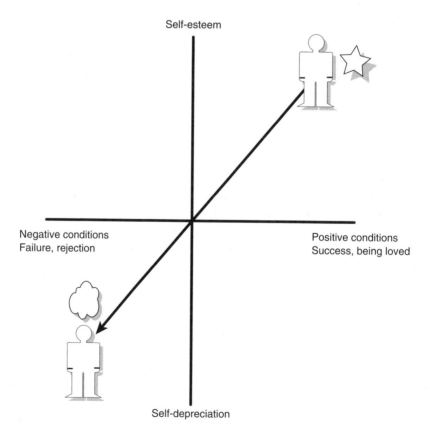

FIGURE 4.2   *Richard Wessler's irrational diagonal (from Walen, DiGiuseppe & Dryden, 1992, p. 200)*

Responsible Hedonism Summary Self-actualisation Handout

Achieving, *not merely endorsing*, a fully functioning sense of self

- Actively choosing self-actualisation
- Disputing absolutist *shoulds* and *musts* that block the achievement of actualising
- Preferring, *not requiring*, solving self-actualisation problems
- Tolerating self and others
- Overcoming procrastination and low frustration tolerance
- Framing problems as something to be redesigned and either solved or not solved
- Moving from either/ors towards and/ors, including ambiguity, paradox, inconsistency, confusion, etc., and then 'pushing' towards an integrated wholeness.

Acceptance of uncertainty
In general, absolute certainties do not exist; one can strive for a degree of order, but not demand complete predictability.

Contentment
Most people tend to be happier when vitally absorbed in something outside themselves. At least one strong creative interest and some significant interpersonal involvement seem to provide structure for a happy daily existence.

Risk-taking
Being prepared to take risks and have a spirit of adventurousness in trying to do what you want to do, without being foolhardy.

Realistic expectations
Accepting that it is unlikely we will get everything we want or avoid everything we find painful and therefore not wasting time striving for the unattainable or for unrealistic perfection.

Self-acceptance
Freely deciding to accept oneself unconditionally (i.e. *I am human, have faults and that is OK*), rather than to measure, rate or try to prove oneself.

High frustration tolerance
Recognising that there are two sorts of problems that are likely to be encountered: those with, and those without, solutions. The goal is to modify the conditions that can be changed and learn to tolerate those that cannot.

Self-responsibility
Accepting responsibility for your own thoughts, feelings and behaviours rather than blaming others, the world or fate for distress.

FIGURE 4.3   *Responsible hedonism summary self-actualisation handout*

Dave: Yeah... I do try not to but it sort of creeps up.

Jeremy: And I guess that receiving compliments from other people feels nice?

Dave: Hell yeah!

Jeremy: And there is a difference between acknowledging that someone has given you clear praise and assuming that because they didn't you aren't praiseworthy.

Dave: Yes, I mean I went out with an old mate last night to see a band. He introduced me to some of his other mates and I felt really awkward and didn't really say much. Just stood around and had a drink until the band came on. I was really surprised afterwards when he told me they thought I was a really nice bloke…

Jeremy: And why do you think that was?

Dave: I assumed they thought I was a loser… a twat.

Jeremy: And they didn't think that.

Dave: No. I wish I was able to think that at the time though 'cause I'd probably have a better time. I ended up feeling pretty foolish and down, and then thought, well, I'm going to experience this from time to time… to be honest, I sometimes hear your voice saying 'it's about really beginning to accept that you will make mistakes… and that is OK; maybe not desirable … but certainly not catastrophic!'

Jeremy: And remember, that's what you're working on.

In this segment I reiterate central elements of the philosophy to assist Dave in his practice outside the sessions and emphasise the progress he is clearly making. I also wish to communicate that I understand that this is a difficult process which requires active participation in developing towards an actualised state.

From Roger:

Bill, a 44-year-old businessman, had been coming to see me because he wanted to stop feeling stressed and out of control. He had presented originally as feeling full of despair about not being able to change the way he was feeling and very scared that if he didn't, he would have a total breakdown and ruin his business and his life. We had worked together very effectively for just over a year and he really seemed to have begun to make some significant changes in himself and in his life.

At the next session he began by saying a bit nervously:

Bill: You know, I don't think I need to come any more. I know I have changed in lots of ways and I'm not scared of having a breakdown and ruining everything any more. I've learned that I have got choices in how I am and how I respond to pressure. After our last session I also realised that even if I do get worse in the future and have a breakdown, I can survive it. It won't ruin everything. It won't destroy me. I'll always have choices of being different and responding differently.

Roger: That sounds like you've made some really big learnings about yourself and how you have changed. It also sounds like you've learned that the best person to help you is you and that you feel more confident about that. You feel you really have grown and I get a sense of that too.

Bill: (*quite strongly*) Yes, that's it…… (*then rather more tentatively*) but can I check that I could come back and see you again if I needed to?

Roger: That sounds like you know that you have changed, you are OK with that…. And at the same time you are wondering about changing in the future…..?

Bill: Yes, will I carry on 'growing' as you put?

Roger: Well, I guess that is mainly up to you and it sounds like you want to take a rest from that for the moment, until you are ready to do some more changing?

Bill: Yes,…. that sounds about right. I've done a lot of changing and now I need to take a rest. I might even fall back a bit but I can choose when I want to do some more work and start changing again.

This seems to me like a good example of my understanding of the process of self-actualisation. For me, it is not a state that can be achieved, but a process that will always need to be worked at. I am concerned about what I see as the 'tyranny of self-actualisation'. That it is like an exponential curve from being dysfunctional to being fully self-actualised. I prefer to think of the process of change interrupted by what I term 'periods of punctuated equilibrium'. It's rather like a series of staircases and landings. My client climbs the first flight of stairs, growing and changing. He then reaches a landing where he can stop, rest, reinforce and stabilise with some equilibrium, before attempting the next phase of change – the next staircase. He may fall back a few steps, as Bill puts it. He can then choose to begin to work at growing and changing again if he wants to. It is not my place as a therapist to put any pressure on him to always be changing and growing.

Directiveness versus a non-directive attitude

All of the CBTs work from the premise that the beliefs or thinking styles employed by humans are over-learned, over-generalised, yet are not adaptive to the demands of life and the environment in which we exist. As such, the extent to which humans experience disturbed emotions follows from the extent to which thinking or beliefs are maladaptive or irrational. Given that this is the case, the CBTs take the approach that therapy requires *more* than passive listening to the client's account and has a clear rationale. As the client remains active in their endorsement of their beliefs and thought processes, this will not only characterise their account of events. Also, the disturbance is precisely why they seek out therapy, and consequently an active-directive approach enables the therapist to begin to guide the client to the source of their difficulties. Providing clients with the ABC model of emotional causality enables them to develop an understanding of the link between their thinking processes and emotional and behavioural responses to this.

From a Person-centred perspective, Rogers was clearly opposed to the notion of intentional directionality by the therapist. While he originally used the term 'non-directive', he later refuted this and instead used the term 'client centred'. Rogers was clear that the term 'non-directive' was dropped because it was misunderstood and maligned, leading to distortions of the approach. He did not use the term after the publication of his book *Client-Centred Therapy* (Rogers, 1951). He used 'non-directive' interchangeably with 'client-centred' for a few pages in this book and then dropped the term altogether. Client-centred and non-directive were presented and left as synonymous terms and his view of non-directivity was later clarified by him in an interview with Evans (1978). Evans asked Rogers:

> Would you say today that you have perhaps qualified somewhat this notion of being non-directive? (1978: 26)

Rogers replied:

> No. I think perhaps I enriched it, but not really qualified it. I still feel that the person who should guide the client's life is the client. My whole philosophy and whole approach is to try to strengthen him in that way of being, that he's in charge of his own life and nothing that I say is intended to take that capacity or that opportunity away from him. (1978: 26)

Non-directivity is defined by Rogers as referring to the central notion that it is the person who should guide her or his own life. In one of his last statements, Rogers (in Baldwin, 1987) cited the suitable goals for the therapist as revolving around the question, 'Am I really with this person at this moment?' (1987: 48). Due to the centrality of the term to the theory, it is important to delineate non-directivity as integrally related to Rogers' theory. It is not, however, Rogers' intentions concerning the term that argue for the non-directive component of person-centred therapy. It is implicit in the theory! It is also important to remember that Rogers was not suggesting being totally non-directive, but rather that the therapist should have a generally non-directive attitude.

The principal canon of Person-centred theory which governs the non-directive nature of the approach is that there is an internal force – the drive to become more fully functioning – in each individual and this is the motivational force for change. This force is always constructive and directed towards developing the potential of the individual. This force is promoted by the client's experiencing of the three central conditions. It is clear that there are no directive intentions to instruct, guide or direct in Person-centred Therapy. Such intentions are antithetical to the theory. The therapist creates an atmosphere of freedom in the client–therapist relationship by embodying the facilitative attitudes and by trusting the natural developmental direction of the client, rather than giving direction to the client. So, the Person-centred therapist needs to have a non-directive or facilitative attitude rather than being implicitly directive.

● ● ● *Examples from practice* ● ● ●

From Roger:

June had been coming to see me for several months, struggling with feelings of inadequacy and of being a failure. She seemed to be really driven to achieve a senior executive position in management in a private sector company, despite regularly making a mess of managing people. Her father had been a chief executive and she seemed desperate to emulate him.

I had explored with her my sense of her 'drivenness' and she had identified where it came from. She had explored the ways in which her father had subtly communicated that she ought to follow in his footsteps and even become his successor.

June: He often tells me he has a dream of handing his job over to me – that I could take it on even further. He follows that up by telling me I've got to be tougher, really prepared to make people do what I want, really take control of my life. I didn't get the senior manager's job last week and he was really cross with me. He said if I didn't get my act together I'd end up with nothing, being a secretary, or out of work, or just looking after some man. As far as he is concerned, I've got to be just like him. I really wish I could be. I'd like the money he earns and the status he has but I don't think I can do it.

Roger: That sounds like you feel you have no choice, that he is the one who is driving you. He has this idea of who and how you should be.

June: Yes, that's just how it is. I know I'm not like him. I don't think I can be so I'm bound to be a failure to him.

Roger: Again, what I hear is your belief that you have no choice. You feel trapped and very uncomfortable with trying to be how he wants you to be. A part of you wants to please him so that he will love and respect you and another part of you knows that you can't be like that. Is that how it is?

June: Yes, I really am trapped.

Roger: Mmmm… I know that is what you feel and yet I have difficulty in believing that. It seems to me that you are choosing to be trapped because you are so desperate for his love and respect and choosing to believe that you have no choice in the matter.

June: Mmmm… yes….

Roger: Well… I know that feeling of being trapped is pretty scary and I don't believe what you believe is true. I believe that each of us can choose who and how we want to be. We don't have to accept what someone else believes about who and how we should be, because that is about them.

(June looks at me quietly, a little puzzled expression on her face)

Roger: I want to make it clear that I am not saying you should or must choose for yourself who and how you want to be. What I am saying is that I believe that you could choose to not be who and how your Dad wants you to be. I guess you would have to live with the consequences of that and you might not be prepared to do that.

June: I don't think I'm prepared to do that. It would be so hard to take the risk of him not loving me or him believing that I am a failure.

Roger: I guess I'm a little sad that you are choosing to remain trapped in this way and I really am OK with you making that choice.

June: Yes… Well, at least I realise now that I have got a choice and it is mine and nobody else's.

June ended therapy eventually without ever resolving that issue. I felt quite frustrated with her choosing to stay in the trap created by her father's introjections and injunctions. At the same time, it seemed really important for me, from a Person-centred perspective, to really avoid being directive. However much I might think it would be good for her to change, it was important from an ethical perspective that I fully respected her autonomy.

From Jeremy:

I am very comfortable with the notion of being active-directive and conceptualise this as a core aspect of therapy given that, from my perspective, it is from the combination of insight and practice that change occurs. Clearly, clients do not attend therapy if they have been able to achieve and sustain insight alone. Steve is a man who has previously experienced bouts of low-level depression and has also avoided situations in which some of his self-damning beliefs can been challenged. As a result, he works to an excessive extent in a job that he believes does not tax him; he can resolve problems and 'smooth out' the problems. It became very clear that Steve spent an inordinate amount of time engaged in work activities to the exclusion of his social life. Indeed, he usually spent most of his weekends and leisure time monitoring emails in a state of heightened anxiety. In short, he is an avoider and acknowledges this in a way that acts as another hammer to beat himself with! We had been meeting for some time and had built up a positive therapeutic relationship. Although Steve had previously attempted some homework tasks, he reported that he found it difficult to make the transition between imaginal and behavioural exercises.

Steve: I never get a chance to relax, there's always so much to do.

Jeremy: How about the evenings or weekends?

Steve: I've always got things that need action… I always keep this wretched mobile on and make sure that I can access my email from at least two sources. (*Laughs*) Yes… silly, isn't it? I like to make sure that I've got a back-up… just in case.

Jeremy: Well, it clearly seems to be the case that you don't experience a time when you're not checking for work, so it is little wonder that you have created a significant concern about not completing something.

Steve: I'd go further… I get beside myself… really anxious. Isn't that ridiculous! That's something that I'd really like to work on! I mean, on Saturday mornings I even make a list of things I've got to do for work and then gradually work through this over the weekend…. I rarely finish them all and end up going in early on Monday!

Jeremy: I notice that you've taken the opportunity to give yourself a kick. However, I wonder if we can come back to that in a moment? Let's think about an active homework task that provides a relatively controlled yet real opportunity for you to experience the anxiety associated with not completing a task.

Steve: Uh oh, what are you thinking of…?

Jeremy: I am wondering that as we've discussed a significant component of the anxiety that you feel is fuelled by your assumption that it will be overwhelming. This seems to combine with your concern that other people will conclude that you're basically incompetent.

Steve: Yes, you're right!

Jeremy: Clearly, the 'Steve-can-never-relax-or-let-anyone-down' approach has had only limited effect.

Steve: You can say that again… in fact, it's been totally counter-productive!

Jeremy: Indeed, and we've already begun to dispute your assumption that not completing a task is tantamount to failing.

Steve: Yep…

Jeremy: And that other people will necessarily conclude that you're incompetent….

Steve: Yes, but that one's harder to really believe.

Jeremy: How about this as a homework assignment to really put this to the test: make a list of 'tasks' and then decide on half of these. These will be the ones you are not going to attempt to complete over the weekend.

Steve: Wow… I'm even anxious just thinking about that!

Jeremy: And that's the point of the exercise… notice what you're feeling and what you're saying to yourself. Exactly just how much awfulising are you doing?

Again, as I noted in the preamble, I am clearly being pretty directive in this segment and this is noticed by Steve in his use of humour. My intention in being quite so directive here is to galvanise him into stopping his higher-level avoidance behaviour. Clearly, this is a man who has very entrenched avoidance strategies!

Necessary and sufficient conditions – necessary but not sufficient

In the previous chapter we have outlined Rogers' (1956: 827–832) necessary and sufficient conditions, which he suggests are both 'definable and measurable' and 'those elements which are essential if psychotherapeutic change is to ensue'. Rogers argues for psychological contact between therapist and client and that the client is in 'a state of incongruence' while the therapist is 'congruent or integrated in the relationship'. Rogers suggests that the therapist 'experiences unconditional positive regard for the client' and 'an empathic understanding of the client's internal frame of reference and endeavours to communicate this experience to the client'. Finally, the therapist's empathic understanding and unconditional positive regard is communicated to the client at the very least to 'a minimal degree'. It is of note that Rogers is careful to state that these ideas are tentative, a hypothesis, which is open to being disproved.

From the fundamental position of the CBTs, it is clearly an interesting contention that a client should be in a state of incongruence, on the basis that our perception of, and consequently experience of, the world is intimately linked to a belief system which is prone to so many biases that this is, in the case of disturbed emotions and behaviours, an exaggeration of our natural state.

Returning to the first of Rogers' core conditions, he provides a very minimal, albeit challenging, notion that this is a relationship at some level between two people. Given that, at some level, this is a pivotal aspect in Rogers' argument for significant personality change, it is clearly possible that an individual may experience significant change in the absence of a therapeutic relationship, or indeed any relationship with another, for example the 'light-bulb' or 'eureka' moment. As such, it is desirable and to some extent necessary (if this is not an oxymoron). However, to argue that this is sufficient does not seem defensible.

In similar vein, while it is desirable that the therapist is congruent and integrated into the relationship and offers unconditional positive regard (UPR) and an empathic understanding of the client's frame of reference to the client, is it true that this is either necessary or, indeed, sufficient? If it is true that people are able to achieve significant positive and fundamental change in the absence of a relationship, then it cannot follow that intra-therapist conditions are necessary or sufficient. Bluntly, the evidence would suggest that change can occur without these and consequently they are not logically necessary *per se*. Rather, these are highly desirable and most likely contingently necessary for positive change in therapy. What is a less semantic issue, and possibly more critical to the therapeutic situation, is the issue that these are not sufficient *in and of themselves*. Most coherent research evidence indicates that a robust and positive relationship between client and therapist exists and that ruptures in this can undermine therapy. Indeed, this has given rise to a consideration of behaviours from the client designed to block therapeutic progress.

It is clear that people get better without therapy and sometimes despite poor therapy. From a person-centred perspective, it may be more accurate to state that the conditions for therapeutic growth are not necessarily necessary, but whenever they are present they are sufficient. This is well argued by Bozarth in *Beyond Carl Rogers* (Brazier, 1993).

For Ellis, at least, a more central issue relates to the notion and centrality of UPR from the therapist to the client in as much as this is likely to maintain an external source of self-evaluation as opposed to the development of a healthier unconditional positive self-acceptance.

● ● ● **Examples from practice** ● ● ●

From Jeremy:

I do not intend to provide a specific example of a session as such, rather a generalised sense drawn from experience over a considerable period of time. I had been working in a service for people who had committed serious offences and who were subject to significant restrictions to their liberty. As part of this they were required to undergo 'therapy' with a psychologist, whom they referred to as the 'head doctor' or 'trick cyclist'. Inevitably, motivation to attend sessions was a significant issue, but this also represented a very significant challenge as review of restrictions placed upon clients was dependent upon engaging in such work and gave rise to a culture within the service that some clients would simply learn to 'talk-the-talk but not walk-the-walk'. At times this developed into a culture of cynicism and suspicion, in which clients were extremely wary of being open as they considered that staff would deliberately interpret their responses as evidence that things had not changed.

Often clients would attend sessions presenting as very hostile and argumentative but would clearly respond by noting when they had acted upon either dogmatic or implicit assumptions about a given situation. Indeed, at times clients would state that they didn't like me because they believed that I was one of 'them' and that therefore I couldn't be trusted ... even if some of the things I said and suggested made sense and were helpful! Although it was an extreme environment, this represents, for me, the ultimate example of where I could offer the necessary components of a collaborative therapeutic relationship but it was the techniques and suggestions which the clients took from it that were important. I often reflect that, in such unusual environments, it is a significant demand indeed to place on a client that they can even begin to accept the most tentative of therapeutic relationships.

From Roger:

Jean was a mature woman, married with three grown-up children and several grandchildren, whom she spent a lot of time looking after so her daughters could work. They were constantly critical of her and could be quite cruel. Her husband suffered with MS and she increasingly had to take on the role of his carer as he became more disabled. She had recently experienced the loss of both her parents and was just waiting for the next thing to go wrong. She presented in a very depressed condition, feeling enormously stressed and full of despair that she couldn't go on in this way and fearful of what was going to happen next. I did not get any sense that she might be suicidal, just that she was worn out and exhausted.

We worked together for several months, in which time I focused on getting a real understanding of how she felt at various levels within herself, and communicating my unconditional acceptance of her and my understanding of her feelings.

For me, I felt very frustrated with the sadness and apparent unchangeability of her situation and quite inadequate in what I had to offer her. In one of our sessions together I felt I needed to be transparent with my feelings so they did not block what I was experiencing from her.

Jean: (*with her head down looking at her lap*) I feel kind of stuck, like I keep going over the same old things and nothing changes. It feels like nothing is ever going to change and it's really frustrating.

Roger: Mmm… I get a real sense of your frustration. You desperately want things to change and it seems like they are never going to. I need to share with you that I'm feeling pretty frustrated too.

(*Jean looked up at me sharply…*)

Roger: Yes, I'm feeling pretty frustrated with me. I feel a bit inadequate. You have all these major issues and things that have gone wrong for you and I'm powerless to help. Part of me wants to sort things out for you and make your life better – and I know I can't do that. All I have to offer you is my time and attention for this one hour a week when I can try to make a safe space for you to be with your feelings and not be judged. In the context of all that you are dealing with, this seems so very little to me.

Jean: (*after a short reflective pause*) It may seem small for you and yet it is huge for me. This is the only place where I feel heard and understood. This is the only place where I feel accepted for who I am and never criticised. I can cry here, I can be angry here and you really understand. I always leave here feeling just a little bit lighter, knowing I can carry on. So it's huge really, what you do how you are……

Roger: (*sitting quietly waiting*) Mmmm, yes.

Jean: And it's really good that you are willing to say exactly how you feel right here, that helps me to do that more easily.

That seems to me to be a good example of the sufficiency of the central conditions of empathy and acceptance from my client's point of view and also shows how essential it was for me to be authentic and transparent with my feelings, in the moment.

Technique – internalised practice

It can be, and has been, argued that the notion that technique is the single most significant contribution to psychological therapy from the CBTs and, ironically, this has, to a large part, undermined the credibility of the model. In essence, the predominance of the technique has surpassed the theoretical underpinning of the CBT model. As a consequence, many proponents of the CBT model do not provide a coherent rationale for the model, its consequences or its conclusions.

Similarly, it can be argued that the 'use of self' can be an equally significant contribution to psychological therapy from the PCA. The proposition that the therapist just being present with those central core conditions integrated in the self is, in itself, therapeutic.

Ironically, in the best of CBT practice the use of techniques would not be experienced by the client in a mechanistic/utilitarian way, but rather would be experienced as a natural distillation of the integration of these within the therapist.

From the PCA, it is very clear that Rogers took significant issue with the use of techniques or the notion of having a toolkit of methods to use with clients. This was completely antithetical to his underpinning rationale that it is the relationship which is paramount. It is the client experiencing the three central conditions as integrated aspects of the therapist's personality which is the facilitating feature which enables the client to grow and change. For Rogers, it is essential to see the client as a human being and to engage with the client at an affective level, rather than seeing the client as an alienated object that things must be done to through the application of techniques. The latter perspective is both philosophically and theoretically diametrically opposed to the Person-centred perspective, which has a very clear rationale for this position, its consequences and its conclusions.

● ● ● *Examples from practice* ● ● ●

From Jeremy:

Sandra has concerns about her body shape and attractiveness and described herself as 'fat' and 'disgusting', and consequently not attractive in any way at all.

Jeremy: I wonder what would happen if we asked 100 people about that.

Sandra: What do you mean?

Jeremy: Well, you said that you believe that you are fat and that this makes you disgusting. In other words, fat equals disgusting!

Sandra: Yes, indeed… fat **is** disgusting!

Jeremy: I wonder what would happen if we asked 100 people if they would believe that if they were fat they were disgusting?

Sandra: Well, some people might not think so.

Jeremy: Might not think what?

Sandra: That they were disgusting…

Jeremy: Would you necessarily think that someone was disgusting because you considered them to be fat?

Sandra: Errm no, not really…. I might think that they're overweight or had let themselves go, but not that they were disgusting for that!

Jeremy: And therefore it seems that you are being particularly harsh in your judgement of yourself then… particularly if you would not apply the same criterion to others.

In this segment I am clearly using techniques that have been extensively outlined in my training and in various publications. However, I believe that my use of them is both 'natural' and coherent within the session and are not experienced by Sandra as contrived or disingenuous.

From Roger:

Rather than a lengthy excerpt from my work with a client, I would like to use two examples of feedback from clients about our work together.

Joe, a 30-year-old man from a solid working-class background, had presented with pretty severe anxiety and anger problems, and we had worked together pretty intensively for a little over two years. At the last session, as we were coming to the end, I asked him:

Roger: So, Joe, before we finish I'm wondering if there is one last piece of feedback you would like to give me on how this has been for you?

Joe: Well, yes there is. (*Pauses briefly*) I don't know if you remember back in the beginning I told you that a mate of mine at work had told me I should come and see you.

Roger: Yes, and you were a bit suspicious of me, as I remember.

Joe: Yes, he told me to come and see you because you do magic. (*Pause*) Well, he was wrong.

(*Roger sits up and stays silent, wondering what was coming next*)

Joe: No, you don't **do** magic, you **are** magic. You haven't actually done anything but just being the way you are with me has really helped. Just the way you have accepted me somehow has helped me to learn to accept and like myself and be different. That's magic.

Similarly, with Mireille, a 40-year-old Frenchwoman struggling with low self-esteem and anxiety, in our last session after three years of working together.

Roger: So, Mirielle, before we finish I'm wondering if there is one last piece of feedback you would like to give me on how this has been for you?

Mirielle: Yes, the best thing of all is that I know I have really changed – and I've done it all for myself.

Roger: That sounds really important to you and I believe it too.

Mirielle: It's true, you didn't actually do anything like other therapists I've had. It was just how you have been with me that has made such a difference. You were just being you, not posing as a therapist and you gave me the space to be me and to learn to be me differently.

Roger: So just my presence, the way I am, has been therapeutic.

Mireille: Yes, and that's been very special

These two examples seem to me to reinforce Carl Rogers' view that the presence of the therapist, being authentic and enabling the client to experience those three central core conditions, is both necessary and sufficient for therapeutic growth to occur.

Introjections versus core beliefs

Although it is within REBT that the notion of the evaluative belief originates, with the more general CBT conceptualisation this has been expanded to the 'core' belief or schemata. It is this evaluation, or statement of value (or worth), that drives the consequential power of an inference. It is of note that, throughout the CBT literature, it is assumed that the specific beliefs and thought processes characteristic of particular emotional disturbances have a history of social influence. Again, Ellis makes reference to the constructivist basis of his REBT model in his *New Directions for Rational Emotive Behaviour Therapy* (2001).

There do seem to be some real similarities about the CBTs' notion of irrational beliefs and Rogers' ideas of conditions of worth caused by introjected values. It may be that they are the same thing with different names! In proposition 10, Rogers states:

> The values attached to experiences, and the values which are a part of the self structure, in some instances are values experienced directly by the organism, and in some instances are values introjected or taken over from others, but perceived in distorted fashion, as if they had been experienced directly.

This suggests that at an early stage the individual experiences being treated by significant others in a way which is highly conditional and leads to the development of introjected values of the self or distorted conditions of worth. These are experienced by the individual as 'I am only of value as a human being if…….' (e.g. I am always smiling and submissive to others), or 'I am only lovable if…….' (e.g. I always do things for other people and never put myself first). These introjected values or conditions of worth seem to us to be no different from the core belief or schemata in the CBTs' language. From the PCA, the experiencing of unconditional acceptance from the therapist enables the client to choose to challenge those conditions of worth or beliefs about the conditionality of their value as a human being and start to develop a more unconditional self concept.

● ● ● **Examples from practice** ● ● ●

From Roger:

Beattie was a middle-aged African Caribbean woman who worked as a care assistant in a social work setting. She was a Catholic by upbringing and was married with four children. She had been put through a disciplinary process at work and found guilty of several misdemeanours, including telling some lies about some work she had failed to do. She had been given a written warning making clear how she had to improve and offered extra support and supervision to help her improve. Afterwards she had been overcome with feelings of depression and hopelessness and could not understand why. She seemed to be totally fixated with the view that everyone hated her now and that she was bound to get the sack. I worked with Beattie for several months and seemed to be getting nowhere until the following exchange:

Roger: So, we keep coming back to this feeling you have that everybody at work hates you because of what you did. In fact, you're saying now that it is everybody, not just the people at work, is that right?

Beattie: (*quietly*) Yes.

Roger: Does that include me?

Beattie: (*more strongly*) Yes, it does.

Roger: (*gently*) Mmm – I can hear that you feel that and I need to say that it isn't true. (*Pauses for a moment*) I'm kinda puzzled about that. I'm wondering what it is you did that you think would make me hate you?

Beattie: (*after a lengthy pause and looking down*) I told lies.

Roger: That sounds like you feel very ashamed of telling lies? So ashamed that you believe everybody is bound to hate you for doing that?

Beattie: Yes, I do. You've got to be ashamed if you tell lies. People who tell lies are wicked and go to hell. It's one of the worst sins of all.

Roger: Mmm, so that's what you think. I wonder who taught you that.

Beattie: (*after a long pause*) Well, I suppose it was my Dad and my Mom, and the priest and my teachers at school, they all kept on about it all the time. I couldn't even tell no white lies or little fibs. (*At which point she cried profusely*)

Roger: So that's what you were taught by everyone who mattered to you, from a very early age – and you still believe that now? That if you tell lies you are a bad person and you will go to hell and everyone will hate you.

Beattie: Yes, that's what I was taught.

Roger: Yes, I understand how you would have to believe that as a little child surrounded by all those powerful adults. And I guess you aren't a little girl any more and I wonder if you might think about what you could choose to believe now as an adult, rather than being forever stuck with what they taught you when you were a child?

This moment seemed to bring about a change in Beattie and enabled us to go on to work on establishing values that she could choose to hold rather than being stuck with the ones that had been imposed on her. It seems to me a very powerful example of how introjections from significant others in childhood could have such a damaging impact on a person's ability to function effectively.

From Jeremy:

I had recently begun to see a client who was a qualified professional who was studying postgraduate-level psychology 'in her spare time' and described herself as being very anxious about getting things right. During the initial sessions she presented as very distressed and made repeated reference to how she had always tried to please her parents yet considered that her performance was never 'good enough'.

Kath:	It's so bloody frustrating, I just want to be able to relax and enjoy things but I end up getting into a state and then worrying that I'll not get it right. I always start to think that he was never satisfied almost to the point that I'm saying well that's no good, is it?
Jeremy:	I notice that when we spoke previously you described how you had gotten angry when you considered that your dad was critical of you and that you decided to go off to college.
Kath:	To spite him... yes... didn't work though, did it?
Jeremy:	Didn't work in what way?
Kath:	Well, I ended up having to do lots of work, pass more exams and get more qualifications.
Jeremy:	I wonder how that follows, given that it sounds like you believed that your dad was never satisfied with what you achieved but you did not agree with that?
Kath:	No I didn't ... I worked bloody hard.
Jeremy:	And I notice that you become very critical of your own performance, even before you've performed whatever task you've set yourself ... to the extent that you simply avoid performing it.
Kath:	(*tearfully*) Yes, I can imagine what he would have thought...
Jeremy:	And it's ironic that the very harsh assumption that your performance will be substandard and that this is unacceptable remains one that you act upon.
Kath:	Yes... stupid, isn't it!
Jeremy:	And there it is again... and I note that although you considered that your dad was never satisfied, you decided to make various achievements regardless of his view.
Kath:	Well, yes I suppose.
Jeremy:	And that relates to your thought processes and beliefs. I guess that we could spend a considerable amount of time revisiting events that you recall in which you concluded that your dad was not satisfied with your performance but these memories will always be influenced by your thoughts and belief as they are now. At one level the belief that you are not able to 'perform' adequately and that this is 'intolerable' reflects part of your thinking now. Our task is to begin to dispute that in order that you can really begin to feel and act differently...

In this segment I illustrate the process by which Kath's negative self-evaluation permeates her life, including the emotional hurt that she causes herself by so doing. In addition, I offer an illustration of the potential tendency to act as a double-whammy in that she engages in very substantial self-downing when her beliefs become activated.

Challenge versus disputation

There seems to be a perception that the CBTs are more active/directive and more challenging and that the PCAs, being wrongly mislabelled as non-directive, are more passive and less challenging. This is clearly a misperception which we want to address.

The client's experiencing of unconditional acceptance can, of itself, be significantly challenging for a client, particularly as this may often be the first time the client has experienced this in a relationship. Rogers suggested that the experiencing of unconditional acceptance would enable the client to begin to accept her or himself. It is also clear that if the client experiences real acceptance, this offers the therapist the opportunity to actively challenge the client's beliefs about her or himself and to sustain that challenge. The best PCA therapists would be very active and robust in this.

● ● ● *Examples from practice* ● ● ●

From Roger:

I recall working with a very depressed client who presented as very 'fragile' and indeed described herself in that way. I responded with:

Roger:	I can really hear how much pain you are in and how powerless you feel. I can really understand how the way your parents treated you has led you to believe that that you are fragile and could easily be broken and that you have no power to change that. It seems like you feel you are incredibly vulnerable and fearful of being smashed.
Client:	(*Nodded quietly in assent*).
Roger:	Yes, I really get that and at the same time I believe something else about you. I experience you as someone who has tremendous potential. When I think about all the things that have happened to you and continue to happen and that you have in one way or another overcome, I get a real sense of your resilience. I don't believe you are fragile, I know that is what you feel and I feel very differently. I experience you as very wounded, very hurt, very scared and, at the same time, I think you're tough as old boots.
Client:	(*smiling*) That's not a very nice description.
Roger:	It sounds like you felt a bit miffed by that description of you? And I wonder if you could hold your feelings of being hurt, wounded, scared and fragile and at the same time be in touch with all that strength and resilience that you have which mean that actually you are pretty tough?

Client: It would be good to feel that way.

Roger: And you could choose to feel differently about your self rather than continuing to believe what other people, including what your parents, have imposed on you.

For me, this seems like a good example of the communication of my acceptance of the client and her feelings, which she really experiences. That then provides a platform for a pretty robust challenge from me, which is also communicated in an accepting way.

From Jeremy:

I had been working with a client, Dennis, who is in his early twenties, for a number of sessions. Dennis had self-referred with a 'diagnosis' of Obsessive-Compulsive Disorder (OCD) and Generalised Anxiety Disorder (GAD). Discussions with him revealed, however, that the basis of his difficulties was a deep-rooted concern that he was 'weird', possibly 'mentally ill' or a pervert.

Jeremy: You seem quiet today. Do you want to tell me what's on your mind?

Dennis: Oh the usual stuff ... but I'm also worried that I'm not telling you the real stuff. The stuff I'm really worried about.

Jeremy: And why would you worry about that?

Dennis: I'm not being honest with you ... or me.

Jeremy: I have two questions for you but it sounds like you've already answered one by deciding that if you don't tell me, you're not being honest. Sounds like you have a problem with yourself over that. Perhaps we can consider that in a minute?

Dennis: Errm. I guess I do because perhaps I'm trying to hide and what would be the point in that?

Jeremy: Hmmm, my second question is this: what's the worst that could happen if you told me?

Dennis: My main worry is that you'll confirm my darkest fears... darkest thoughts.

Jeremy: And that would be...

Dennis: Terrible, truly awful.

Jeremy: Sounds pretty serious. Can I ask you about what it is you're not telling me?

In this brief segment, although not directly challenging, I am clearly encouraging the client to chain the cognitive consequences of his belief as my suspicion is that this is a fine example of discomfort disturbance interacting with his intense anxiety and intolerance of his discomfort.

Unconditional positive regard and unconditional self-acceptance

In giving consideration to unconditional positive regard (UPR), it is first necessary to comment upon self-esteem (SE) as this can be either unconditional

(USE) or conditional (CSE). In the latter, self-esteem is dependent upon some criterion (e.g. performance). This is really a form of the Protestant work ethic, which can be construed as a motivator in as much as effort and commitment are likely to be highly prized in some societies. Owing to our fallibility, however, it is not possible to always achieve, and consequently the conflation of outcome (success/failure) with self-esteem (high/low) inevitably leads to lowered self-esteem and, according to Ellis (2005), emotional disturbance.

The concept of UPR is not a topic that is widely written about within the CBT literature *per se*. Greenberg (2007: 44) refers to it as 'a genuinely prizing, empathic relationship and on the therapist being present, respectful and responsive to the client's experience'. This can, of course, be a tricky enterprise, as Gilbert (2007) identifies, and is often confused with an over-identification with clients which effectively becomes the therapist making considerations from their own frame of reference. Ellis has written (2005) more about the necessity or otherwise of the therapist's regard for clients.

Ellis (2005) rightly acknowledges Rogers' early prominence as a pioneer of unconditional self-acceptance (USA) through the concept of UPR. Ellis objected to his perception that Rogers made this a necessary component of therapy. Rather, he hypothesised that psychological contact was not necessary for people to experience a fundamental insight.

Ellis often voiced his contempt of the concept of SE and instead promoted the concept of acceptance, particularly unconditional self-acceptance (USA) as our behaviour, no matter how despicable, is, to paraphrase Korzybski, a part but not the whole of us. Similarly, his inheritance from the humanist philosophy of Tillich is clear; all humans always have the potential to do things differently and therefore they always have value. Ellis considers acceptance to be threefold – Self, Other and Life – and therefore it is the development of all three that becomes critical for self-actualisation.

In his writing, Ellis also attacked the notion that clients are always in a state of incongruence and that therapists needed to be congruent with them. Perhaps his most scathing critique of Rogers can be seen in his contention that, within the relationship, the therapist does not need to be a congruent, genuine and integrated person; rather, this is *preferable* but certainly *not necessary*.

Ellis also criticised Rogers' notion that the therapist *must* experience UPR for the client, suggesting that it was possible to make very positive therapeutic progress without the therapist experiencing UPR for the client. Furthermore, that therapists do not *necessarily* need to empathically understand clients and that it was possible for therapists who did not to do so.

Ellis argued that Rogers presented these in a dogmatic manner which is, on reflection, a characteristically polemical manner of interpretation to which, not surprisingly, Rogers reacted with similar gusto. It is of note that Ellis wrote of the definition of acceptance in *On Becoming a Person* that it is 'very clever – and the same as the REBT position' (Ellis, 2005: 27).

● ● ● *Examples from practice* ● ● ●

From Jeremy:

Kate is young graduate who sought CBT following intermittent attempts at counselling with a number of therapists over the preceding three years. She had problems with anxiety and experienced panic attacks at times of key stress. She had been regularly taking anxiolytic medication and reported considerable problems with interpersonal relationships. At this stage, we had been meeting for a number of sessions. Her partner, whom she had strongly wished to marry, had recently and unexpectedly ended the relationship, and it appeared that he had been covertly in a relationship with a friend. This had, somewhat unsurprisingly, resulted in a re-emergence of Kate's self-doubts and a temporary increase in her anxiety.

Kate: And that's just it… he thinks I'm useless and I am pretty useless!

Jeremy: We've spoken before about how it does not follow that because we believe something it is necessarily true.

Kate: That's all very well but this is real evidence, isn't it? I mean whether or not I think I'm useless, he certainly does …and that **really** hurts!

Jeremy: I can see how much the thought of that distresses you Kate, and again I wonder where is the difference between you assuming that because you think something it must be true and because anyone else thinks something it must be true?

Kate: How do you mean?

Jeremy: Well, I could sit here and declare loud and proud that this office is in the centre of the French Riviera!

Kate: (*laughs*) But it isn't, that would just be mad!

Jeremy: It would be a rather strange thing to say… and certainly not true. What would happen if I **sincerely** believed it…? Would that make it any more true?

Kate: (*laughing*) No, not at all… you might try and convince yourself but it is still utter rubbish!

Jeremy: And the same is true about the belief that you're useless. Even if lots of people believe it, say 100 people, it doesn't make it TRUE, does it?

Kate: Well, no I guess… Let's face it, lots of people believe all sorts of strange nonsense.

Jeremy: Exactly, an opinion remains simply that… an opinion, which is different from **the truth**! It seems that you might have to adjust that 'perfect Kate' prototype you are so keen to set up as a standard as it is unachievable, isn't it?

Kate: (*Nods her assent*)

Jeremy: Unless you can begin to accept that you are who you are… along with the aspects of you that you don't particularly like. It may be that there are some elements that you can change, but until you can begin to accept yourself as a fallible human being without applying criteria, then this will remain an Achilles heel for you…

In this segment it is clearly not my empathic acceptance of Kate that is of effect. Indeed, simply offering this or acknowledging her distress would not provide an opportunity to expose the trap of 'emotional thinking' in which she automatically assumes that her emotional conclusions must be correct, and consequently her distress is insurmountable.

From Roger:

Annie was in her early thirties, working in quite a good job but with very few social relationships and no intimate relationships. She had been married for a short time and then divorced and had two young children. Her parents had died some years before and she did not have much contact with the remaining members of her family. She had been referred by social services because she was self-harming. We worked together for several months and we had identified that she had serious problems of self-doubt and felt very unloved and unlovable. She desperately wanted to be accepted.

Annie: I just can't work out what to do to get people to accept me and I feel like I never will.

Roger: (*tentatively*) I get a sense that you think it is something you have to do to other people that will get them to accept you. Like you think there is a magic answer that you are never going to discover.

Annie: Well, yes.

Roger: Well, I think maybe there is an answer but it probably isn't the one you might expect. (*Pauses a while*) I think the answer is in you and it's about you being different, not about you doing something different.

Annie: How do you mean?

Roger: Well, my sense is that the most important person who doesn't care about you is you! (*Pauses again*) If you don't accept, care about, even love yourself, how is anybody else going to be able to do that?

Annie: (*after a short reflective silence*) Mmm, you could be right, that sounds like it makes sense…. But what do you mean, 'care about myself'?

Roger: Well, it's a bit hard to explain, but perhaps I can share with you how it was for me, how I discovered it for me?

Annie: OK.

Roger: Do you remember when you had your first baby and that first few moments when you held her in your arms? (*Annie nods quietly*)… Well, I remember when that happened for me. I suddenly felt so overwhelmed with how much I loved and accepted this little person. I was completely, totally accepting of her, just as she was.

Annie: Yes, I remember that and how scared I was of the responsibility.

Roger: Yes, I felt that too.

Annie: (*thoughtfully*) Mmmm, yes, I guess that's just how it feels like you accept me. No questions, no ifs and buts. You just accept me as I am and perhaps that is what is helping me to begin to accept myself.

Roger: That is how I want it to feel for you and I'm wondering if you could begin to choose to start accepting and loving yourself in that way?

Annie: (*after a long pause*) I think I could try…

Over the next few months Annie struggled hard with learning to accept herself and it seemed to me that the more I focused on enabling her to feel fully accepted by me, the more she was able to begin to do that. This seems a useful example of the importance, from a Person-centred perspective, of the client's experiencing of unconditional positive regard, or complete acceptance as I prefer to call it.

Unconscious – unattended

Although the terms 'unconscious' and 'attended' or 'implicit' and 'constructive' are differentially and interchangeably applied within the canon of CBT literature, they are rarely adequately defined. This is, in many ways, a shortfall and potentially provides an opportunity to dispute the robustness of the model. However, it may be that this reflects one of the central problems of meta-cognition.

The notion of the unconscious has a long tradition within abnormal psychology and particularly within the psychotherapeutic literature. Despite this, it remains a contentious concept within contemporary psychology. The idea of the implicit theory has gained prominence during recent contemporary debates and this is evidently more associated with the notion of a belief system than the unconscious, which carries a significant abundance of neo-Freudian theory and associated surplus meaning.

One of the more critical aspects of the unconscious is that this has the teleological consequence regarding the extent to which the individual has both the capacity to choose to 'be different' and the will to counteract fundamental forces. Conversely, if we accept an unconscious, then this also contains the predicated ontological assumption of motivational elements that defy any level of coherent awareness. The concept of implicit theory is, however, more applicable as this assumes that human reasoning may not *necessarily* consider the logical antecedents of the conclusions drawn, and consequently that the principles may be vulnerable to the *reductio ad absurdum*. All of this can be seen to offer opportunities for both harmony and dissonance.

● ● ● *Examples from practice* ● ● ●

From Jeremy:

I guess that I have always struggled with the notion that we are motivated by unconscious motivation; I have found the psychological concept of implicit theories motivating behaviour more theoretically satisfying. Jon has been in a relationship for many years that he describes as unsatisfactory. He states that this is not satisfying and that he has considered ending it many times. When he has previously mooted the idea, his partner has reacted angrily and he responds in a conciliatory way and states that he simply 'doesn't know why'. Similarly, he reports having excessive occupational stress and that he finds work overwhelming. Furthermore, he desperately wants to leave, has the financial resources to leave work, no longer enjoys his job yet continues to work very long hours. The following segment relates to a session considering his sense of being 'trapped' by both work and his relationship.

Jon:	So I thought, bugger this, I'm going to say that's it... we're just not making each other happy.
Jeremy:	And...
Jon:	(*laughing*)...Well, you know what's coming next don't you... I sat in silence and she commented... so I apologised and took her out for a meal.
Jeremy:	I wonder why you decided to apologise and offer her a meal?

Jon: Well I just felt guilty… really awkward and terrible.

Jeremy: What were you feeling guilty about?

Jon: Honestly, I have no idea…. I guess I was anticipating that she might be angry.

Jeremy: I wonder what was going through your mind at the time? What are you telling yourself as you were considering ending it?

Jon: Well, obvious that she wouldn't cope so I had no choice but to carry on.

Jeremy: No choice?!

Jon: I knew you'd pick up on that!! Well she would be upset and…

Jeremy: Exactly, she would be upset and…

Jon: Errm.

Jeremy: Is it within your gift to control someone else's distress?

Jon: Well no, but…

Jeremy: But what? If we can presume that this is not news that she wishes to hear, then it is reasonable to assume that she might be a little upset by this….

Jon: **Ohh** yes… and more than a little…

Jeremy: And I wonder how experiencing or anticipating someone else's distress becomes so unpleasant to you that you assume that you have no choice about your own actions.

Jon: Well, it's horrible to think that I've caused her distress, isn't it?

Jeremy: It almost seems that you are implicitly assuming responsibility for her distress.

Jon: Well, yes I suppose I am … when you put it like that I guess I am sort of saying that… and obviously…

Jeremy: And I wonder what you might imply about the sort of man you are if you **were** causing hurt to her?

Jon: Not nice, not nice at all … something of a shit really… Although I don't think I've ever consciously thought of myself as a shit in that sense.

In this segment I have utilised an inference-chaining method to encourage Jon to voice the implicit connection between the emotions between his experience and his own irrationally exaggerated beliefs about culpability. The voicing of these was an emotional experience for him, and something of a 'light bulb moment' in his therapy.

From Roger:

I'm pretty clear that an important function I have as a PCA therapist is to notice evidence of what might be going on in the unconscious world of my client, in all the phenomena they present. Noting these is often not enough. I need to be prepared to enable my client to consider what might be going on in them at a deeper, hidden level and to try to draw these into awareness. Working phenomenologically is not a passive process of just noticing. It has an active purpose of enabling the client to develop insight and awareness of what might be going on in them.

I was working with Jane, a 40-year-old teacher, who was rather reserved by nature and concerned about her inability to develop and maintain an intimate relationship. She had been openly a lesbian since she was at university and had had a series of short and unsatisfying relationships. Each one had ended with her being 'dumped' as she put it, and left her feeling very rejected and abandoned.

We had worked together for quite a few sessions and I found myself really struggling to get a sense of her feelings. So I found myself paying rather more attention to how she was being as she sat in her chair, rather than listening intently to her story.

Jane: I keep saying that I want to get to the deeper stuff that was buried in me, to really find out what it is in me that leads to me always being dumped, never being able to really engage. And... why does it hurt so much to be so alone?

Roger: I can hear that pain of feeling abandoned... perhaps even a fear that you might actually be unlovable, that no one will ever stay with you?

Jane: Yes,... It's... (*and then she folded her arms and sat back silently*).

Roger: (*paused for a moment*) Jane, I really heard you get in touch with that feeling for a moment and then I noticed that you folded your arms across your chest and sat back and went silent. I guess I'm wondering what that was about?

Jane: (*looked at me rather sternly*) Did I really do that?

Roger: Yes, you seem to do that quite often. It feels to me like you start to get in touch with your feelings and then you sort of 'lock me out'. I don't know if that it what is happening but it feels like that to me.

Jane: Mmmm... Yes, come to think of it, I think I probably do that a lot.

Roger: Including in your relationships with your friends?

Jane: (*after a long, long pause*) Yes, I really do shut people out, don't I? (*After an even longer pause*) No wonder I get dumped. I guess if I don't allow any one in, they will never want to stay with me.

That seems to me a fairly common example of the way I work phenomenologically to enable a client to reflect on what might be going on with them at an unconscious level and to raise it into their awareness so they can begin to think about what they might choose to do about it.

A link to the next chapter

In the next chapter we will explore some examples of our practice to show what we see as differences and similarities in our approaches. We will look at particular presenting problems, such as depression, anxiety, anger, aggression and mental health issues.

Recommended reading

Ellis, A. (2005) *The Myth of Self-Esteem*. New York: Prometheus.
Wilkins, P. (2010) *Person-centred Therapy: 100 Key Points*. London and New York: Routledge.

CHAPTER 5
CBT AND PERSON-CENTRED COUNSELLING IN ACTION

In this chapter our intention is to draw from examples of beginning our work with clients to exemplify what we see as differences and similarities in our approaches and practice. We will not be describing individual clients in ways which might break confidentiality, but we will look at particular presenting problems. For example:

   a A client suffering from anxiety and depression.

   b A client experiencing difficulties with anger and aggression and alcohol use.

My assessment and contracting process – Roger

Before I describe my work with a new client, perhaps it would be helpful to give a brief outline of how I usually start that process of working with a new client.

As my client and I sit down for the first time, I want to avoid the client splurging their story before it is safe enough for them to do so. I want to help them to feel safe and contained straight away. I have already begun to do some phenomenological assessment of them as a person and to notice how I am experiencing them. I am usually nervous at meeting someone new, so I gently disclose that and go on to wonder how they are feeling.

I usually say something like:

'I'm feeling a bit nervous about this, because I'm always nervous at meeting new people. I wonder if you're a bit nervous, a bit anxious, and if you are, that is OK. I think it can often take quite a bit of courage to come and see a stranger and talk about your feelings, even if you really want to do it.'

Clients usually nod in response to this and often seem relieved.

I go on to say:

'In order to make it safe enough for both of us so that you can talk freely, there are some things I need to do before you begin. I need to take some formal details first, and then I will tell you something about me and my background and a bit more about the way that I work. I will then explain what this counselling process is about and then we will have some time for you to talk about anything you feel you need to.'

I also say:

'This first session is an assessment session for both of us. On the one hand, for you to assess if I am the right kind of person to be your counsellor and to check that you feel that you can work with me. On the other hand, for me to assess if I am competent enough to work with whatever you may be bringing. At the end of this first session, if we decide that we are going to work together, then we can make the next appointment. I only make one appointment at a time because I think that you have the right to choose to end whenever you want.'

I then pick up my folder, in which I usually have a sheet made out with the client's name, address and telephone number on it. I check their name, and how they would like to be called, their address, postcode and telephone number and if it is alright for me to call them on that number should I need to.

The next thing I ask is for their date of birth (DOB). I always ask this because hospitals usually use the DOB as the first field they search on their database. There have been times when I have needed to consult the client's psychiatrist or doctor at a hospital. I've learned that if I don't have the DOB, the hospital may not be able to find the client on their patient database. In addition, I am really bad at guessing ages and I don't want to make assumptions about the client's age based on how they look. I usually tell the client this last reason.

I go on to ask for the name and telephone number of their GP. I make it clear that I will never contact the GP without their expressed approval. I tell them that sometimes it can be useful if a client is on medication, for instance, to check with their GP what they actually take. I usually also check at this point if they are currently on any medication and, if so, what it is.

If they have not been referred to me by a doctor or psychiatrist or other source of referral, I usually check how they found out about me and make a note of that.

I ask them if they have seen their doctor recently and if they have, I ask them to tell me what that was for. I then ask them if they have any medical condition that it might be useful for me to know about. I also ask them if they have any history of mental health issues and, if they have, I ask them to briefly tell me about those. I also ask them if they have had an experience of seeing a counsellor and, if they have, to tell me a little about that.

I then tell them that this is all the formal information I need at this point. It will get transferred on to an index file on my computer in a coded file and nobody else can get at it. I then tell them:

'I do make some notes at the end of every session after you have gone. Those notes will be about how I have been working with you. They won't say very much about your story but it will be predominantly about the way that I have worked with you and the processes involved in this. The purpose of my notes is for me to share with my supervisor how I have been working with you in order to help me keep my counselling work at a high level. Those notes will be kept in a secure place and if you want to see them at any time, you only have to ask.'

I then go on to say:

'What I would like to do now is just tell you a bit more about the counselling process, a bit more about me and my background, and about the way that I work. Before I do that I would like you to have a look at my Counselling Agreement, which gives you some detail of what you and I can expect from each other.

So here is a copy of my Counselling Agreement. I'd like you to have a look through this now, as it covers all the main aspects of how we might work together.'

I read through my copy of the agreement (Figure 5.1 on p. 83) while the client is reading their copy. When they have finished, I ask if they have any questions about it and then tell them that if we agree to work together at the end of this session, then we can both sign and keep a copy.

All the time we are doing this I am carefully observing the client in a phenomenological way and trying to get a sense of how I am experiencing them at this time. I then go on to say something along the following lines:

'So just to let you know a bit more about me. I have been a therapist for over 40 years now and in that time have worked with a wide variety of presenting problems and concerns. I won't say that I have heard everything because that would be tempting fate, but I have heard an awful lot and I think I am fairly un-shockable. In addition to my work as a therapist, I teach other people how to become counsellors at Warwick University and I do some consultancy work with a variety of organisations up and down the country on the management of change. I am 70 and I am married with two grown up children and two young grandchildren and they are a very important focus in my life these days.'

I then ask them if there is anything else they would like to know about me.

Then I ask them if they know anything about counselling before I go on to briefly outline how I work and the differences with other approaches.

I tell them that I am trained in the Person-centred Approach which is based on the belief that people will always try to do the best for themselves and that, given the right conditions in a helping relationship, they will 'heal' themselves. I also believe that they are the only expert in their own internal world. They are the only one who really knows how they feel. I will usually say something like:

'This approach places great importance on the relationship between therapist and client and has a strong focus on what you are feeling in the present moment. In this relationship, I will be very present with my feelings and may, from time to time, want to look at what is happening between you and me. I need to tell you that I will not analyse what you are saying or thinking and neither will I set out to teach you how to think differently. I really am not here to tell you what to do; I am not an expert in you. I will listen to whatever you tell me and try to get an understanding of what you are experiencing. I don't have any solutions to your problems. I sometimes have the occasional solution which works for me – and I believe that the only answers to your problems, if there are any, lie within you.

What I am here to do is to be very accepting of you, by trying to get a real understanding of how you feel and to provide you with some safe space in which you can talk about anything that concerns you. This is a place in which you can really be yourself, with all of your feelings, a place in which you don't have to pretend. This is a safe place, where I will not judge you, though I may not necessarily agree with everything you say and do. My job is to listen and try to understand your feelings and, through that, help you to understand them better. I will not probe or pry, and the only questions I will ask will be to check that I have understood what you have said or to check my understanding of your feelings. If you want me to know something, you will have to tell it to me. I am very used to long silences and also to strong feelings being expressed.

You may find this process very challenging at times and sometimes therapy can make you feel worse before you begin to feel better.

As I said before, if we choose to work together, I only book one session at a time and it will usually be for an hour. Because no one except my clients ever sees me working, I believe that it is important for me to get feedback from you as to how each session has been. So there will be five minutes at the end for you to give me some feedback on how the session has been for you and if there has been anything you would have liked me to have done differently.'

I usually finish by asking:

'Is there anything else you want to know about how I work?'

This is my way of 'contracting' with my clients. I feel it is important to have some formality to this process. I like to do it as warmly as I can and I also like it to be formal, clear and explicit. For me, this enables clients who are often feeling vulnerable and anxious to feel safe and contained. It lets them know that they are in a professional relationship in which I will take responsibility for managing the boundaries and they can take responsibility for themselves.

For me, I believe that my contracting process has little, if anything, to do with my modality. It is primarily about good ethical practice, regardless of theoretical approach.

CLIENT RIGHTS AND RESPONSIBILITIES

In counselling, both the Counsellor and the Client have rights and responsibilities. It may be helpful for you to read these few notes before we begin our session together and to clarify any concerns you may have about coming for counselling before we start.

As a client you have certain rights. You have a right:

1   To dignity as an individual human being. You have the right to equal consideration and treatment and I will work with you in a non-judgemental way and value any social, cultural or physical differences you may have.
2   To be provided with professional and respectful care by me.
3   To be accepted as you are, and to be listened to in a non-judgemental way.
4   To know my assessment of the problem or concerns that you are presenting.
5   To refuse to comply with recommendations, even though I may strongly suggest you take some form of action or seek some other form of help. You may choose not to follow my guidance. Alternative resources may be available and you have the right to know what these are.
6   To confidentiality within counselling, providing that what you tell me does not put me in the position of breaking the law or may make me aware that you are contemplating causing serious harm to yourself or to others. You should also know that I am bound to comply with the Ethical Framework for Good Practice of the British Association for Counselling and Psychotherapy.

Along with these rights you have certain responsibilities. These are:

1   To be honest, open and willing to share your concerns with me.
2   To ask questions when you don't understand or when you need clarification.
3   To discuss any reservations you have about your future options with me.
4   To report changes or unexpected events to me as related to your problem.
5   To keep appointments or to give at least 48 hours advance notice when you need to cancel or reschedule an appointment and to pay the agreed fees. This includes payment for sessions cancelled with less than 48 hours notice.

You are responsible for your own thoughts, feelings, actions, and for your own personal growth.

I am here to help you identify ways to help yourself, to the best of your abilities.

As your Therapist I may wish to discuss the work that I am doing with you with my Supervisor, in order to monitor and improve my practice. This will be done in such a way as to protect your identity and not breach any confidence. I would be grateful if you would confirm that you have given me permission to do this.

Signed...   Date...........................

Signed...   Date...........................

FIGURE 5.1   *Roger's Counselling Agreement*

My assessment and contracting process – Jeremy

As with Roger, the initial session with any client is one in which there is a degree of trepidation for me as therapist, but also for the client. I attempt to provide an atmosphere in which the environment is both safe and businesslike, in as much as the content of our discussion is related to the distress or disturbance the client is experiencing. As such, it is both natural and commonsense that this will be associated with some anxiety as therapy is an unusual interchange between relative strangers. My motive, similar to that of Roger, is to facilitate an environment that is 'safe', but also to communicate that this relationship is different from other relationships as it is fundamentally motivated by the discomfort or distress, as opposed to other primary motivating factors providing the foundations for relationships.

Unlike Roger, I do not spend time attending to my own phenomenological process as this reflects my belief systems... and their attendant irrationalities! At this stage, I offer clients an introduction that focuses upon the business of therapy, such as:

'What is it that brings you to speak to me today?'

Or

'Can you tell me about what led to you wanting to come in to discuss your problems?'

As with Roger, I always start my assessment session by outlining who I am, the length and purpose of the session, and that the initial session enables both of us to ask the awkward question, *'Can I work with this person?'* Furthermore, I am explicit in stating that if I do not believe that I am either the right person to work with the client at this time, or that the type of therapy I offer is not appropriate, then I will state this. I also indicate that I will write to my clients after our initial session to outline my initial formulation and opinion about what might be a way forward, even if I do not believe that I am the most appropriate therapist to work with the problem. Thus, there are basic demographic details, including GP details and an emergency contact, that are necessary, along with my outline of the basis of confidentiality in that my understanding of this is that what is said in therapy remains confidential within therapy unless this relates to harm or risk of harm to either the self or others, even where this is historical and not previously disclosed.

If I detect that my client is anxious or uneasy, I might indicate that I experience them as presenting as such. However, my practice is almost always driven by a motive to encourage the client to use their own script and, consequently, I actively avoid offering cues and use questions to move the client towards defining and describing these feelings, such as:

'Can you tell me what that means?'

Or

'What would you say the emotion is that you are feeling?'

I might enquire as to any previous contact with health services, counsellors or therapy that the client has had and, similar to Roger, I usually enquire as to how people have come to see me. At this stage I also collect basic information (contact details and GP details) and outline the boundaries of confidentiality. I am very explicit about the circumstances in which I might have to communicate with a third party, particularly in the event that I have grounds to believe that a client may either hurt themselves or someone else, or in the event that the client has committed, or is intending to commit, a serious interpersonal offence.

Similar to Roger, I will enquire about whether they have received any diagnosis or formulation of their difficulties and, further, if they have been prescribed any medication.

I outline that I do make notes as an *aide-mémoire*, although unlike Roger this is something that I complete as part of the process of therapy. In addition, I sometimes use either a whiteboard or flipchart. Unlike Roger's note-taking, my purpose is to punctuate elements within the session and clarify particular points, to highlight the links between beliefs, emotions and behaviour, and to explain aspects of the model and consequently introduce the client to the theory. I do use the notes for discussion in supervision, but also as an opportunity to begin the process of formulation and to begin to tailor elements of potential homework assignments.

I always explain that my therapeutic style is active and directive in as much as I will ask questions, clarify and even ask clients to restate things and then notice any change in their experience.

I then explain that my practice is to hold an initial assessment session to achieve a number of objectives. Primarily this is to identify whether we can work together or indeed whether the problem is one that is likely, or requires, therapy. Although this may seem like an unusual point to consider, I have had clients whose spouses, family or employers have strongly suggested that they 'self-refer'. I always explain that psychological therapy involves considerable active involvement and that it is necessary for clients to want to engage and not simply comply with the requirements of others. I then explain that, following the initial session, I will write a brief letter including an initial formulation and an outline of how I propose to work with them, but also I will attempt to identify local alternative practitioners in order that the client can make an active and informed choice should they wish to proceed with therapy. The letter also includes a requirement for the client to sign and return a copy of the letter, which acts as a basic therapeutic contract.

Similar to Roger, I briefly outline my background and training, but take more time to explain that I have heard a wide range of presentations and concerns, and that I consider one of the most liberating aspects of a therapeutic relationship is that this is an opportunity for clients to consider and address those aspects of their lives which which they struggle most. Similar to Roger, I explain that therapy does not involve any judgement or any requirement to impress me.

When I introduce the basic model to clients, I outline the notion of emotional responsibility alongside the role that belief and perception plays in emotional and behavioural disturbance. I explain how I will encourage the client to engage with their own thought and emotional process, but particularly on the thoughts and beliefs that characterise particular difficulties. I usually ask the question to begin the session:

'Tell me, what problem brings you here today?'

I will make a point of outlining to clients that I may ask what appear to be very obvious or somewhat silly questions, however, I am doing this because I am motivated to understand their problems and difficulties, and I wish to help them make changes. I do stress that change is challenging, difficult and that ultimately this remains a choice.

What follows next are an example from Roger and an example from Jeremy of their beginning to work with two quite different clients.

Unifying themes

It is clear that in both approaches we have a structure to our assessment and formulation processes that has less to do with our modalities than what we see as good and ethical therapeutic process. What is clear as a unifying theme is our commitment to being carefully phenomenological in our meeting with and beginning to develop a working alliance with clients. Also, we note that in this beginning stage of forming the relationship we both give something concrete to our clients.

Roger – Working with a client suffering from anxiety and depression

Bernie

Bernie was referred to me by her GP, who felt that for medical reasons to do with her health history, he did not want to put her on medication for her depression and anxiety attacks. He suggested she try one or two sessions with me and talk through the options. He agreed to get Bernie to telephone me to make an appointment. I agreed to meet her and to do an initial assessment session to see if we could work together.

When she arrived at my consulting room she was clearly very anxious and quite stressed. I confirmed that this was an assessment session for her to find out if I was the right therapist for her and for me to check that I was competent to work with the issues she was bringing. I went through the usual contracting process that I have outlined above, setting out to enable her to feel safe enough to be open with me and to experience me as a real person. I then invited her to begin to tell me about herself and why she had come to see me.

Bernie began by telling me something of her life history, where she came from originally, her difficult childhood with parents who were always fighting until her father left when she was 9 years old. She had been married for 26 years and had three daughters all living at home. Just over three months ago she had discovered that her husband had been having a sexual affair with a young man and this had horrified her. They had a number of very angry rows, from which she knew that he was completely unrepentant about it and had no intention of ending the relationship. She had tried to get him to leave the house, but he refused to go. He did, however, agree to move into the spare bedroom.

So they continue to live in the same house in what she described as 'a very icy silence, punctuated by occasional red hot outbursts'. She said that she felt totally distraught, disgusted, terrified and powerless, almost like her perfect little world had been torn apart. Over the last three months she had felt increasingly despondent and disconsolate, unable to cope with the three children, and was terrified of what the future was going to be like. She had begun to have some really intense panic attacks, which were immobilising her, and was scared stiff by that experience and feeling really out of control. She was also having real difficulty sleeping and eating, and didn't feel that there was anyone she could talk to about it because she was scared of what they might think. She hadn't even told the doctor what had happened; she just told him how she was feeling and that she didn't know why she felt that way.

I responded empathically, tentatively working hard to get a clear understanding of how she was experiencing each of the feelings she had talked about, from her frame of reference. I told her that in addition to the feelings she had shared with me, I also had a sense that she felt really disgusted and betrayed by her husband and powerless to change things. At the same time, I communicated my acceptance of her feelings and my acceptance of how she had responded to what had happened and was still happening to her.

I was very concerned about her experiencing of the panic attacks and her sense of being out of control. So once I was sure that she felt really heard and understood, I told her what I was feeling about what she had shared with me. I said that I wasn't qualified to diagnose her as being depressed, but it did seem to me that she was suffering from a number of depressive symptoms, as a reaction to a highly traumatic event. I felt that I was competent to work with the issues she was presenting if she felt that she could work with me.

From my perspective, we had not started therapy yet so it was appropriate for me to try to be therapeutic and provide her with some information that she would find helpful. I needed to be careful how I did this so that I was not being directive and was not experienced as being an 'expert'.

I then went on to say that I was concerned about the symptoms that she was experiencing and wondered if it would be helpful to have some information about how she might manage those symptoms more effectively. If I could do that, it would then give us an opportunity to explore the underlying issues that were creating these symptoms and reactions. And then might be able to begin therapy.

Bernie said she thought that would be helpful. So I shared the following information with her, stopping so she could check and clarify what I was saying.

'Panic attacks are not a bad thing or something to feel ashamed of. They can be frightening but they are a part of our natural survival kit, usually stemming from a response to something we are scared about. When you get a fright, or feel threatened in some way, the normal response is to 'fight or to fly or to freeze'. A panic attack is usually just an extreme version of that fight/flight/freeze response. The only trouble is that it is often an unconscious response to a fear that we are consciously unaware of. It is also important to remember that a panic attack is very unlikely to kill you.

It can be really helpful to talk to someone about the attacks to try to uncover what is causing them, what it is that you are anxious about deep down. What was the thought or feeling that occurred immediately before the panic began? If you can identify what the feeling/thought was that the panic attack is taking you away from, that can be very helpful, particularly if you can allow yourself to try to experience and stay with that thought or feeling without going down the panic attack escape route.

Talking to a counsellor can be really helpful for this.

It can also be important to do some very practical things to help you to manage the attacks.

Did you know that your lungs, when spread out flat would each cover an area of space as large as a football field?

Most of us do not use our lungs properly. When we panic or get stressed, we tend to breath in short, shallow, rapid breaths. This tends to make us take in too much oxygen and leads to an increase of adrenalin, which makes us feel more panicky.

For those who suddenly feel panicky or anxious, learning to breathe with your diaphragm is very helpful. To learn to manage panic attacks and not be overcome by them, we need to teach ourselves to breathe differently.

First of all, when you get up in the morning, slowly take in one full breath, filling your lungs as much as you possibly can, then slowly release the breath. Breathe normally after this. This will open up all the millions of small capillaries in your lungs and they will stay open for about four hours, allowing you to use your lungs to their full capacity. Repeat this exercise about every four hours, making the last one just before you go to bed. Do this on a regular basis every day.

Then, at any time when you start to feel anxious or panicky concentrate on slowing your breathing down and breathing with your diaphragm, rather than with the upper part of your lungs. This will help you to teach your lungs to operate more efficiently and will help you to reduce the incidence of panic attacks. In addition to developing a strategy for relaxation, you may also need to manage yourself better when a panic attack begins, using the following process.

If you suddenly begin to feel wound up or panicky or very nervous, start doing diaphragmatic breathing straight away and slow your breathing down. As you may not be used to doing this, it will take a bit of practice. Just gently but firmly push your diaphragm out and you will find that the air comes easily into your lungs. Then gently but firmly pull your diaphragm in and you will find that air is expelled from your lungs. You will find that this will reduce your intake of oxygen to the level you need, it will stop you hyper-ventilating and will enable you to calm down and feel less anxious. Do not try to stop the attack by taking deep breaths with the whole of your lungs – this will only make the situation worse. Slow yourself down, focus on your diaphragm and make it do your breathing for you.'

We talked about this to clarify that I was not telling her to do this. This was something she could choose to try out to see if it worked for her. I gave her an information sheet to help her remember what to do.

I then suggested we talk a bit about the depressive symptoms she was experiencing and began with:

'When you talk about your depression, I get a sense of you experiencing it as something which is happening to you. Something which is invading you and which you have no control over?'

Bernie nodded slowly in agreement…

I continued:

'Well I believe that it is something that you are doing to yourself. There are very good reasons why you are depressed. You're scared and feeling very lost and powerless, and retreating into a depressed state inside yourself seems like a very natural reaction. I'm wondering if it perhaps feels unhappy and quite unpleasant in one way and yet at the same time it feels quite safe and comfortable.'

'Mmm…yes', Bernie replied, 'That's just how it is – and I can't shift it.'

'That's what it feels like, that it has control over you?', I asked.

She nodded and I replied:

'Well there are some things you could try, which might just reduce some of those symptoms a bit and might help you feel you have got back some of the control over yourself. Would you like to explore those with me?'

Bernie tentatively agreed and then listened intently as I explained how brief and regular exercise every day and a longer more sustained exercise once a week, would both promote the production and circulation of endorphins in her system. We explored what she might do to improve her sleep pattern and the importance of having a healthy nutritious diet. We also explored things she might do to help her to sleep better and looked at the importance having someone to talk to about her feelings so that they were not being repressed.

I explained that if she did all of these things then this might help her to shift her depressed mood and be able to begin to look at making some changes in her life, so that it would seem more bearable. Again, I gave her a fact sheet with the information on it and repeated that I was not telling her to do these things, but suggesting that she might like to choose to try some or all of them.

Bernie replied:

'Just talking about things has really helped, especially as I know you really understand how I feel and you're not telling me I shouldn't feel this way. The information sounds useful too, although it all sounds pretty hard to do, but it's given me a bit of hope that I can change how I feel and I can take responsibility for myself.'

I said:

'That's great because you're the only one who can do that. It will take time and it will be hard work and may at times be very painful. I'll be happy to work with you if you feel up to it?'

She nodded and said:

'OK. Can I make another appointment then?'

Jeremy – Working with a client with alcohol and anger problems

Steven initially referred himself, stating that his partner and family had demanded that he:

'Come to speak to a psychologist or therapist' regarding his 'issues to do with my partner's infidelities'.

On meeting with Steven, it was evident that he was a very intellectually able individual who experienced considerable difficulty with his alcohol consumption and he reported having previously 'done the whole AA thing' and found this 'useless'.

In our initial session, Steven described that he had been with his partner for approximately 25 years, having met him at university and that he *knew*

'I should have left him years ago' owing to his sexual affairs and generally 'unacceptable behaviour'.

When we spoke, Steven was very self-deprecating and made reference to how he was

'not able to think anymore'.

or that he had

'not made anything of my life'.

Steven described that when they met his partner had just graduated from a very prestigious university and, on meeting him, Steven had fallen in love,

'more or less there and then', but that he had 'thought he was out of my league'.

At this time Steven was just beginning to experiment with relationships and had moved away from home for the first time. Steven described his home environment as

'claustrophobic'.

and recalled the end of his parents' marriage owing to his father having left his mother for another woman and that, consequently, he had become

'increasingly aware that history was repeating itself' and he was 'turning into my bloody mother!'

Steven detailed that his partner had made the commitment to remain with him and they had set up home together, however, his partner had many sexual liaisons outside their relationship which he found very distressing. Steven commented that friends had suggested that he do the same, but he stated that he did not wish to do that as he was in love and that

'it just isn't me'.

When I asked about what he hoped to achieve through therapy, Steven explained that he wished to *be calmer* and to stop being *nasty* and *angry*, which became particularly apparent after drinking alcohol.

A very characteristic element of Steven's presentation was the extremely negative and self-deprecating language he used to describe himself, such as being

'consumed with bitterness'.

It seemed that Steven's problems were twofold. First, he experienced very significant anger associated with his belief that his partner had betrayed him by his previous sexual encounters and intrigues, and Steven reasoned that his partner did not consider him to be

'emotionally important'.

and he described this as being

'intolerable'.

The second aspect of his difficulties concerned his use of alcohol. Steven described his personal relationship and sex life with his partner as

'Never good'.

describing himself as

'more needy'.

than him. At this stage it was notable that Steven reiterated his belief that his partner was

'not as interested in a personal relationship with him as I am with him'.

Steven described his partner as 'a workaholic' and that he would routinely spend the week living in a separate flat in a different city as this was closer to his workplace, but nevertheless would often not finish his working day until late evening. At weekends Steven described that his partner would spend a significant amount of time dealing with administrative work and that he was 'never uncontactable'. As a consequence, Steven reported that he felt very lonely and isolated and that the relationship was deeply dissatisfying as he found it 'almost impossible' not to reflect on the lack of intimacy and that he was 'unable' to forget his infidelity, which fuelled his distress and inspired his drinking alcohol. This, in turn, fuelled his anger and resulted in aggressive outbursts and behaviour, although Steven was clear that this was directed to objects and not individuals. When I enquired about the consequences of these alcohol-fuelled outbursts, Steven described that his partner found his intoxi-cated behaviour highly aversive and would be rejecting and avoided further contact with him. At times it seemed that Steven's partner would leave their home to stay closer to the office, although Steven believed that this was, func-tionally, a means of avoiding contact with him. Steven described this pattern of behaviour as

'a vicious cycle. He ignores me and I end up hating myself just a little bit more.'

Through our discussion of his alcohol use, it became evident that this had ini-tially developed as a means of relaxing and socialising, however, Steven had increasingly come to the realisation that he consumed alcohol alone and that this became more frequent when he was

'angry at him'.

At the time of coming to see me, Steven commented that he felt 'worried that I can't have a day without at least a bottle of wine'.

Steven detailed that he had recently started to secrete alcohol in different rooms in the house and would

'nip off for a sneaky drink'.

I enquired as to whether this included times when he and his partner were in bed, and Steven acknowledged that this was the case, and I enquired as to what effect this had on their intimacy, to which Steven commented:

'He's usually fallen asleep by the time I get back into bed so I end up feeling more rotten and lonely.'

I noticed that Steven's anger seemed not only to be directed towards his partner but also towards himself, highlighting that he made many very self-deprecating remarks. Furthermore, I noted the reference that he had made that he, 'should have left him' and asked him, 'What sort of person doesn't leave someone when they should?', to which he answered:

'Someone with no worth… pathetic!'

I noted that this seemed not only to be a very harsh, but also a global judgement and opined that this might be a beneficial course for us to address first in therapy as reframing this might enable him to experience reasonable and healthy anger towards his partner for behaviour he considered to be contrary to the boundaries of their relationship and that this could be expressed as opposed to avoided. I also noted that Steven's definition of himself as someone who needed his partner more than his partner needed him contained an implicit assumption that he would be rejected, and that if this were the case, then it would represent a clear covert motivation to engage in indirect anger and that this was unlikely to address the issue.

I outlined my belief that as he detailed his alcohol use, it was not only damaging to his physical health, but also appeared to increase his evaluation of the lack of intimacy in their relationship. In addition, this facilitated recall of how betrayed he felt and therefore resulted in him avoiding intimate situations while concluding that it was his partner who did not seek intimacy.

We agreed that we would spend time working on identifying times when he noticed that he 'needed' a drink, and that he would complete an ABC diary and that we would then begin to focus on any implicit beliefs he held regarding his own worth. We also spent a considerable time discussing the implication of remaining in a relationship with a partner who had sexual encounters outside this relationship, and I encouraged him to dispute his conclusion that this held a necessary implication regarding him. Rather, it was decision arrived at by his partner and was more linked to his desire to have sex in the moment as opposed to representing a 'lack of respect'. Steven was able to acknowledge with some degree of ironic humour that his partner

'hadn't signed a legally binding contract to respect me in the way that I define!'

Steven was also able to acknowledge the link between his thought processes and his emotional and behavioural responses, suggesting

'I guess I really need to think about this differently, don't I?'

Conclusion

We are not suggesting that these are examples illustrating the differences between the PCA and the CBTs. These are descriptions of how each of us works, which we believe are rooted in our theoretical understanding of our approaches. At the same time we see this as good therapeutic practice, irrespective of modality.

A link to the next chapter

The process of assessment and formulation is already a requirement within the IAPT service and will become a requirement in the wider profession when regulation of the profession takes place. This will cause some difficulties for some Person-centred therapists, who will have an antipathy towards diagnosis and assessment and the 'medical' model. The next chapter will set out to show how formulation and assessment can be carried out from a PCA perspective, drawing on experience in CBT.

Recommended reading

Casemore, R. (2011) *Person-centred Counselling in a Nutshell* (rev. edn). London: Sage.

Dryden, W. & Mytton, J. (1999) *Four Approaches to Counselling and Psychotherapy.* London and New York: Routledge.

Ellis, A. & Dryden, W. (1999) *The Practice of Rational Emotive Behaviour Therapy.* London: Free Association Books.

Mearns, D. and Thorne, B. (2007) *Person-centred Counselling in Action* (3rd edn). London: Sage.

Neenan, M. and Dryden, W. (2011b) *Rational Emotive Behaviour Therapy in a Nutshell* (2nd edn). London: Sage.

Nye, R.D. (1996) *Three Psychologies: Perspectives from Freud, Skinner and Rogers.* New York: Brooks-Cole.

Trower, P., Jones, J., Dryden, W., & Casey, A. (2011) *Cognitive-behavioural Counselling in Action* (2nd edn). London: Sage.

CHAPTER 6
FORMULATION AND ASSESSMENT

The processes of assessment and formulation are already a requirement within most psychological therapy services. They are seen to be strong formative aspects of good therapeutic practice regardless of theoretical approach. The language used to describe these processes, and to some extent the philosophy behind them, can cause some difficulties for some PCA therapists, many of whom who will have an antipathy towards diagnosis and assessment and the medicalisation of therapy. Ironically, for CBT practitioners, the use of a diagnostic label or framework is counter to the basic philosophy, although this is often overlooked. In this chapter we will begin with an overview of formulation and assessment and our understanding of the rationale and purpose for undertaking these processes. Then we aim to show how formulation and assessment can be carried out from a person-centred perspective, drawing on experience in CBT. This will include incorporating how case notes, assessments and 'treatment plans' may be seen as good therapeutic practice from within the CBTs and the Person-centred approach.

We would like to begin with simple definitions of the processes.

Assessment

There are different types of assessment, each serves a different and distinct purpose, and each has its place. Clinical Outcomes for Routine Evaluation (CORE) is an example of a summative assessment instrument.

Assessment can be defined as the process of making a judgement, or forming an opinion, after considering something or someone carefully and within a theoretical framework.

Formative assessment	Summative assessment
Happens all the time in the therapy room.	Is carried out at the beginning, at key stages in therapy and at the end of counselling.
It is rooted in self-referencing; a client needs to know where s/he is and understand not only where s/he wants to be but also how to 'fill the gap'.	It is often rooted in level or clinical descriptions and may often be given a numerical value. It is a valuable part of the data held and used for management purposes.
This involves both the counsellor and the client in a process of continual reflection and review about progress.	It is usually carried out by the counsellor.

FIGURE 6.1   *Types of assessment*

Diagnosis and formulation

Psychiatric diagnosis is fundamentally a rule-bound system concerned with symptom-based models. As such, it is reliant upon correlations between individual cases and concentrates on current symptomatology, making predictions (prognoses) based on hypothetical model cases (e.g. 'classical depression'). The origins of diagnosis are essentially atheoretical, and research driven by this is, frankly, tautological. Indeed, it has been argued (e.g. Phillips, 2005) that current psychiatric diagnoses serve the purposes of biomedical research rather than clinical use. Phillips, along with other dissenters from the diagnostic model, argue that clinical work requires idiographic models in which it is the task of the therapist to understand the meaning of the client's distress as contingent, unique and subjective phenomena.

This being said, the adoption of a purely ideographic approach to understanding distress, which ignores data gathered by multiple sources, is at best, rather daring; at worst, cavalier. A more defensible approach would be to focus conceptualisation on the individual and their presentation and phenomenology, as this utilises knowledge of hypothetical prototypes yet is not constricted by them.

Formulation is an application of an ideographic approach that is designed around the unique presentation of the individual but draws additional information from clinical research studies. There are many models of formulation and it is not our intention to advocate for any particular approach in this book. Rather, we encourage readers to develop their knowledge and understanding in this most essential of therapeutic skills. For both of us, this is not a matter of theoretical orientation, but rather one of good clinical practice. It is recognised internationally that best practice in formulation is that it should be congruent with the theoretical orientation of the practitioner and should be carried out in collaboration with the client. While we would not advocate the integration of PCA and CBT, we would suggest that a more integrative approach to formulation could be helpful, as advocated by Eels (2009).

A formulation can be very proximal and immediate but also longitudinal and cross-sectional. At best, this provides a hypothetical model to account for the original onset, maintenance and future likelihood of any given presentation or set of symptoms. At its most effective level, psychological formulation should draw on considered and established psychological, as opposed to purely bio-medical or psychopathological, research so that it remains fundamentally theoretical in nature.

For many people experiencing psychological distress, the most fundamental difficulties concerns their apparent inability to make sense of what is often a confusing morass of symptoms. Psychiatric diagnosis can provide an instant 'explanation' of these symptoms, but may offer a longer-term problem as it represents a label or very disheartening future prognosis. On the other hand, a coherent and collaborative psychological formulation of these difficulties provides a theoretically-guided method for structuring the information concerning an individual problem, and consequently a logical and coherent basis upon which someone can make sense of their experience. Although often considered to be empowering in and of itself, the limited research available suggests that the psychological formulation may even present a challenge (Chadwick et al., 2003), maybe as it implies the need for self-change. Also, the assertion that interventions based on psychological formulations have a better chance of success than those based on diagnosis or a generalised 'treatment programme' remains to be demonstrated empirically. It is ironic that little published work exists within the literature concentrating on the impact or efficacy of such a central skill. Indeed, empirical evidence of improved treatment efficacy from formulation-based intervention is not clear. From the limited literature available, individualised treatments appear to be little better than the standardised treatments (Emmelkamp et al., 1994; Jacobson et al., 1989; Schulte, 1997; Schulte et al., 1992).

Diagnosis and assessment in PCA and CBT

As noted before, at worst, a diagnosis represents a statement that identifies an illness or disorder through examination, medical tests or other procedures. Bluntly, it is difficult to see how any therapist, regardless of modality, can object to the first two processes. Clearly, those processes may well be carried out differently in different theoretical approaches to therapy, but we would assume that they would be part of the start of any therapeutic relationship and would be maintained throughout the continuing engagement with the client, regardless of modality.

Diagnosis in relation to physical illness may be appropriate. However, psychological diagnosis is a different matter. It is the process which may be the most difficult for person-centred therapists to accept, particularly as it is rooted in a medicalised model of illness requiring treatment or cure.

We have all been used to the terms 'assessment' and 'diagnosis' being used within the therapeutic world. In more recent times, a new term, *'formulation'* has begun to be used. Agreeing a systematic formulation with a client is now pretty much a requirement in all NHS counselling settings. We suspect that in due course there will be an expectation on every therapist to be able to demonstrate that they have carried out a clear and explicit formulation with each client with whom they work, regardless of their modality.

In respect of clinical effectiveness, we also believe that there is a need for a caveat or cautionary perspective in carrying out formulations and in using outcome evaluation measures, which recognises that measures of symptom severity may provide *some* evidence of the effectiveness of the planned intervention, but do not necessarily provide evidence of change in the client. What is important is the clients' experiencing of change in themselves.

Formulation

Put simply, formulation is the development of a plan, system or proposal as to how to proceed. This covers a wider area than 'assessment'. It is a process which, ideally, is carried out with the client and provides a focus on what the client wants to work on and how that will be carried out.

Rogers (1951) suggested that therapist expertise has social and philosophical implications that need careful consideration. He saw diagnosis, for instance, as partly a form of social control and as placing the locus of responsibility for treatment in the hands of the expert. Diagnosis, he believed, also risked placing emphasis on problems and problem resolution rather than on the person. He was opposed to most traditional forms of diagnosis and wrote that 'psychological diagnosis as usually understood is unnecessary for psychotherapy and may actually be detrimental to the therapeutic process' (1951: 220). He expressed concern about the imbalance of power created when the therapist is in the position to diagnose. He was concerned about 'the possibility of an unhealthy dependency developing if the therapist plays the role of expert, and the possibility that diagnosing clients places social control of the many in the hands of the few' (1951: 224).

However, Rogers (1951: 221) also suggested that there was a client-centred rationale for diagnosis, which he summarised as:

- Behaviour is caused, and the psychological cause of behaviour is a certain perception or way of perceiving.

- The client is the only one who has the potentiality of knowing fully the dynamics of his perceptions and his behaviour.

- In order for behaviour to change, a change in perception must be experienced. Intellectual knowledge cannot substitute for this.

- The constructive forces which bring about altered perception, reorganisation of self, and relearning, reside primarily in the client, and probably cannot come from outside.

- Therapy is basically the experiencing of the inadequacies in old ways of perceiving, the experiencing of new and more accurate and adequate perceptions, and the recognition of significant relationships between perceptions.

- In this very meaningful and accurate sense, therapy is diagnosis, and this diagnosis is a process which goes on in the experience of the client, rather than the intellect of the clinician.

It was pretty clear that Rogers was eschewing the use of the usual clinical diagnostic procedures, with the therapist taking an expert position in deciding what was wrong with the client. At the same time, he was not opposed to the processes of assessment and formulation. He was very much in favour of working with the client and making a judgement or forming an opinion with the client about what they wanted to work on. He would also clearly be in favour of formulating a plan with the client as to how they would work together.

The BACP *Ethical Framework for Good Practice in Counselling and Psychotherapy* (BACP, 2010) makes it clear that counsellors must know their limitations and capabilities in working and should actively monitor the limitations of their own competence. As an absolute minimum, a counsellor should assess (a) whether a potential client is suitable and/or ready for counselling, and (b) if they are competent to work with that client.

The client and the counsellor need to decide:

I Can we work together at this time?

II Should we work together at this time?

In order to make that decision, assessment evidence is needed about:

1 The client and their issues, concerns and their context.

2 What the client wants to achieve.

3 Any possible signs and symptoms of psychopathology in the client.

4 Any history of a mental health diagnosis or condition in the client.

5 The competence of the counsellor and their known limitations.

6 The early formative stages of the relationship between the counsellor and the client.

7 The involvement of significant others, including health professionals, with whom the client may be engaging at this time.

A more general view, irrespective of modality, would be that assessment needs to be a part of counselling as it formalises the process of selecting who the therapist is going to work with, and whether the client is within the therapist's current boundary of competence. Assessment for counselling can be carried out as a separate session, sometimes called an 'intake session', or as part of the first or first few sessions of therapy. It may involve taking a formal history of any previous contacts with the mental health services, noting any current medication, and recording clients' addresses and GP details. The dilemma in assessment is whether to ask direct questions to get the details that are needed, or whether to let clients unfold their history in their own way. PCA therapists would generally prefer to take the latter course. Assessment can be a very detailed, even a mechanised, process, requiring various forms to be completed by the client and the therapist. This is particularly so in health service settings or in agencies working with clients presenting with mental health issues and psychiatric disorders.

The full spectrum of psychiatric disorders can be split into four broad categories. The first is all those who may be described as having a *mental health condition or illness*. Those labelled in this way come from all races, cultures, classes and family constellations. The word 'illness' is only partially suitable because it refers to behaviour, personality and abilities, and is not an illness at all. There are those who can make a full recovery through medication, general life changes, counselling or psychiatry. But some people do not respond, and the changes for them are irreversible, or they deteriorate despite all the help that can be provided.

The second can be labelled as those with *psychotic illnesses*. This is believed to be less than 1 per cent of the population, of whom 10 per cent will commit suicide as an escape from torment. The third are those who are labelled with *depressive illnesses*. About 1 per cent of the population can be diagnosed with this label and between 10 and 15 per cent will kill themselves. The fourth major psychiatric category is *personality disorder*, and over 1 per cent of the population are like this. They may kill themselves on impulse or in an attention-seeking gesture that goes wrong.

Therapists need to be aware of their competence in deciding to work with a client who falls into any of those four categories, and in order to make that judgement a carefully thought out formulation process is essential.

A formulation can:

- Partly be 'needs led' and largely from the client's perspectives. It also allows counsellors to identify areas of unmet need and issues on which clients may need to focus.

- Provide clients with choice, flexibility and information so that they can make an informed commitment to counselling.

- Be orientated around the principles of monitoring the quality of care being provided, and 'helping, not harming'.

- Include setting the boundaries of the counselling relationship, assessment of the type of intervention required, and perhaps consider the need for psychiatric or other assessment and referral.

- Formulation will be ongoing as counsellors largely monitor their own performance. Through supervision, counsellors will monitor their client's progress and review the ground covered, while being open about their own limitations.

- Lead to a formal written agreement (sometimes referred to as a 'Contract') and a formal written formulation (sometimes referred to as a 'Treatment Plan').

Formulation of cases within the CBTs

It is ironic that, until recently, while less developed in REBT than in CBT, formulation has been considered to be central to CBT (Kinderman & Lobban, 2000; Persons, 1989). However, as noted earlier, it is essentially a cross-modality principle common to all psychological therapies. At the core, formulation should enable communication and understanding between client and therapist. Some authors (e.g. Harper & Moss, 2003: 9) note that it should, 'help the client and therapist make sense of the client's difficulties in the context of their lives and lay out key issues to be addressed'. As such, a formulation must be explicit, understandable, based in evidence, contextual and clearly outline a model to explain what is happening, how it has developed and how it is maintained.

As a key skill in psychological therapy, formulation is clearly distinct from diagnosis as it results in an ideographic psychological model. Although different modalities will generate different formulations of a client's presentation, at the basic level these usually contain fundamental areas of complementarity.

Although historically developed from a medical-diagnostic model in early psychoanalysis, it was the development of applied behavioural models that enabled practitioners to conceptualise clinical presentation in a very structured format. The development of functional analysis provided an empirical framework for observing and recording what a client may be presenting and then systematically generating plausible models to account for behaviour that was, at a superficial level, apparently beyond comprehension. A key feature within applied behavioural theory is the deconstruction of episodes (behavioural or emotional) into smaller, more discrete aspects (antecedents–behaviours–consequences), and it is from these that the functional links between events can be postulated. As the dominance of behavioural psychology began to wane, it became evident that it was necessary to develop more phenomenological models of distress that retained the core methodological elements of applied behavioural analysis (observation, recording and hypothesis-testing).

Functional analysis: a brief reminder

Functional analysis uses a central concept of the functionality of behaviour (Goldiamond, 1974). Another key feature is that this does not require structural diagnosis as this is not necessarily considered to be the most functionally dependent aspect of the behaviour. This represented a powerful shift from more deterministic models of intention and behaviour, despite the irony that behavioural theorists were often accused of deterministic reductionism.

The common general features of applied behavioural analysis involve systematic consideration of the behaviour/s themselves and often requires a very precise description of the target behaviour (sometimes referred to as an operational definition), setting events (to identify the most predictive of these), the ways in which the behaviour is responded to and the behavioural response to these. In essence, these become the antecedent, behaviour and consequence (ABC) and usually involve the following questions in one form or another:

- Where does the problem occur?

- Where is the problem worse?

- Are there any circumstances in which the problem occurs at the same time as a different problem?

Functional diagrams

These were originally used in biology but were adopted by radical behaviourist practitioners as it was applied to emotional and psychological disorders. The functional diagram was strongly influenced by the notion of 'cybernetic systems' in which the functional elements feed back into each other. The adoption of these feedback loops enables co-dependent and complex direct functional relationships to be described in a relatively easily accessible manner.

Figure 6.2 shows the simple negative feedback loop between the cue to eat and hunger. Eating is driven by the sensation of hunger and the cue to stop eating is driven by satiation. Applying this to more complex psychological and emotional problems involves a similar approach.

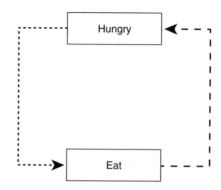

FIGURE 6.2   *An example of a simple negative feedback loop*

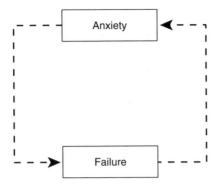

FIGURE 6.3   *A feedback loop demonstrating the dynamic relationship between a belief that one is a failure and anxiety*

Figure 6.3 illustrates the dynamic relationship between a belief that one is a social failure and anxiety. Consequently, the greater the anxiety, the more profound the sense of social failure and subsequently the more this increases anxiety. More subtle functional relationships between interlinked elements in complex presentation can be represented by identifying distinct, yet systemically interlinked systems. Figure 6.4 shows how binge eating is linked to depression, specifically how in this example feelings of depression are temporarily relieved by bingeing. However, this process leads to an increased fear of loss of control. The increased fear of a loss of control exacerbates the dynamic system of depressed affect and binge behaviour.

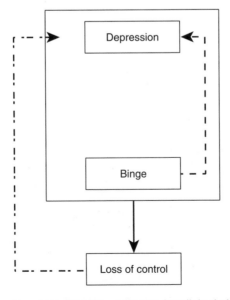

FIGURE 6.4   *The functional relationships between interlinked elements in complex presentations*

This use of the functional diagrams enables the representation of the feedback dynamics that operate both within and between different elements systems, alongside the relationships that increase and decrease the different elements or symptoms. More sophisticated models can be used to differentiate between long-term and short-term consequences and antecedents.

The functional analysis can then begin to consider two very important issues, the first of which is, aside from the apparent consequences, do these increase or decrease the probability of future behaviour? If this is the former, then it is likely that the actual versus intended consequence is strengthening the functionality of the behaviour. Any parent or dog owner will undoubtedly have insight into the inadvertent effects of failing to consider the potential reinforcing effects of their responses to problem behaviour.

Figure 6.5 gives a diagrammatical representation of a hypothetical client who was described as 'paranoid' and 'suffering from persecutory delusions'. This individual was a regular user of amphetamine and cannabis, which not only involves social connection with criminal activity and consequent attention from law enforcement agencies, but is also linked to disrupted physiological arousal patterns and consequently disturbed sleeping. Prolonged sleep deprivation associated with amphetamine use increases arousal which, in turn, links to a vicious cycle of vigilance/ avoidance of circumstances in which concerns (i.e. being watched or monitored) may be reinforced regardless of the innocuous nature of the perceived situation.

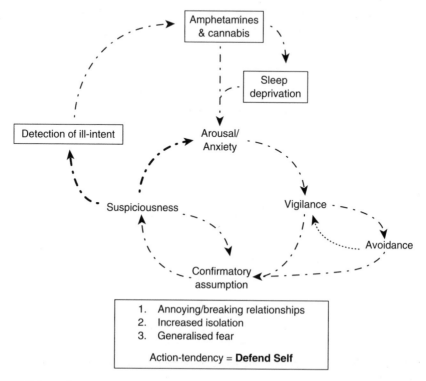

FIGURE 6.5   *An example of a complex cybernetic feedback*

When key situations are detected, this confirms the assumptions underlying the vigilant behaviour and these, in turn, lead to behaviour that increases a sense of fear and anxiety, provocative behaviour in relationships which inadvertently undermines these and ultimately increased isolation. These elements ultimately increase the probability of substance use as a means of 'escape' from an ultimately punishing world experience.

Another very strong and influential aspect of applied functional analysis was the consideration of how other elements within the system may be influencing the behaviour. Therefore, is this a feedback-based cybernetic system?

With regard to the identification of formulation as a robust alternative to diagnosis, Owens and Ashcroft (1982) argued that the basic principles from functional analysis could be applied to all modalities and that this provided a truly trans-theoretical model to use the analysis to explain aetiology, predict progress, and design interventions that will address the problem by any one of a number of means and routes. This is generally more complex than other approaches, but tends to be more effective once appropriately applied, and Turkat (1990) argued that this process has a threefold aim:

1 To develop a hypothesis about the relationship between various problems of the individual.

2 To develop hypotheses about aetiology.

3 To make predictions about the future problem.

It is also reasonable to develop this further to include a secondary element in number 2, that of identifying the most critical elements and those that need to change in order to minimise or reduce the likelihood of future re-occurrence. The model also allows the practitioner to develop both clinical skills (*how to deal with particular problems*) and intellectual skills (*how to understand a problem in its context*). Sturmey (1996) opined that the integration of functional analysis into clinical psychology practice represented a great strength of the profession, but that the non-behavioural and cognitive orientations were slow to adopt the model. It is ironic that the development of cognitive behavioural formulation does not give prominence to the behavioural aspects in functional analysis *per se*. It is of note that formulation across modalities has received precious little research attention (Eels, 2009; Sturmey, 2009).

Despite the paucity of research in what is, arguably, the most obvious and core of skills, a trans-theoretical model of formulation poses core common questions with regard to a presentation:

1 What is the key element of the presentation that is the problem?

2 Which variables change the probability or severity of the problem?

3 Which variables are antecedent and which consequent to the problem?

Tudway (2007) suggests a series of essential questions to 'test' the viability of a formulation. These include:

1 Does it make theoretical sense?
   a Whatever your model, does it hang together coherently?
      i If not, do you need to change your model or formulation?

2 Does it fit with the evidence gathered during the assessment?
   a If not, consider changing or reassessing your conceptualisation.

3 Does it account for predisposing, precipitating and maintaining factors?
   a If not, then this will be of limited use.
   b Are these factors specific enough to be of use?

4 Does it make sense to peers?
   a Do your colleagues or supervisor follow your conceptualisation?

5 Is it possible to generate predictions about the client's thoughts, emotions or behaviours?
   a If not, then revise.

6 Can you test these predictions by safe experimentation?
   a Again, if not, revise.

7 Does the past history fit?
   a If not, revise and check your understanding of events.

8 Does it suggest an intervention and does this progress as the theory would predict?
   a If not, then be honest with the client.

9 Can it be used to identify future sources of risk or difficulty for this person?
   a If not, then check your understanding of events and history.

10 Are there important factors left unexplained?
   a If not, then be honest with the client.

Within the CBTs, the following elements can be considered to be common to the model:

1 History and development of the problem, limited demographic data.

2 Identify *at least one* target behaviour (crying), or cognition (thoughts of worthlessness) or physiological (feeling tense).

3 Identify *at least one* operationalised antecedent that must include examples (crying), or cognition (thoughts of worthlessness) or physiological (feeling tense) often occurred when alone (morning) or after assertion failure (giving in to bullying).

4 Identify *at least one* operationalised consequence that must include examples (positive social reinforcement of comforting attention, trips to the GP and negative reinforcement by the use of anxiolytics, driving avoidance and avoiding certain social situations).

5 A stated distinction between onset and maintenance (began at school, worsened after failing at work).

Phase 1:	Definitions of problems
1	Obtain statement of the problem from those involved
2	Clarify initial objectives of those involved
3	On the basis of initial information received, specify problems
Theme:	A process of growing awareness aimed at a therapeutic consensus
Phase 2:	**Exploration***
1	Hypothesis of cause and maintenance are generated
2	Multilevel CBT assessment is conducted
3	Data are collected to test hypotheses
Theme:	**The process is one of increasing refined observations**
Phase 3:	**Formulation**
1	A formulation and intervention hypotheses are established
2	Discussion with participants and redefinition of objectives takes place
3	The adequacy of the hypotheses are checked and verified
Theme:	**The process is one of testing the hypothesis until an adequate explanation is available**
Phase 4:	**Intervention***
1	The procedures to be used are specified
2	An intervention contract is established
3	The agreed programme is enacted and monitored
Theme:	**The process is one of structured practice**
Phase 5:	**Evaluation**
1	Accomplished outcomes are evaluated
2	Any gains made are supported and enhanced, the programme is optimised and further objectives, if suggested, are pursued
3	Continuing evaluation and review. Generation of further ideas to consolidate progress
Theme:	**The process is one of monitored achievement and support**

*These elements in the model assume that evidence is drawn directly from empirical research or extrapolated from a credible, existing knowledge base. In the absence of clear evidence to support the use of an intervention or assessment, care must be taken and support and advice from senior colleagues should be sought.

FIGURE 6.6 *The University College London (UCL) Case Formulation Model, Bruch and Bond (1998), p. 26*

6   Identify factors that increase and decrease the behaviour.

7   Identify secondary gains.

8   Identify possible functions (agoraphobia keeps family at home more often than otherwise, avoidance of having to take responsibility).

9   State an intervention strategy for the problem by linking to 2, 3 and 4.

Ironically, the importance of the contribution of behavioural theory is obvious. However, this provides a significant structure by which we can enable an understanding of the range, direction and intensity of behaviours, symptoms and disorders across therapeutic modalities.

Bruch and Bond (1998) propose a very useful structural framework for CBT formulation (see Figure 6.6).

Formulation and Assessment Form

Figure 6.7 is an example of a form which has been produced for use by a person-centred counsellor.

Practice exercise

As a practice exercise, readers might like to attempt a simple formulation of how they might set out to work with a client who presents as follows:

Exercise 1

Geoff

Geoff is 44 years old, tall, pleasant looking, slightly overweight and he has a rather 'flushed' countenance (blotchy red face). Geoff is casually dressed in good quality clothes and shoes, and seems a bit 'low'. He reports that he went to see a counsellor via an Employee Access Program (EAP) as he was feeling very miserable. The EAP referred him on to you after he had undergone six sessions. The EAP informed you that at the last of his six sessions he had told his EAP counsellor that his doctor had said that he may have Bipolar Disorder. Geoff refused medication from his GP and did not want to see a psychiatrist for a full assessment.

When you meet him for the first time, Geoff presents as very quietly spoken and seems quite shy – he has difficulty making and maintaining eye contact.

Geoff tells you that he has always suffered from periods of very low moods but that he rarely feels elated. He also has attacks of very low self-confidence at work.

Client..........….....................   **Code**..................…...................................…....... **Date**..........…..................…...
(a) **How do I experience the client on arrival?** (briefly)
(b) **Presenting issue/problem**
(c) **Contact level** in relation to me and within themselves (consider Prouty's *reality, affective* and *communicative* functions[1])? **How available are their own feelings to them? How aware are they of mine? Will sufficient psychological contact be possible?** Motivation to work on themselves?
(d) Is the client affected by **drugs, alcohol, or medication?**
(e) **Support:** significant others, family background or issues of isolation
(f) **Psychological – past and current**: Psychiatric involvement? Previous or current therapy? Are any other health professionals involved with the client?
(g) **Medical conditions**
(h) **Risk behaviour**: Suicide attempts: Self-harm: Violence to others: Drug misuse: Alcohol misuse: Eating disorders:
(i) **Am I mentally and emotionally fit or competent to work with this person, with their presenting issues, in this setting, at this time?**
(j) **What does the client want, or expect, from counselling?** What do they expect from me?
(k) **How have I experienced the client in this initial session?**
(l) **What is my therapeutic intent with this client at this stage?**
(m) **Outcome of assessment**:   Contracted   Declined   Referred on   Not appropriate

1 Prouty, G. (1994) *Theoretical Evolutions in Person Centred/Experiential Therapy: Applications to Schizophrenic and Retarded Psychoses.* Westport, CT: Praeger. pp. 40–42.

FIGURE 6.7 *University of Warwick Person-centred Formulation and Assessment Form*

Geoff says that he has never been in a proper relationship with a woman, although he would very much like to. The only relationship he had was in his early twenties when at university. That lasted six months and then she became fed up with his moods and left him.

Geoff says he has almost no friends other than a couple of colleagues whom he gets on well with at work and he does not have any social activities.

Geoff describes his childhood as OK but he never had any affection from either of his parents, who are now both dead. He has no siblings and no other relatives living.

Currently, Geoff lives on his own in a 'bachelor flat'.

Geoff has a good management job in a government agency which he quite likes, but gets into a panic when he has to take very senior officials on site visits. These attacks can result in him taking days off work.

Geoff says he is not suicidal but often feels that life is not worth living. He says he would never take his own life, although he often thinks about other people committing suicide, usually other people that he knows.

Geoff's main concerns are:

- That he is so unhappy so often and can't seem to stop it.

- That he says he is frightened that he might be bipolar.

- That he can't find a way to get into a relationship and desperately wants to be in one.

- That he spends lots of days feeling very lonely and just stays home alone, eating junk food, watching TV (porn) and masturbating.

QUESTIONS

1 What would your key interests be in quickly trying to understand this client, his needs and how you might work with him, if you agree to enter into a therapy relationship?

2 On the basis of the information provided above, are there any tentative hypotheses that you might consider regarding Geoff's difficulties and concerns?

3 What questions might you ask or what information do you think you would need to obtain from him to enable you and Geoff to proceed to an effective formulation?

4 How would you set out to work with Geoff?

Exercise 2

Liz

Liz is 28 years old, tall, attractive, with long blond hair. She is smartly dressed in a blue trouser suit, and wears no makeup. Liz seems a little shy, although engages with good eye contact and a firm handshake and she has been referred by her employer via the Occupational Health Unit because she has been feeling very low and is having difficulty with her manager, who she claims is bullying her.

In your first assessment session with her, Liz tells you that she married Tony, a professional musician, last year. They met at university, when Liz was 18 and when she was experiencing severe depression. Liz reports that Tony 'looked after her' and supported her, enabling her to complete her degree. She achieved a first-class degree in Business Administration.

Tony's career has now taken off and he is very absorbed in his music. He gets very irritated with her low moods. Liz feels their relationship is rocky at the moment and she has experienced a number of depressive periods since leaving university, but this has not stopped her from gaining promotion to a fairly senior post in a government agency. Liz says that she drinks a bottle of wine every evening and also regularly smokes cannabis in the evenings and weekends and snorts cocaine at parties.

Liz tells you that she had a difficult childhood, as an only child. Her parents were both psychiatrists who had what Liz describes as a loveless marriage. They were only interested in her academic achievements and she never experienced any love or affection from them. Liz feels she was driven, particularly by her father, to achieve academic success.

Liz reports that she was never allowed to play with other children and was only allowed to play on her own with 'serious' toys. Liz described that she spent a lot of time in their large garden, playing fantasy games, pretending to be a 'Princess locked in an Ivory Tower'. If she misbehaved, they would lock her in the hall cupboard for several hours. Then they would 'send her to Coventry' for weeks at a time. At no time did they physically abuse her and she has no recollection of ever being smacked.

After some time, Liz changed from talking to you as a mature adult and began to adopt the posture of a small child in the chair and to talk with a 'little girl' voice. When you notice this out loud to her and wonder what it is about, she responds in the little girl voice, 'That's because I have to keep myself hidden, while she gets on with our life.' Liz went on to say that she didn't want any one to know just how frightened and lonely she was, after which she sobbed quietly in a childlike way and then became quiet, curled up in the chair.

After several minutes of silence, she seemed to reassert her earlier, confident adult self, sat up straight and sat quietly.

Questions

1   What would your key interests be in quickly trying to understand this client, her needs and how you might work with her, if you agree to enter into a therapy relationship?

2   On the basis of the information provided above, are there any tentative hypotheses that you might consider regarding Liz's difficulties and concerns?

3   What questions might you ask or what information do you think you would need to obtain from her to enable you and Liz to proceed to an effective formulation?

4   How would you set out to work with Liz?

Exercise 3

George

George is 29 years old, tall, quite well built and well proportioned. He is smartly dressed with short hair and has some slight acne on his face.

George seems very nervous on meeting you, blushing strongly and does not find it easy to talk. He appears to be very self-conscious or shy.

George was referred by his GP because of some depressive symptoms and some problematic behaviours, and describes periods of low mood, difficulty in sleeping, and attacks of shyness accompanied by uncontrolled blushing on face, neck and hands. George says that red blotches appear on his neck and chest.

George admits that he goes on some binge drinking expeditions on his own.

George reports that his mother suddenly left home when he was 7 years old, after years of a very abusive relationship between his parents. George described hiding under the kitchen table many times, as they rowed and threw things at each other, and he claimed to have had no affection from either of them.

George describes how he came home from school one day to discover Mum had left while he and his younger brother continued to live with Dad, who never talked about his mother again. George reports that he has never seen his mother since and has no idea if she is alive or dead. He also tells you that he has no interest in finding out about her.

George now lives on his own in a small flat and says that he has a reasonable relationship with his Dad, whom he visits from time to time, and they go out for Sunday lunch.

George reports that he has no personal friendships, although he is friendly with a couple of female colleagues at work.

George reports that he feels dreadfully lonely and would like to be in a relationship. However, he won't go out to meet people because he is so ashamed of his uncontrollable blushing.

George says that he can't eat out in restaurants because some foods bring on the blotches on his neck and then he starts to blush all over.

George also thinks he 'looks strange'. He feels he is 'misshapen', particularly his head. He says quite strongly that 'People are bound to think I'm not normal'.

As soon as he wakes up he has intrusive thoughts that people will think he is weird because of the way he looks. These thoughts keep re-occurring throughout the day and keep him awake at night, and he says he is really obsessed with seeing his reflection in mirrors, shop windows or any reflective surface.

1   What would your key interests be in quickly trying to understand this client, his needs and how you might work with him, if you agree to enter into a therapy relationship?

2   On the basis of the information provided above, are there any tentative hypotheses that you might consider regarding George's difficulties and concerns?

3   What questions might you ask or what information do you think you would need to obtain from him to enable you and George to proceed to an effective formulation?

4   How would you set out to work with George?

A link to the next chapter

We have a particular interest in the way in which many therapists get 'stuck' when they are unable to establish psychological contact and 'relational depth' with clients. The next chapter presents an exploration of a way of differentiating between 'therapy', for which psychological contact, the first of Rogers' core conditions (which he described as an essential 'precondition'), must be present, and 'working therapeutically', which we will define as 'psycho-social therapeutic education'. The authors believe that this will free up PCA therapists to draw on cognitive behavioural methods in order to work differently from within their own therapeutic modality. This will also enable them to operate within an economically-driven model for short-term and stepped care services in the IAPTs. This will include some examination of the use and misuse of research evidence.

Recommended reading

Eels, T.D. (ed.) (2007) *Handbook of Psychotherapy Case Formulation*. New York: Guilford Press.

Johnston, D. & Dallos, R. (2006) *Formulation in Psychology and Psychotherapy*. Hove: Routledge.

Milner, J. & O'Byrne, P. (2004) *Assessment in Counselling: Theory Process and Decision Making*. Basingstoke: Palgrave.

CHAPTER 7
THERAPY VERSUS WORKING THERAPEUTICALLY: AN ECONOMIC AND PRACTICE ISSUE FOR BOTH APPROACHES

We have a particular interest in the way in which many therapists get 'stuck' when they are unable to establish psychological contact and 'relational depth' with clients. This chapter presents an exploration of a way of differentiating between 'therapy', as defined by Rogers in his core conditions, and 'working therapeutically'.

Therapy versus therapeutic support

Rogers described his core conditions as an essential 'pre-condition for therapy that must be present in order for therapy to take place'. We differentiate between this and what Roger has termed 'Psycho-social Therapeutic Education' (Casemore, 2011), in which therapeutic progress can be achieved even though this does not meet the standard set by Rogers in his core conditions. We believe that this will free up therapists from both the CBTs and PCA to work differently from within their own therapeutic modality and enable them to operate within an economically driven-model for short-term and stepped care services in IAPT. In examining these elements, we are aware that empirical studies supporting the use of the latter of these approaches may reflect the type of data collected, which may limit the potential generalisability of this.

From a CBT perspective, we have a concern about the 'manualisation' of therapy, which is increasingly at risk of becoming an end in and of itself. Research evidence clearly exists to support the use of very structured adaptations of the CBT model and this appears to be the case not only for training in CBT to enable practitioners to deliver manualised packages consistently (Williams et al., 2011), but also for providing information on interventions for 'common mental health conditions' drawn from the CBT model (e.g. Cavanagha et al., 2011). Evidently, there is a benefit from maintaining the integrity of a model and practice standards. However, adopting such a model also runs the risk of a type of psycho-therapeutic 'Fordism', in which limiting the cost is the principal factor determining the nature and duration of therapeutic interventions. This can result in both client and practitioner becoming lost among generic protocols.

While the current economic and political climate has galvanised attention to the issues of scarce resources and the need to ensure maximum effect for the maximum number of people, the notion of time-limited therapy is not unique to the present. Indeed, both Ellis and Beck noted that their dissatisfaction with 'traditional' psychotherapy was, in part, associated with the amount of time this consumed, suggesting that this approach enabled clients to achieve more in a shorter space of time. Historical research by Rush et al. (1977) noted that much of the therapeutic change in CBT occurred within the first few weeks of treatment, which supports the notion of time-limited therapy.

Although usually associated with the CBTs, the notion of very brief interventions is neither unique to, nor does it characterise, the CBTs. There have been various incarnations of time-limited therapy, including psychodynamic models (e.g. Davenloo, 1980; Malan, 1979), which can extend up to 30 sessions as an effective way to achieve positive change. It was in the mid-1980s that very brief treatments, sometimes referred to as the CBT two-plus-one model, were initially outlined. This was strongly influenced by behavioural therapy and is rooted in self-help and skills-based interventions. As noted previously, there is little doubt that, at times, targeted application of techniques or skills can have clear and life-improving benefits. However, whether this very specific change is equivalent to the more generalised shift associated with formal psychological therapy remains a moot point.

As noted, time-limited or time-sensitive therapy is not the exclusive preserve of the CBTs, and Bryant-Jefferies (2003) has written usefully on this topic in relation to the use of PCA in primary care settings.

It is of note that some empirical evidence does indeed suggest that time-limited therapies have proven useful (e.g. Barkham et al., 1999) and the literature contains reference to clear benefits from the CBTs over other modalities. In this regard, despite the obvious financial assumption that core CBT interventions intended to 'treat the whole system' would be more 'cost-effective', research evidence suggests something different. Indeed, work by Bodden et al. (2008) and Voncken and Bogels (2006) suggests individual CBT is not only as effective but less costly than family CBT for this client group. Conversely, Evans-Jones and Peters (2009) report that a greater number of sessions is linked to client ratings of the therapeutic relationship. As with all research evidence, it is essential to consider the generalisability of such studies as careful scrutiny of these data may suggest a more conservative interpretation.

It is tempting to assume that developments in health are made independently of the economic circumstances in which they exist, but this is clearly not the case and we contend that clear parallels exist between the risks of single-market monopolies in business and those in psychological therapy. As CBT has become identified as a preferred treatment by statutory services, this has led to a proliferation of training in a generic model of CBT based around diagnosis-led interventions for specific common mental health problems. It is our contention that this initially apparent 'golden age' also contains a potential risk that might ultimately hinder the further development of the CBTs and also other therapeutic modalities.

We understand the financial imperatives that drive the move towards 'time-limited' therapy. However, we would prefer to use the concept of 'time-sensitive therapy', rather than time-limited. No therapist should work on a basis of a completely open book in relation to the duration of therapy, but should always bear in mind the financial pragmatics of availability of resources. These financial constraints should not be the sole determinant of the duration of therapy and should be a factor that is borne in mind.

In an article in the *Journal of the British Association for Counselling*, Casemore wrote:

> I would like to begin by taking the slightly heretical view that a substantial amount of the activity which many people call counselling is no such thing at all. I believe that this results from a 'deification' of the process of counselling and an implicit belief that it is both a universal panacea and that it occupies the foremost position in a hierarchy of helping activities. This demeans all the other helping strategies which are therapeutic and lead to change in the individual. Just because two people are sitting down in a room together and one of them is identified as 'Counsellor' and the other as 'Client', doesn't mean to say that 'Counselling' is taking place. (Casemore, 2002: 6–8)

It is our belief that this remains pertinent today not only to therapy generally, but more particularly to much of the practice within IAPT. This is not to say that working therapeutically has neither benefit nor reduced efficacy – not only does the evidence base but also common sense reject such an argument. A more significant issue rests with the notion that psychological therapies are intimately linked to the individual phenomenological world of the client. The saying:

> 'All people are like all other people in the same way that all people are like some other people in the same way that all people are like no other people'

paraphrases Kluckhohn and Murray (1948), who identified the three levels of personality analysis summarised above, seems particularly apt, albeit a little confusing to those not *au fait* with academic psychology. In essence, every human being is alike at the 'nature' level, yet at the individual and group difference level these comparisons are less robust. Finally, at the level of individual uniqueness, they are, frankly, not alike. It seems obvious to state but distress is, for the individual, unique and consequently diagnoses based on a broad-based correlation will reference the second level at best. Consequently, it is our contention that the adoption of diagnostic-based interventions based around between-subject comparisons as opposed to tailoring the model to individual characteristics inevitably results in a 'general fit'.

The term 'CBT' has proliferated in statutory services and is evidently the preferred intervention option of services and politicians alike. However, as the popularity of CBT has grown, so has the need to standardise in order to preserve model integrity. This has given rise to a plethora of books detailing the particular adaptations of the model to particular diagnoses. While it is not our intention here to suggest that there is benefit from clarification of core issues associated with particular generalised presentations, it is our contention that this has led to a misconception that CBT is easy or something that anyone able to read a book 'can do a bit of'. While there is an impressive empirical literature supporting positive outcomes following CBT, clearly this is dependent upon exactly which questions are asked and what is measured as an outcome. Although formulation remains a key element within the CBTs and, as noted earlier in the book, all psychological therapies generally, it remains grossly under-researched and there is very little empirical study detailing the impact of formulation upon clients (e.g. Chadwick et al., 2003; Kuyken et al., 2005). However, it has retained an assumed importance and resultant presence within practice that is so public in its avowed statement that empirical evidence is necessary.

In reality, there really is very little difference between the CBTs and PCA with regard to the importance of the therapeutic relationship. Rather, the emphasis is that in the CBTs this is not the therapy, but is another vehicle in which therapy journeys. As such, the over-emphasis on the learning of the 'technique' has, to some extent, dominated and this is succinctly noted by Wills and Sanders (1997: 55):

> Traditionally, the technical aspects of therapy have been felt to be the active ingredients. If the therapeutic relationship was a car, the cognitive therapist would use it to travel from A to B, whereas the psychodynamic or Rogerian therapist would be a collector, spending hours polishing and fine-tuning each vehicle.

Following considerable research, Rogers (1957) identified what he referred to as six necessary and sufficient conditions which are required in order for therapeutic change to take place. Today, other modalities accept the necessity for those conditions, but disagree that they are sufficient. So what we have to say applies to all the counselling modalities and not just the PCA.

It is important to concentrate on the first of those six conditions of a therapeutic relationship, which is that the counsellor and client must be in 'psychological contact'. Originally, Rogers used the term 'contact' but later he restated it as:

> The first condition specifies that a minimal relationship, a psychological contact, must exist. I am hypothesising that significant personality change does not occur except in a relationship. …

> …All that is intended by this first condition is to specify that two people are to some degree in contact, that each makes some perceived difference in the experiential field of the other…

> …If each is aware of being in personal or psychological contact with the other, then this condition is met…

> …Without it, however, the remaining items (the other conditions) would have no meaning and that is the reason for including it. (Rogers, 1957: 95–103)

Rogers himself, did not go on to further define the nature of 'psychological contact' or how it might be achieved or measured.

At a naïve level, it seems almost illogical to question the notion of the central necessity of therapist skills and demeanour as a therapist perceived as non-accepting and uncompassionate is unlikely to provide a sound basis for a client to confide in regarding complex and distressing experiences in anything other than a highly problematic manner.

Research into psychological therapy has consistently found a positive relationship between the quality of the therapeutic relationship and outcome (Martin et al., 2000; Zuroff & Blatt, 2006) and, despite some of the assumptions of the very brief or self-help approaches, evidence suggests that the symptom change in the initial stages of therapy does not account for the interaction of the therapeutic relationship and positive outcome (e.g. Klein et al., 2003; Zuroff & Blatt, 2006). Consequently, it seems hard to account for all of the claims made by the two plus one models of very brief CBT. On a logical note, if it were the case that all clients actually required was information and technique, then it would be predicted that the provision of systematised information via a public access forum such as the internet would then be associated with a general reduction in psychological distress. Clearly this is not the case as there are significant amounts of material (from the sublime to the ridiculous) available, yet the need and demand for psychological therapy remains.

With regard to Rogers' core conditions, it has long been acknowledged within the CBTs that certain therapist characteristics are necessary. Indeed, Beck et al. (1979) make reference to therapist factors and the need for attention to be paid to the relationship. However, it was assumed that practitioners would have undertaken initial training in therapy and, consequently, this received little attention in the literature. Despite this, Beck et al. (1979) noted that warmth, accurate empathy and genuineness were necessary and that a therapist needs to be 'honest with himself as well as with the client'. Beck et al. also caution:

> If these attributes are overemphasised or applied artlessly, they may become disruptive to the therapeutic collaboration. ... [W]e believe that these characteristics in themselves are necessary but not sufficient to produce optimum therapeutic effect. (Beck et al., 1979: 45)

Furthermore, they elaborate that the techniques of CBT should be 'applied in a tactful, therapeutic and human manner by a fallible person – the therapist'.

On the dearth of attention paid to these factors, Wills and Sanders (1997: 56) comment:

> Although the 'necessary but not sufficient' view of the therapeutic relationship has been central to cognitive therapy, more attention is now being paid to the importance of the therapeutic relationship itself. It comes as no surprise that the research in cognitive therapy supports what our humanistic colleagues have been saying all along: that the quality of the relationship is central.

It is perhaps an ironic consequence that the CBTs have not only tended to conceptualise emotional sequences and episodes in a componential manner, it seems that this has been repeated to some extent in the research and training. It seems ironic that the safety of the boundaries and acceptance within the therapeutic relationship, enabling powerful emotive and behavioural practice as a means of practical disputation, has been largely overlooked as opposed to the technical aspects of the procedures themselves (e.g. Rational-Emotive Imagery, Emotion-Induction, etc.).

The empirical study of therapeutic factors in the CBTs suggests that key elements form the relationship, including empathy, experience and confidence (Ackerman & Hilsenroth, 2003) along with expertness, attractiveness and trustworthiness (Strong, 1968), acceptance (Pierson & Hayes, 2007) and compassion (Gilbert, 2007), are likely to be factors in the quality of the therapeutic relationship. Evans-Jones and Peters (2009) found that client ratings of therapist empathy, expertness, attractiveness and trustworthiness, along with more sessions and a formulation, were linked to a better therapeutic relationship and engagement. With regard to the necessity of transparency, Dryden (1995a) illustrates the point about the uniquely interpersonal nature of the therapeutic relationship when he considers Bodrin's concept of the bond by reference to the reaction of a client to a personal disclosure. This point is given further support by the empirical work of Hardy et al. (2007), who suggest that self-disclosure can be considered to represent a potential threat to the therapeutic relationship as well as resistance from the client. Again, this conceptualisation represents a significant difference between the two modalities. From the Person-centred approach, resistance and self-disclosure are conceptualised as necessary components of the therapeutic relationship to be experienced and not overcome or challenged.

Gilbert and Leahy (2007) note that collaboration does not obviate the need for the therapist to at least be perceived as possessing expertise, knowledge and the capacity to set the agenda. They continue to consider Gilbert's 10-stage model:

- Developing rapport.
- Exploring possible fears, concerns and expectations of coming for counselling.
- Shared understanding and meaning.
- Exploring the story and eliciting key themes and cognitive emotive styles: (a) taking a historical perspective; (b) working in the here and now.
- Sharing therapeutic goals.
- Explaining the therapy rationale.
- Increasing awareness of the relationship among thoughts, feelings and social behaviour.
- Moving to alternative conceptualisations.
- Monitoring internal feelings and cognitions, and role enactments.
- Homework and alternative role enactments.

From his experience of over 40 years as a therapist, Roger suggests that establishing psychological contact is difficult to achieve in the first place (Casemore,

2011). Indeed, he suggests that although it may occur fleetingly in the first or early sessions with a client, it takes on average in excess of six weeks to occur in any meaningful and sustainable way. It is also difficult and both emotionally and physically exhausting to maintain. Most experienced therapists would have difficulty describing how they experience the condition and how they achieve it. As previously noted, the therapeutic relationship has always been considered important in the CBTs and this has been particularly the case for those clients with more long-term problems.

Prouty (1994) conducted research into therapeutic work with clients diagnosed with severe psychopathology, and although working from a person-centred approach, he concluded that psychological contact is a necessary pre-condition for counselling. Other authors have undertaken work relating the therapeutic relationship to engagement and therapeutic effect. Bordin (1979) attempted to develop a pan-theoretical model of therapeutic relationship which suggested three factors:

- Goals
    Mutually agreed between client and therapist.
- Tasks
    Agreed assignment of tasks.
- Bond
    The development of the relationship into a complex attachment in which Bordin emphasises the need for hope to be introduced at an early stage.

Within this model, therapeutic goals and the tasks required to meet them are mutually understood and mediated by an interpersonal bond between client and therapist. Hardy et al. (2007) developed this further to include both therapist and client experiences of past relationships. Bordin (1979) speculated that effective therapy occurs when therapist and client have an appropriately bonded relationship, mutually agreed goals from the enterprise and both understand and agree to carry out their own and the other's tasks in therapy. An emphasis made by Dryden (1995b), but also implicit in the CBTs generally, is that the bond is intended by the therapist to encourage the client to implement goal-directed therapeutic tasks, an emphasis that Rogers would have found very difficult.

Prouty (1994) hypothesised that the client needs to experience three forms of 'contact' within the relationship with the therapist in order to be able to enter into psychological contact with the therapist. Specifically, he suggests that the client needs to be in:

---

a '**Reality Contact**' – contact with the actual reality of their world (as opposed to their perception of the reality of their world);
b '**Affective Contact**' – contact with their internal affective self; and
c '**Communicative Contact**' – contact with the affective self of the therapist.

Psychological contact is made up of three elements:

1 A set of therapeutic techniques or interventions;
2 A set of psychological functions necessary for therapy to occur; and
3 A set of measurable outcome behaviours.

Perls (1976) suggests that there is a functional relationship between human beings and their environment which forms a 'contact boundary where psychological events take place'. Polster and Polster (1973) suggests that this boundary is the point at which clients experience the self or 'me' in relation to the non self or 'not me', and that contact at this boundary enables both to be more clearly experienced. Similarly, Safran and Segal (1990) argue that human beings are motivated to 'maintain relatedness' to other human beings and that support for this process is rooted in our biology and, consequently, core beliefs and assumptions are likely to be interpersonal. Gilbert (1992) offered a similar theory relating to the evolutionary aspects of depressive thinking styles. As such, then, for Safran and Segal, the therapeutic relationship is conceptualised as a specialised aspect of other human relationships that can be used in therapy as opposed to something that can be achieved *per se*. Within the CBTs, the therapeutic relationship has been conceptualised more as a concentrated arena in which the client's underlying beliefs will emerge. This enables *in vivo* change and disputation to occur in a safe and empathic way.

Within the PCA, clients who are disturbed or distressed and may be described as being *in a state of incongruence*, and are likely to have some difficulty with some or all of the three forms of 'contact' which Prouty (1994) describes. The greater the degree of incongruence, the more this is likely to be true. Clients who are experiencing severe mental disorder or psychopathological conditions are even more unlikely to be able to experience the three essential forms of contact, thus making a full therapeutic relationship impossible. For example, those clients who are unable to be in touch with their actual reality will find it impossible to experience a mutual 'here and now' reality with the therapist. This may also be true for clients on significant doses of anti-depressant or anti-psychotic medication, and for clients actively involved in alcohol and substance misuse.

Prouty's theory predicts that, if it is difficult to establish and maintain psychological contact, then it is likely that both client and therapist are going to experience feeling stuck in the therapeutic process. By definition, this also suggests that much of what goes on in the therapy room really is not 'therapy' if psychological contact is not present.

From a Person-centred approach that does not mean to say that other effective forms of therapeutic support cannot work and be really valuable. However, guidance, advice, support, teaching, active listening, behaviour modification, debriefing (to name but a few) do not need to be defined as 'counselling' or 'therapy', and these are effective strategies which can be really helpful in enabling change to take place. Similar to the techniques so well described and defined within the CBTs, these elements often constitute aspects of CBT within the process and therapeutic relationship.

Prouty (1994) suggests that 'pre-therapy', which is designed to enable a client to reach a position where they may be able to begin to establish and experience a psychological contact relationship, is another important strategy, but one which requires therapists to acquire extra knowledge and to undergo extra training in order to practise.

The therapeutic equivalence paradox

Any consideration of the nature of therapy and therapeutic change cannot avoid the implications of the therapeutic equivalence paradox. All the therapies are the same in what they are setting out to achieve and paradoxically they are all different in how they are setting out to do it. Data from this are well established and continue to produce results supporting these findings, and the growing significant body of evidence suggests that similarities between therapeutic modalities are more evident than might seemed to be the case (e.g. Osatuke et al., 2005; Stiles et al., 2008). We would suggest caution about applying simplistic interpretations of these data to the effect that there really is little difference between 'types of therapy' and research indicates that practitioners were clearly working within their models (e.g. Elliott et al., 1985; Osatuke et al., 2005; Stiles et al., 2008). With regard to specific aspects of therapeutic interaction and the use of interpretation, studies suggest that, although clients generate their own insights, therapist interpretation is necessary for client insight. While this may involve a more complex relationship and definition of insight, for example, specific 'questions' leading to reflection on the issue of the timing of interpretation, it is clearly very important to a positive therapeutic outcome (e.g. Elliott, 1984; Elliott et al., 1985, 1994). All of these studies have generated trans-modality models which offer promise in the evolution of psychological therapy, for example, the five-stage trans-theoretical model of insight in therapy (Elliott et al., 1985) (see Figure 7.1) and Stiles et al.'s (1996) seven clusters of therapist intentions – treatment context, session structure, affect, obstacles, encouraging change, behaviour and cognition-insight – which are important across modalities, but the patterns and timing of these differ according to the modality of the therapist.

Despite the overall therapeutic paradox it seems that the content and pattern of process is different in different modalities. For example, negative emotional content of insight-orientated therapies is different from the CBTs. This may provide some evidence that different modalities activate different emotional-processing systems (Mackay et al., 2002).

1	Contextual priming in which earlier sessions provide therapists with relevant thematic information and allow a therapeutic alliance to develop and the client narrates a recently experienced painful problematic life event.
2	Novel information in which therapists present clients with new information that is both relevant to the recent painful event and in keeping with more general themes about the client's functioning. This new information generally takes the form of therapist interpretation.
3	Initial distantiated processing in which the immediate reaction of the client is to agree the accuracy then mull it over in a fairly unemotional manner.
4	Insight in which the client makes a clear connection or reconnection which is conveyed to the therapist in the form of an observable emotional expression of experience of newness.
5	Elaboration in which the insight stimulates the client to further exploration and elaborates the emotional or other implications of the insight and indicates that the insight is not merely intellectual.

FIGURE 7.1   *Five-stage trans-theoretical model of insight in therapy (Elliott et al., 1985)*

0	**Warded off/dissociated**. Client seems unaware of the problem; the problematic voice is silent or dissociated. Affect may be minimal, reflecting successful avoidance. Alternatively, the problem appears as somatic symptoms, acting out or state switches.
1	**Unwanted thoughts/active avoidance**. Client prefers not to think about the experience. Problematic voices emerge in response to therapist interventions or external circumstances and are suppressed or actively avoided. Affect involves unfocused negative feelings; their connection with the content may be unclear.
2	**Vague awareness/emergence**. Client is aware of the problem but cannot formulate it clearly – can express it but cannot reflect on it. Problematic voice emerges into sustained awareness. Affect includes intense psychological pain – fear, sadness, anger, disgust – associated with the problematic experience.
3	**Problem statement/clarification**. Content includes a clear statement of a problem – something that can be worked on. Opposing voices are differentiated and can talk about each other. Affect is negative but manageable, not panicky.
4	**Understanding/insight**. The problematic experience is formulated and understood in some way. Voices reach an understanding with each other (a meaning bridge). Affect may be mixed, with some unpleasant recognition but also some pleasant surprise.
5	**Application/working through**. The understanding is used to work on a problem. Voices work together to address problems of living. Affective tone is positive, optimistic.
6	**Resourcefulness/problem solution**. The formerly problematic experience has become a resource, used for solving problems. Voices can be used flexibly. Affect is positive, satisfied.
7	**Integration/mastery**. Client automatically generalises solutions; voices are fully integrated, serving as resources in new situations. Affect is positive or neutral (i.e. this is no longer something to get excited about).

FIGURE 7.2   *Assimilation Model of Psychotherapeutic Change (Stiles et al., 1991)*

Given these general findings, then, it seems likely that those modalities with the closest philosophical lineage, such as the CBTs and PCA, are more likely to have distinct similarities. Indeed, it is of note that, despite their avowed antipathy towards the classical interpretative phenomenology of the therapist, both the CBTs and PCA use a form of interpretation (e.g. Elliott et al., 1985; Stiles et al., 1996). The Osatuke et al. (2005) study applied Stiles' Assimilation Model of Psychotherapeutic Change (Stiles et al., 1991) (see Figure 7.2) to matched clients undergoing CBT and PCA and it was evident that the process differences resulted in different patterns of assimilation that were consistent with the predictions of their models. It is of interest that each was 'successful'. All of this begs the question: *'Is it not so much the course that needs to match the horse, but the horse that needs to match the course?'*

Within our current social context, it seems to us that there is something important about our attitudinal stance as therapists, about the value of what we are actually doing. For example, it often appears that therapists adopt an attitudinal stance which regards counselling as being at the top of a hierarchy of helping strategies. For others, psychotherapy is considered to hold the topmost position and the term 'cognitive behavioural psychotherapy' is an oxymoron that can illicit an almost Pavlovian response of ridicule! It seems more important and realistic to see counselling and psychotherapy as processes on a continuum of helping strategies, any of which can be the most important at any given time, depending on the client's needs. It is perhaps useful to envisage a wheel, the rim of which constitutes the whole range of helping and coping skills, methods and approaches. The spokes might include the following.

All of the elements shown in Figure 7.3, and many other helping strategies, will be important to the individual who needs help. A very important element is the active involvement of the individual in making a choice about the most appropriate form of help for them at the time they require it. Ironically, although it may be the case that others may take the view that someone would benefit from, or needs, psychological therapy, unless the individual is self-motivated then little change is likely to occur. This is a universal principle within psychological therapy. However, this was somewhat lost by the adoption of a CBT model for the involuntary 'treatment' of offenders, many of whom are neither willing nor prepared to be engaged in such therapy.

Counselling and psychological therapy are very important processes but these are not *the* most important. Consequently, these cannot be considered as any more important than any of the other helping processes. In short, the talking therapies are not a universal panacea for all ills. Sometimes just being listened to is all that is required, and it is more important to be allowed to sort out one's concerns on one's own. It may be helpful for the individual to know that someone else is available if they need help, to help them to help themselves.

For many authors on psychological therapy, the therapeutic relationship is of central importance, although this is given far less prominence in the canon of CBT literature than in PCA. Carl Rogers established very clearly his view

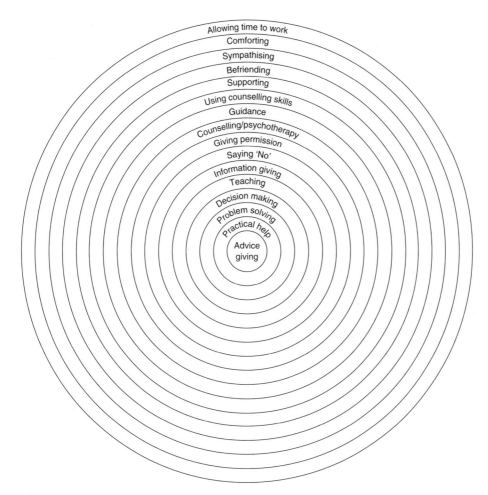

FIGURE 7.3   *The pie chart of helping strategies*

that the therapeutic relationship begins with the establishment of the first condition of psychological contact. Rogers also suggested that the counselling
relationship was no different from any other relationship and that psychological contact could only occur if both parties had an intention and a willingness
to be in contact with each other. From a CBT perspective, the establishment of
rapport within an appropriately empathic relationship forms the basis of the
therapeutic process and there really is no direct corollary with the notion of
psychological contact *per se*. It is interesting to speculate that it is perhaps the
lack of concentration upon these aspects within the CBTs literature that has
given rise to the notion that this is an over-mechanistic and prescriptive
modality that has little truck with emotions and tends to lose the client. There
is little doubt that the very wide and significant published literature regarding
how the model can be applied, or its summarising techniques, has contributed

to the proliferation of the CBTs. However, as its application expands, so too does the risk that the relationship elements become lost and that the model is reduced to little more than a collection of techniques driven by diagnostic categorisation.

Roger suggests that in recent years he has become even more aware that there have been many times when he realised that he wasn't really 'counselling' a client. Somehow, for whatever reason, the client and he were not able to engage. There did not seem to be any psychological contact present. At the same time, what he was doing seemed to be therapeutic and helpful to the client. This could have been described as 'working in a counselling way' or even 'using counselling skills'. Because he so dislikes the notion of counselling 'skills', which seem so antithetical to the person-centred philosophy, he has taken to referring to this work as 'psycho-social educational support' or 'therapeutic support'.

A link to the next chapter

The next chapter takes the form of a dialogue between Roger and Jeremy on the points of similarity and difference between our approaches. Through working together on designing and delivering the course we have been running at Warwick University, we have been very challenged and stimulated by our experiencing of parallels and divergence between the two approaches. The following chapter explores our learning and deepening understanding of theory, philosophy and practice from the two perspectives.

Recommended reading

Gilbert, P. & Leahy, R.L. (ed.) (2007) *Compassion: Conceptualisations, Research and Use in Psychotherapy*. London: Routledge.

Safran, J.D. & Segal, Z.V. (1990) *Interpersonal Process in Cognitive Therapy*. New York: Basic Books.

CHAPTER 8
A DIALOGUE ON SIMILARITY AND DIFFERENCE

Originally, we thought we would have an invited chapter from two well-known exponents of the two approaches, to dialogue their responses to the views we are putting forward. As we became more involved in writing the book, however, we recognised that it would be difficult to harmonise such a chapter with the rest of the book. We were also increasingly engaged with our own dialogue and our learning from that, and had started to write separately the first two parts of this chapter. We then decided that we would have a spoken dialogue about whatever we saw as arising from these two submissions. In looking at our work on this chapter, we decided to try to identify some of the omissions from what we put in, and reflect on the key points of dissonance that are used against the models.

The dialogue

So, this is where we began.

Techniques versus a way of being

Jeremy: We are both aware that our (perhaps) omissions from the submissions that we put in reflect key points of dissonance that are used against the models. And if we think for a minute about your (RC's) omission of Rogers' antipathy towards skills, or the tools of the therapist, where do you think that came from?

Roger: Where do I think my not noticing that came from?

Jeremy: No, where do you think Rogers' antipathy came from?

Roger: I think what he says in his writings is that, his own experiencing as a client, of a therapist who used a very technique-orientated approach left him feeling uncomfortable and unsure of himself. What was really important for him emerging from this experience was the development of the notion of the attributes of a good therapist being integrated in the self. So, in particular, those three central conditions of empathy and acceptance and authenticity were really about how the therapist is being with a client, which might be seen as an amplification of how the therapist is being in everyday life. He was really uncomfortable with the idea of using a set of tools or techniques, like you might find in another approach, such as the technical way of interpreting transference for instance, or the technical way of using inferential chaining. Rogers was really very opposed to that notion from a philosophical viewpoint. He wasn't saying that the use of tools and techniques by those therapists who do that in other modalities was wrong. What he was suggesting was that it doesn't fit with the underlying philosophy of the Person-centred Approach, particularly of the philosophy that the client needs to lead the therapy. It really doesn't fit with that early person-centred philosophical stance that he originally called non-directive and later very explicitly changed to 'client-led', rather than non-directive.

Jeremy: And it's interesting to consider that that is almost a point-of-principle position that is to do with the inauthenticity of the therapist, I presume?

Roger: Yes.

Jeremy: Essentially, if you have someone who is digging into a bag of tricks, then they are not concentrating on the process; they are not concentrating on the client and where they may be.

Roger: And that's not to say that from a PC perspective Rogers wouldn't attempt to work with transference or inferential chaining. He would, however, work with them in a much more tentative way, if it felt like the right thing to do within the relationship. For instance, he would be very unlikely to directively suggest that a client might do some homework between sessions. Rather, he might tentatively ask the client: 'I wonder if it might be helpful for you to do some work on this issue we've been talking about, between this session and the next session when you come and see me?' He wouldn't tell the client that they must do it. He would tentatively check out that the client actually wanted to do it, and it wouldn't be done as a technique, but it would be done through Rogers' felt sense that this was appropriate at that moment with this client.

Jeremy: And I guess that the understating of that is that Ellis, of any of the cognitive therapists, would for me have been more likely to have thought about, and concentrated on, therapeutic process issues. Whereas the others (Beck, Michenbaum, Young) make an assumption that those process elements need to be present. I guess the failure to concentrate more effort in the canon towards process has left the CBTs open to the criticism that therapeutic process is ignored, which it isn't. It's just that it has occupied a lot less space in the literature. Perversely, the technique and the skills-based elements have risen more to prominence than perhaps has been advisable, and particularly so when thinking back to the radical behaviourists like Michenbaum, who actually described the process as 're-skilling' people. One of the jobs of therapy is to technically re-skill people and this highlights that, within a radical behavioural model, there is first of all an agenda for the therapist to identify and utilise an element of skill to then enable the client to challenge themselves. So actually where those techniques are coming in, if they're done inappropriately, can become prescriptive, but where the therapist is fully integrated within the model, I think that that reduces the likelihood of that happening. But it's a serious omission within the CBT literature and I'm intrigued by why that, in particular, happened.

A reaction to Adlerian and Horneyan analysis and the medical model

Jeremy: I am also intrigued myself about where Rogers comes from and where Ellis comes from in that both reacted very strongly against the dominant tide at the time, which was Adlerian and Horneyan analysis. Interestingly, Ellis' concerns were more that the model used to explain why people experienced difficulties seemed wrong and that there was no scientific underpinning as to why therapy had to progress down a particular route. Whereas my understanding of Rogers was that he embraced the philosophical position of valuing the person, I get a sense that he reacted against what he saw as a dehumanising process.

Roger: Yes. Not only dehumanising, but very grounded in the medical model, where the client is 'ill' and needs to be 'cured' by the doctor, who is the expert and in control of the treatment. His decision to change from calling it person-centred counselling to client-centred counselling was really quite important, and also the change of term from 'patient' to 'client'. That, too, was to done deliberately to get away from the medical model and to put the focus on the client as the centre of the process. He suggested quite strongly that the client is the only expert in their own internal world; a position which I think the CBTs and, interestingly, psychodynamic therapists would agree with. I'm not sure that the other approaches would go as far as Rogers and state that the client should take the lead in therapy. The other thing for me that is interesting in looking at the two submissions we have written is this notion of structure and the criticism that the person-centred approach doesn't have any structure. Actually, that's not true – it has very clearly got a structure that is implicit in the theory, whereas in the CBTs the structure is very much more explicit.

Jeremy: Yes.

Different kinds of structure

Roger: This led me into seeing that there seems to be a real parallel between the PC approach and the CBTs, in the sense that they are both clearly structured but in very different ways. In the CBTs there is the structure of the ABCDE model, which is usually explained to the client and is used, in my experience, in a fairly explicit but fluid way. In the PCA there is Rogers' structure of the seven stages of therapeutic change. They are not about the same thing, but they are both structures, and Rogers described them as seven stages, but actually that was for description purposes. He saw it as a continuum that the client moved backwards and forwards along with the therapist. And I guess my understanding of how the structure works best, within the ABC etc. model, is in that fluid way. It would seem to me that in the CBTs the client needs to actively choose to use the structure that is being given to them, of their own volition, and that you as a therapist can't force them and you wouldn't attempt to. And yet there seems to be the mythology around that the CBT therapist would make their clients use structure in quite a forceful way.

Jeremy: And I think the irony is that Ellis, yet again, talks about the three insights: the acknowledgement of that essential AC model of emotional and behavioural 'causality'; emotional responsibility; and then finally, owing to the tendency to reinforce irrational beliefs, even though at an intellectual level clients can see that they are 'irrational' (and I guess there is the parallel there with the introjected value), most clients experience the 'light bulb moment' and make a connection.

In therapy, clients are able to say about their irrational beliefs: '*This is daft – this doesn't work and it's not true*'. However, often when they are faced with adversity again in any other context, they disturb themselves again. They fall back on those belief systems which seems almost like an inherent naïvety or that they 'forget' the fact that they know what was irrational in the first place. Now, if what Ellis was saying is that all you need is the technique and nothing else, then clearly that insight alone would be crazy. However, it is clearly stated by him that this is not sufficient. I wonder what Beck's position is on this point? The pathological model, at times, holds the seed of its own difficulty because this starts from the assumption of a pathological process within the individual and not that this represents an exaggerated function of normal human experience and psychology. Ironically, despite Beck's claims for scientific credibility, it is Ellis' model that seems to hold true for a more empirical research from general psychology. In as much as human perception and interpretations of events are flawed, we have a natural tendency to see things in uniquely self-serving ways. Taking the pathology position assumes that there is something 'different' inherent in those individuals experiencing disturbance as opposed to a more humanistic conceptualisation that this is an exaggeration of more general human phenomenology and that it is belief fuelling the disturbance that is the problem and not something about the person. Furthermore, the pathology model contains an *a priori* assumption that the perception, or 'seeing', is always flawed (for example, in so-called paranoid interpretations) whereas we know that the perception of a set of events may, in fact, be correct and people may evaluate us negatively and intend to do us harm or the world is, essentially, indifferent to our wishes. The real key is, therefore, not to disturb ourselves about the possibility that this is the case. The experiencing of reality – a shared concept.

Roger: Oh, absolutely. And I think that one of the clear parallels for me between the CBT ideas and practices of Beck and Ellis and Rogers is this existential notion that each of us has our own experiencing of our own reality, and nobody else can actually have that. I am the only one who can know how I experience my world, and it's not up to anybody else to interpret that for me.

Jeremy: No, and I guess one of the difficulties would be, and we have often had these discussions, where we strike a parallel between inappropriate application of the therapeutic model. Let's face it, this can happen in any modality and inappropriate model. None, from my reading of them, would suggest that what the therapists does is effectively talk-down the client by saying your experiencing of that is wrong (although there are some applications of the CBTs model which almost suggest this). I think all therapies to a certain extent introduce this quizzical notion of 'could your interpretation of that experience be wrong?'

Roger: Or could there be another experience?

Jeremy: Exactly.

The fallacy of directivity

Roger: I think there is this kind of mythology or misbelief around that CBT is directive and Person-centred is not directive, and that is just not true. We both of us, as therapists, work very tentatively and we both have a strong desire to understand how the client experiences their feelings. Rogers very much wanted to suggest that this approach is about enabling the client to understand and take ownership of their feelings, through the use of empathic clarification and communicated acceptance – very much in the same way that a CBT therapist encourages a client to take responsibility for their feelings. It seems like it is much the same thing. Neither approach would be setting out to tell a client what to do with their feelings, but we would both be wanting to enable a client to recognise that they have choices about the ways in which they experience their feelings, but we would be offering a client some choices that they might think about. I guess, also in your case, by encouraging the client to recognise the ways in which their thinking affects the way they feel.

Jeremy: And I guess, yet again, if we accept the premise that the insights Ellis talks about follow on from each other. Essentially, what we are saying to clients is: 'You need to carry on practising this because knowledge by itself is meaningless … it's not enough.' And I guess at that stage this is all we can do as therapists. It doesn't really matter how skilled and how integrated you are. Essentially, it is as irrational to assume that you can do that as it is to assume that you can change the weather. I guess one thing that I do find profoundly interesting is that maybe a lot of the disagreements that were so frequently made were, in fact, straw men. That we became set-up because what we are talking about in Rogers and Ellis is two very strong personalities who were trail-blazing at a time when they not only kicked against the establishment, they were heretical to the extent of being latter-day Luthers. They both turned accepted wisdom on its head but not in a quiet and polite kind of way.

Roger: A very direct way.

Jeremy: A very direct way. Interestingly, the pair of them have been criticised as being brash at times, and I think perhaps there might be an experience of each of them as being brash. In order to do that they both sacrificed a very significant amount. Each of them was ostracised by the establishment, yet were so in tune with the models that they had forged and maybe made a greater emotional investment in their respective models than they necessarily were prepared to reflect on at times. I wonder that maybe the great men sometimes saw larger differences between things than were really the case. And if we go back, it would seem to me to be a very strange thing indeed for anyone to say, 'I am a humanist and I believe that clients needed to be treated in a technological way.' That seems to me to be a daft thing to say.

Roger: It's an oxymoron, isn't it?

Jeremy: Exactly. So, therefore, any of those therapies that are essentially humanistic in nature must have a genuineness to the therapeutic interaction.

Roger: And is part of the key to what you and I have been … jousting with is probably the right word, in terms of trying to be respectful, no, not trying, of actually and actively being respectful towards each other's approaches and valuing each other's approaches highly; that somewhere in there, there are important points. One is what we believe, two is what we do, and three is probably the connection between what we believe and what we do, and four is how we are. Because one of the things I get a sense of, for instance, is that many of the really effective CBT therapists that I meet, I can tell that they are CBT therapists from the way they are. It's integrated, their responses are natural and there is an almost automatic way in which they start to do inference chaining in ordinary everyday conversation. And so it's not a technique, it's just that it is well learned and practised, it's part of them – in the same way that the best PC therapists are very natural in their authenticity. I know that you have described me as 'here comes authenticity in a wheel barrow!' – which I see as a compliment?

Jeremy: Absolutely.

Differences and similarities in fundamental beliefs

Roger: But, underneath this somewhere, what are the similarities and differences between the belief systems? If Rogers' view of human beings was a potentiality view, that seems to me to be critically important in driving everything, in that his notion that the most important tendency in human beings comes from the capacity to have limitless potential and the drive to achieve that potential all of the time.

Jeremy: I think that I can see that as being close to the notion that all humans have value because they have the potential to do something different. Whether or not that necessarily equates to a drive, and I think this is a difference that is very fundamental. Whereas the notion that, as a fundamental part of us being human, we have this tendency to make presumptions about the world that are necessarily biased and that the more strongly stated and disturbing of these give rise to our upset. Also, we then show a tendency to go and find examples of this, because we have those inherent biases in our judgement and in our reasoning. Logically, therefore, we must have a tendency to irrationality and part of that, funnily enough, holds the notion that we must counter that with a tendency to rationality; we must have the capacity to be rational otherwise we would never be able to be so.

Roger: Absolutely. If one of the beliefs that I have, one aspect of human nature that I find fascinating, is the drive to make sense, the drive to understand, that is clearly present in all human beings in order to enable them to survive. If you have to understand, then you have to have a rational aspect to yourself to enable you to do that. Therefore, I cannot believe that we are innately irrational.

Jeremy: And I guess my counter to that is understanding about where irrationality comes from. We have an interpretative framework that we apply, whether or not that's necessarily rational. I'm not convinced because I guess the fact that we do so is pretty fundamental. As such, I absolutely agree with you that we have that tendency to try and make sense of something. The irony is that an awful lot of the time we will make sense in a way that reflects and reinforces the rather peculiar beliefs we have, many of which will cause us distress. For example, when someone believes that a particular group of people are somehow responsible for their economic hardships, it is not surprising that they are very strongly motivated to see news stories that reflect that. When they read those news stories, they experience yet another wave of anger and resentment towards that group, regardless of whether or not they have bypassed 90 per cent of other stories actually in the same news sheet which totally contradict this. I guess in that sense I am intrigued by the notion that this form of 'making sense' would necessarily be rational. There is a 'rationale' to it, that is to say there is a logic, but I would say that is what irrationality is about in that the strong disturbed emotions are based on the 'logic' the person has used. Even though, when you argue it through, they can say, 'Yes you are right, that doesn't make sense.' Whether or not we use the term 'unconscious' or 'non-attended to' or 'implicit', those are the ones that seem to prevail. I guess, for me then, the difference at a very fundamental level is that Rogers has almost an optimistic theory about human growth potential whereas the CBTs might baulk at such an idea. For me, there is not so much a pessimism to it, rather there is a realism to it. We have this tendency to disturb ourselves and it is the effort that we invest to counter this that enables us to maintain a degree of balance and become non-disturbed.

Entropy versus the formative tendency

Roger: And I guess this raises one of the aspects of Rogers' theory that I've changed my thinking about in recent years, which I see written about in so many places. This is about Rogers making a statement that there is one fundamental drive in human beings. And I am frankly puzzled by how he changed to saying that from a position where he recognised that entropy is a drive in every atom of the universe and paradoxically at the same time there is the formative drive. Those two drives are present, and somehow, in later writing and in the writings of others, the drive for entropy just seems to get denied. I guess, for me, with the partly scientific background that I have, and my real fascination with the notion from physics that for every force in the universe there is an equal and opposite force, I can't see there only being irrationality or rationality. I think both have to be present in human beings. Like the drive for entropy and the drive to the formative tendency, they both have to be there. What I think Rogers was really getting at was that, given the right conditions, the formative tendency will always prevail, until it reaches the point at which it can't fight entropy any longer because, as a human being, eventually entropy will prevail because of our biological frailty. It would be nonsense to believe that I can go on forever just being formative (what I might call the tyranny of self-actualisation!) and I think those two tendencies are present in every human being and I don't think that's contradictory for any modality.

Jeremy: No, I would agree.

Roger: As therapists, we both know that as clients come to see us, they may have a strong drive to change. They also at the same time will have huge resistance: in your case, often 'below awareness'; in my case, 'in the unconscious'. Again, this is interesting in that we have a language that, on the face of it, people say means we don't agree. Actually, when you talk about 'below awareness' and I'm talking about 'in the unconscious', we are talking about the same thing. We are just using different language.

Jeremy: Absolutely, and I find it interesting that some of the conceptual frameworks do, for me, have complementary parallels within neo-Freudian theories. To a certain extent I think you are absolutely right in the notion of the balance between entropy and the organismic formative tendency versus our tendency to irrationality, with the capacity to become more rational from that with Eros and Thanatos. Now I guess it would not be a surprise, where Ellis, Beck and Rogers came from, that there are going to be elements of that fundamental training that they would have carried with them. It seems to me that the very practical and lived prominence of Rogers' philosophical position in his therapeutic writings and his practice from the outset is something that appears to give rise to a major difference between the modalities. For me, whether we require a new set of terminology or not, I think what we need is to begin to identify those complementary elements and then investigate where the complementary elements begin to run out.

Roger: Yeah, and there is something really important for me about really keeping a fix on what are the philosophical differences and what are the philosophical similarities? Are Ellis' and Beck's views of humanism the same as Rogers' view of humanism, or are there significant differences in that?

Jeremy: Essentially, certainly with Ellis, I don't think there are any fundamental differences. I think that they are singing from the same hymn-sheet. Interestingly, there are times when REBT and Ellis, in particular, are lampooned as being *über*-existentialists because of the very clear prominence of emotional responsibility, and the evolved enactment of the theory was that this was offered very quickly to the client on the basis that 'Well, the theory would suggest a profound philosophical change will necessarily lead to a change in your experiencing of yourself and the world, and that therefore emotional responsibility comes in from that.' With Rogers, that is clearly there in the theory but takes less prominence.

Roger: It's the doing that's the difference. I think that the philosophy is the same, that it's about a potentialist view, a positivistic view of human nature and about enabling clients to understand how they experience their reality and to recognise that they have a choice in that. I think then we hear a very strong existential position from Rogers that life is full of choices and for every decision we make it will have both negative and positive consequences. So if you choose to experience your reality in this way, there are both negative and positive consequences to that, which, I think, in fact, enables Person-centred therapists to be accepting of the positive aspects of something like depression, rather than having to see depression as something that is bad and that shouldn't exist.

Jeremy: And I think one of the interesting things is that there is, I think, a significant difference between Beck's point of origin, which is from a psychopathology model, where depression is seen as the pathology state that has those components that therefore warrant change. Ellis, I think, sees it as undermining and demoralising but not necessarily a pathology state – effectively as the consequence of maintaining irrational belief systems – and has a strong wish to say, 'I would like as a therapist to help you not to experience that distress.' I think you almost get a gradated difference from Beck's model, where it seems that the pathology state through to the dysfunctional and undermining state, through to an experiencing of that client's position and the acknowledgement that there are those positive things about it; inevitably, whether or not we fall on the notion of the secondary gain to say that there would be positive aspects about it.

Choice and the right not to choose

Roger: And I guess that there might be underneath that, one of the differences that I experience between you and me, for instance, and between the approaches, is that we would both want to offer to the client the opportunity, the knowledge, that they can be different. They don't have to experience their reality in this way. You, from your perspective, would work with them and you would see your responsibility as to get them to work with it, and I wouldn't be that directive. I would want to offer to the client the notion that they could choose to experience their reality differently, and I would in no way be implying that they should. I'd be saying they could, and I would be very accepting of them choosing not to. I think this is a very significant, although subtle, difference between the approaches.

Jeremy: I think there is, although again it becomes a point of gradation because at that stage, if I have a client, I will say, 'If you choose not to shift on this, I'm not going to frogmarch you into the consulting room and go through it. However, I wonder what you will benefit from being here?' There comes a point where I will then say, 'This form of therapy is not for you because without that shift you are not going to move into it.' Which I guess at one level, I think it would be a valid criticism to say ... the CBTs are being disingenuous in their valuing of where the client's decision is. On the other hand, I think that that's where the CBTs are equally transparent and in touch, on the basis that the implicit message is, 'No one can force you to change into this. I have, as a therapist, a very strong desire for you to move to this point. I believe very firmly that this will open up horizons to your world and self that you are currently closing. If you are not prepared to put in those aspects of work to do this and challenge that, and dispute it, then nothing will change for you and, bluntly, at that point therapy is not going to be effective.' I'm often intrigued by Roger being able to describe and almost to get the essence of frustration tolerance for therapists in this aspect of his therapy.

The client is the only expert in their own internal world

Roger: There is something in there about a conflict with what I see written in one or two places. I also hear a lot of people claim that Rogers said that the client always knows best, and he didn't say that. What he said was the client is the only expert in their own internal world. He said the client knows best in a televised interview on one occasion, and it is one of those things that people completely misunderstood. It's very clear that the client can't always know best. The client knows best how they experience their reality, but what seems to be inferred from that is the therapist's wisdom isn't of any value.

Jeremy: Which is crazy!

Roger: Which is nonsense. People go to see a therapist because they want the therapist to have some understanding, to have some knowledge. I know that you might say where appropriate, 'Well, you are choosing to do that and if you do that the consequences are likely to be this, this and this. You need to explore what all the consequences are. It's your choice at the end of the day what you do.' I would say much the same thing. For example, 'You are choosing to drink a bottle of whiskey every day, you know what the consequences of that are likely to be, particularly as you are driving and you are going to school everyday and picking your grandchildren up and taking them home with a bottle of whiskey in the glove compartment which you have a regular sip from. I think that's a rather unwise thing to do. I'm not going to tell you not to do it because I'm not your keeper, but I am going to point out to you there are some serious consequences to that and I think you are being very unwise in doing that.' In this instance, the client clearly does not 'know best'.

Jeremy: Indeed.

Roger: And I don't think in that situation and lots of others like it, that the client knows what is best. The client knows what they want to do. That isn't always the best for them or the best for other people.

Jeremy: And I suppose inherent within that is that the client will also have an implicit theory about what to do and why they are doing what they are doing. Because they are stuck within their distress or they are stuck within their incongruent *sense of* being (*I think there is a clear complementarity between those two things*) for whatever reason. Therefore the notion that the client knows best just seems to me to be something that Rogers would have quickly withdrawn back from, even if he meant that when he said it at the time. It is rather like the almost religious adherence to unconditional positive regard … that is a kind of non-thinking adherence to it.

Roger: Yes, Rogers said himself, completely unconditional positive regard is impossible. We are human beings; there is always some form of conditionality. For me, what I want is to be as accepting as I possibly can be. I want to prize this individual as a unique human being who has huge potential. And that is a very different position from saying I must totally and unconditionally and absolutely accept this person and everything they do. I don't think Rogers was that stupid.

Jeremy: No, not at all. I have been intrigued myself, more recently, over the notion that I think what has happened with the separation between the different camps has more to do with wanting to preserve the sacred objects.

Roger: The tablets of stone.

Jeremy: Exactly. It is more to do with that than it has to do with actually moving things forward. And this is an ironically irrational, non-thinking, non-actualising way of being!

Roger: Absolutely, and for me, in a sense, one of the important things is that Rogers was always very careful always to say 'I am hypothesising…', 'I am wondering if…', 'I am suggesting that…', and this needs to be disproved or proved. Even if there is a very strong statement about the importance of the six conditions as necessary and sufficient – that was a hypothesis he was suggesting – it wasn't a tablet of stone.

Jeremy: Going through the various writings of the individuals, I am struck by the fact that Beck has historically criticised Ellis for being too tied up in a philosophical position and not coming from an empirical tradition. I think there are philosophical issues around that, not the least of which that Immanuel Kant suggested that we can have *synthetic knowledge* about things and therefore we don't necessary need to demonstrate everything empirically. Also, there is the danger of reductionism through such an argument to the effect that to say that the only way forward is a positivist way and that will get us to '*the* truth'. Actually if we go back to that fundamental, although unstated, position that human beings have that tendency to irrationality because they are biased, then a positivist approach to analysis is inherently biased and will not get us anywhere near to that 'truth'.

Roger: Yeah, it must be.

The importance of the therapeutic relationship

Jeremy: I guess if we go to this notion of the centrality of the client and the paucity of attention that has been paid to that, I am genuine in my belief that Beck, Ellis, Michenbaum, Young, Padesky, and all of the names as it were in the CBTs, firmly believe that the relationship must, first of all, be therapeutic. Ironically, I believe that it is the inattention that had been paid to therapeutic elements and the tendency to concentrate on the model, the disorder, the distress or the technical elements of how these might be challenged is the result of an assumption that those therapeutic conditions are already met, whereas one of the great contributions to the canon of psychological therapies is made by Rogers in as much as he spent a lot of time distilling and describing stages in therapeutic relationships. To a certain extent his concentration on that element meant that it was clearly paradoxical not to think about technique, whereas had he continued living and continued writing I wonder now whether or not he might actually have started searching for a different terminology.

Roger: Yeah, I think that may be true. Rogers was very clearly opposed to a focus on using techniques and more concerned about the relationship and developing a way of being that was facilitative. I'm also very clear that what he never did was to describe a single, unilateral way of being. He did put forward a view based on a principle of: this is how I am, this is the way in which I will be in therapy with a client, and each of you needs to be yourself. You can't be a clone of Carl Rogers. You must be person-centred in a way that fits you. I think that is a very clear opposition to the technique-focused approach, that there is no single technique that will work for everybody. In the Person-centred Approach, each of us has to be ourselves in the way we are, in a way which is therapeutic with the client. I recognise, for example, that as a part of my natural way of being, I quite often use inference chaining within myself and within my life. It's an intuitive process that I use naturally, a part of how I am. I don't do inference chaining as a technique, and I don't do it in the very sophisticated and subtle way that a good CBT therapist does, but I have my way of doing it, which fits in everyday life and in therapy.

Jeremy: I think that that works for therapists who are comfortable in their skin, who have integrated the philosophical aspects of their model and then have been able to operationalise within the model. The irony is that that it is an almost nebulous concept, and it seems almost metaphysical to try to describe it. I guess that one of the areas that the PCA has fallen foul of is that it is very difficult to summarise that. It is very difficult to communicate that to people, particularly if we are in an ethos that is concerned about training and validation and regulation, because essentially it is a realisation that people achieve as individuals and then become therapists with that. And that's not something that you can necessarily legislate for.

Not necessarily necessary but always sufficient

Roger: And one of the difficulties I often meet as a PCA trainer is the attitude of: 'Prove to me that the conditions work.' I respond with: 'Well, I can't. No one can prove that they work. You have to make what amounts to a leap of faith and when you are *being* in those conditions and the client experiences them, you will discover that it works.' Another statement from Rogers which causes some disbelief from other modalities is his statement that the conditions are necessary and sufficient for personality change to occur, as though that is an absolute. Bozarth (in Brazier, 1993) very succinctly challenged the inference that the six conditions are necessary and sufficient, full stop. That seems to me to be a very bald statement that really does need to be challenged. I believe that the six conditions are not necessarily necessary. People do get better without therapy. People do get better despite bad therapy. What I think is a more reflective position on that is that while those conditions are not necessarily necessary, where those conditions are present they are sufficient. That has been my experience in more than 40 years as a therapist. For you, I guess there would be a different philosophical position.

Jeremy: Indeed, and the irony, as I read some of Ellis' criticism of Rogers' position, was that it is Ellis' interpretation of what he perceived to be Rogers being dogmatic about the use of the term 'necessary', whereas my understanding of Rogers' condition in context is that it is a logical necessity.

Roger: Yeah, and I think that was part of the politics at the time.

Jeremy: Indeed it was.

Self-actualisation – process or end state?

Roger: I think he made a political decision to take the focus off entropy and to put the focus on the formative tendency. I think that was politically necessary at the time. I think we need to come back from that now and say, well, those two forces are both present. One force can't be present in isolation; there will always be an equal and opposite force present. The other significant difference, I think, between your philosophy and mine, if we can own those, is around the notion of self-actualisation. For Rogers, self-actualisation was a process which was about becoming fully functioning in a world which is becoming more complicated, as a person who is becoming more complicated all the time. He saw self-actualisation as an expression of the formative tendency. Because that tendency is formative, it cannot be absolute. It can never be fully achieved because in a potentiality philosophy the moment I achieve potential, my ultimate potential becomes greater. I am in position A, for example, my aim is to get to position B, the moment I get to position B, it becomes position A, and I have a new position B above me that I can seek to aspire to. So potentiality means I am always seeking to self-actualise. I can never actually achieve it, and that is a very different position I think from that held by the CBTs.

Jeremy: Yes, and certainly if I come back to the necessary sufficient thing for just a minute. I would hold, and agree with Dryden in this regard, that those conditions are necessary but not sufficient. To a certain extent the acknowledgement of the insight requires an explanation of where those things are. There is a *de facto* introduction of the idea that there are things that you need to do in order to achieve that change. You need to learn new ways of doing that, and that is a very big difference. My suspicion is that, essentially, in the Cognitive Behavioural Therapies those are distilled elements of good therapeutic practice and a good therapeutic relationship that are then taken and labelled. One of the dangers of this approach is that the therapy becomes too focused on the technique and will be evaluated by reference to *how much*, *how frequently* and *when* the technique is used and therapists become hung up on that. That is not therapy *per se*. Rather, it becomes an adherence to a series of manualised statements within a specified timeframe.

Roger: Which is not therapy.

Jeremy: No, quite what that is I'm not entirely sure. With regard to the other point…

Roger: Becoming self-actualised?

Jeremy: I think that there is a point at which it *is* possible to become actualised. I've thought more about this recently, having been heavily influenced by your view on this, and wonder perhaps that the point of becoming actualised for the individual is both the recognition and integration of the fact that this is an ongoing process. In order to achieve change I must challenge and dispute those irrational tendencies, and that I need to go out and assertively practise this because if I don't, to quote Windy Dryden, 'It'll bite ya!'

Homeostasis and resistance to change

Roger: Well, homeostasis will prevail, won't it? I don't know that Rogers said a great deal about this. I do know that he recognised the power of what a psychodynamic therapist would call the 'mental mechanisms', sometimes referred to as defence mechanisms, and in particular resistance to change. I have a particular interest in accepting a client's internal resistance to change as a choice they are entitled to make. Schön (1971) suggested that 'homeostasis' is the preferred state of any organism and therefore resistance to change is an active process, which he called 'dynamic conservatism'.

This process can be seen at work in individuals and is well known to counsellors and psychotherapists. The most unhappy or disturbed individual ostensibly comes into therapy seeking change from their disordered or unhappy condition. However uncomfortable their emotional or psychological state maybe, it is known and familiar to them and therefore is secure. The therapist who offers them the chance to change, and begins to enable them to do so, draws them away from their secure familiar state (however uncomfortable or unpleasant it might be) towards a new and unknown state. In human psychology, there is nothing more fearful than the unknown. This gives rise to feelings of threat and insecurity and will be resolutely resisted by the client at both an unconscious and a conscious level. Therapists need to recognise this and also to recognise that their own fear of the unknown may well lead them to collude with the client's resistance as a part of their own dynamic resistance to change in the relationship, in the client and in themselves!

Roger: But just before we stop, there seems to be something about recognising that there are some, in some ways, quite subtle philosophical differences and a lot of similarities between our approaches.

Jeremy: Oh yes.

Roger: Which express themselves in practice differently. It's like it's a kind of different wisdom about the wisdom.

Congruence in the relationship and congruence in the model

Jeremy: Yes, and I think that the more I come to it I think there is a *Zeitgeist* at the moment. Perhaps what we need to do is to begin to look at an understanding of the process of integrating theory and philosophy as a way of being within the PCA and how that enables someone to become therapeutic. It seems to me that the emphasis is on *the being*, that experiential element. With regard to training in CBT or REBT, for example, if all this is, simply, '...read this, read this, read this and then practise all the stages you've read...', then why do we need training courses in it?

Roger: That's a million dollar question!

Jeremy: It is a million dollar question and one of the ironical things is that it is a double-edged sword: the optimistic reliance based on an ideology that there will be growth. What happens when the person-centred therapist slips back and becomes incongruent with themselves? There is an implicit reliance on the belief that the therapist is going to self-monitor responsibly.

Roger: Absolutely.

Jeremy: And we know that they don't always do that.

Roger: Well, none of us does.

Jeremy: No, exactly.

Roger: But it's that thing that Rogers stated that the therapist must be congruent in the relationship, and for me he probably meant congruent enough!

Jeremy: And similarly, I suppose, that's where Ellis comes in about where you need those necessary conditions. You need a bit more than this because people do get better by themselves. Also it is palpably obvious that you can do therapy with someone who: (a) you certainly don't connect with and (b) you have difficulty finding anything other than enmity towards.

Roger: And heaven forbid that I should be so perfect as a person, and so absolutely congruent as a therapist, because I don't think my clients would trust that, or me, for a moment.

Jeremy: I would certainly hope that.

Roger: They would expect some incongruence in me, but they need enough congruence that I am together enough to actually be with them in their pain.

Jeremy: Yes, it's an interesting journey doing this because I go back and I think that in the past I have wrongly assumed, and perhaps following on from where

Ellis was, that integrating responsible hedonism at an intellectual level was where you were at for actualising. Now I think that I'm likely to screw up on a regular basis, and I know that there are things that I can do to stop that happening but I need to keep reminding myself of that, … and sometimes that means I need to (metaphorically) fall on my backside.

Acceptance, challenge and disputation

Roger: I mean, I had a client very recently who said:

'Do you know what the most amazing thing was last week? I said: "I am incredibly needy" and you just raised your left eyebrow and held the palms of your hands out and what you were saying was "so?" And actually, I went away from that session thinking: "I am very needy. So? What's wrong with that?" And I really experienced the acceptance in a non-verbal way that enabled me to accept my own fallibility.'

Jeremy: Yeah, isn't it funny? I had a light-bulb moment this morning with a client who is worried because his dad has diabetes and this is a life-threatening condition that is killing him. Bluntly, my client doesn't want his dad to die and finds him not keeping to his dietary regime… When I asked, he described that he: 'Keeps on finding his dad having "doorstops of bread with huge amounts of butter on"'. In response to this, I said: 'Well, how are you finding that at the moment? In the past you would have found it really difficult', and he said: 'Well, I got really angry with him and I shouted at him and I haven't spoken with him properly for a week.' To which I suggested: 'Well, that's not real anger though that's going on there is it?' And he said: 'Well, no', and became tearful, at which point I said: 'Sounds like your worried … what's your worry?', to which he replied: 'I want him to live as long as he can actually live. I don't want him to die.' I then asked him: 'Well, what would you happen if you told your dad that?', to which he responded: 'It wouldn't be done.' When I asked him why it wouldn't be done he responded: 'Well, he would probably get angry with me and think that I was being arrogant.' I suggested: 'It's interesting, if that's what you're thinking, and I don't see how that fits with the degree of anxiety and then frustration.'

We did some inference-chaining and it became evident that his anxiety was associated with a concern that he might be exposed as being weak and over-emotional, to which I opined: 'This is about shame isn't it?' I then asked: 'Is this really about the fact that you don't want to be seen as an arse?' (Because that has come up as a reference in previous sessions relating to lots of different situations and this became a real light-bulb moment for him.) I summarised: 'If we just hold for a minute, now, do you think that you really are an arse who is incompetent and this that and the other?' To which he answered: 'No, because I can do things about it.' At that stage I suggested that he could hold that but returned to a more pragmatic disputation: 'Why are you getting yourself so anxious when I suggest that you could say to your dad "Dad, the reason I got angry with you and shouted at you is because I am worried that you'll die." If you cry, you cry. Even if you're dad does think that you are an arse in that situation, does that make you an arse?' The client was able to laugh and acknowledge that this did not make him an arse!

A link to the next chapter

In the next chapter we will explore our perception of possible future changes and challenges, including those arising from the regulation of the profession. We have also invited several practitioners who had participated in our course on 'The Advanced Diploma in Cognitive Behavioural Practice for Person-centred Therapists' at Warwick University to contribute some reflective accounts, identifying what they learned and how this had impacted on their practice.

Recommended reading

Kirschenbaum, H. & Henderson, L. (1990) *Carl Rogers Dialogues*. London: Constable.

Nye, R. (1996) *Three Psychologies: Perspectives from Freud, Skinner and Rogers*. New York: Brooks/Cole.

Shlien, J. (2003) *To Lead an Honourable Life: Invitations to Think about Client-centred Therapy and the Person-centred Approach*. Ross-on-Wye: PCCS Books.

CHAPTER 9

REFLECTIONS, PREDICTIONS AND HOPES FOR THE FUTURE

This chapter will include some reflective accounts from person-centred practitioners who undertook the Advanced Diploma in Cognitive Behavioural Methods for Person-centred Therapists at Warwick University, run by Roger and Jeremy, identifying what they gained and how this has impacted on their practice. This will be followed by an exploration of the authors' perception of possible changes and challenges in the future, including those arising from the regulation of the profession. It will include an exploration of the possible evolution of different models of therapy using synergy from the existing approaches and dissolution of the conflict and the wars between the tribes.

Reflections from practitioners

In order to look forward and try to have some sense of how therapeutic practice might develop from within our two approaches, we have chosen to draw on the experiences of therapists who participated in a course we run. This is the Advanced Diploma in Cognitive Behavioural Methods for Person-centred Therapists at the University of Warwick. At the start of the course we explain:

This course is aimed at counsellors and psychotherapists who have trained in the person-centred approach and wish to remain true to their core modality, and at the same time wish to develop the ability to draw on methods used in Cognitive Behavioural Therapy, to inform their work with clients, where this is appropriate.

This course is not designed to teach you how to practise as a cognitive behavioural therapist. *This is not a skills training course.* In order to become a cognitive behavioural therapist you would need to undertake a significant training course, which would be as rigorous as your training as a person-centred therapist. Jeremy and I are both opposed to the notion that someone can 'do a bit of person-centred' or 'do a bit of CBT'. This course very clearly does not set out to enable therapists to become 'integrative'. We hope this course will:

- Reinforce your understanding of and renew your belief in the person-centred approach

- Enable you to get a clearer understanding of and respect for the cognitive behavioural approach

- Help you to understand the differences and similarities in the philosophy and theory which underpins the two approaches

- Help you to understand the things that person-centred therapists and CBT therapists do that are exactly the same or very similar

- Try out some cognitive behavioural methods

- Help you to identify the irreconcilable differences in the two approaches

- Enable you to find ways to use CBT practice to inform your understanding of your self, your clients and your counselling practice.

The course aims to enable therapists who are secure in their core modality to have a stronger knowledge and understanding of cognitive behavioural philosophy, theory and practice in order to be able to make an informed choice to use these methods from within the person-centred relationship.

The course will focus particularly on the philosophy and theory of the CBTs, examining differences and similarities with person-centred philosophy and theory. There will be opportunities to learn about and to practise a range of techniques and methods used in the CBTs and how these may be used within a relationship based on the six necessary and sufficient conditions for therapeutic growth in the person-centred approach.

What follows are individual personal reflections from seven experienced person-centred therapists who have completed the Advanced Diploma in CBT Methods for Person-centred Therapists at Warwick University.

Deb Laxton's reflections

I trained originally as a person-centred therapist and then subsequently engaged in systemic and psychodynamic training. However, I still considered myself person-centred in my approach. Knowledge and understanding of CBT theory and practice was the hole in my therapeutic training. Looking back on where I was before I did the CBT for person-centred therapists course, I was… well, perhaps a little belligerent and, underneath that, I had some fear about being *evangelised* by the popular CBT message. As a therapist I had experienced condescension from CBT therapists who clearly didn't rate person-centredness – one even calling it the 'nodding donkey' method. As a client with postnatal depression, I experienced CBT as an adversarial approach and ended each session feeling that it had just been an extended argument between the therapist and me. My experience had not seemed valued. However, every modality has good and bad therapists!

The course allowed me to explore CBT without defensiveness and to experience a subtle shift in my understanding of CBT philosophy. I was relieved to discover that I wouldn't have to throw out all that I had learned in order to reconsider CBT.

Learning to separate *thoughts* and *feelings* more formally clarified my person-centred practice. Prior to this course, I had been sloppy and interchanged the terms 'thoughts' and 'feelings', missing the importance of distinguishing between them, probably through a lack of appreciation of the role of thoughts in driving and maintaining feelings and behaviours. Thoughts can be challenged and feelings accepted – it was helpful to be clearer about this.

It was refreshing for me to experience some training on formulation on this course, which I had not had in my person-centred training. Taking the principles of formulation from CBT, I learned to formulate my clients' issues in order to agree the direction of our work together. More importantly perhaps, I learned a language and framework that improved communications with colleagues from other modalities and with differing roles.

The simplest ideas are usually the best and I found the ABC structure is great for enabling clients to understand the roles of their beliefs in their distress. Using paper and pen in sessions to identify the client's ABC was extremely uncomfortable at first, having previously refused to use what I had thought of as 'props'. My experience on the course was pivotal and now working with the pen and paper has become a natural extension of my practice, which I believe does not conflict with my person-centredness.

Since the course with Roger and Jeremy I have been appointed as a High Intensity Therapist for IAPT and I'm sure my success was in part due to my ability to describe how a Person-centred therapist could use CBT and my understanding of how the modalities fit together and complement one another. Since then, remembering the shared phenomenological and existential roots has enabled me to maintain my professional integrity as a person-centred therapist working in IAPT.

The two approaches are both about noticing and being curious about the client's experience and expression through listening to words and non-verbal cues. Both approaches seek to understand the client's meaning rather than imposing an analysis. CBT makes more use of Socratic questioning as a formal technique than does the person-centred approach, although I certainly had used Socratic type questions as part of my practice unwittingly before the course. Both approaches have a positive view of the client's capacity to change and the importance of their engagement in that change.

On the topic of 'agenda' there is divergence. The CBT therapist will negotiate the goals with the client and keep to the agreed agenda. The Person-centred therapist will follow the client's agenda, encouraging wider and deeper exploration. The CBT therapist will attempt to overcome resistance; the person-centred therapist will be curious about a client's resistance and explore the meaning of it with the client but not try to *overcome* it.

In the short-term, outcome-driven work in the NHS, these more directive aspects of CBT are helpful – frustrating but pragmatic – within the constraints of the service. In self-employment, I am free to ditch the agenda, although I find the habit of clarifying the goals of the client has stuck rather more than I like to admit. I recognise a strong resistance to having a written agenda laid down at the start of each session. Perhaps I find myself somewhere between the two approaches here.

The training course for my current role caused a greater appreciation of my person-centred training – community times, personal development, personal therapy alongside skills and knowledge development. There was a cursory nod to the core conditions on the IAPT CBT course I subsequently undertook. There seemed to be an assumption that the conditions should be present but were insufficient on their own. CBT training emphasises knowledge, techniques and maintenance cycles whereas person-centred training teaches theory alongside the use of self – with the development of reflexivity, processing, staying with the difficult emotions, challenging the self towards greater transparency, working with blocked empathy, or unpicking some reaction to a client based on adverse judgement. In CBT training, there seemed to be little appreciation of the skills of being in a therapeutic relationship. In my view, something essential is missed because both camps acknowledge that 'it's the relationship that counts'. It was the relationship that I missed when I had postnatal depression and experienced CBT firsthand from the client's chair. That therapist may have known all the theory and techniques, but failed to know me and reach me – and that's the whole point… isn't it?

Deb Laxton *BSc (Hons), Dip. PC Couns., Adv. Dip. Supervision, Adv. Dip. CBT, Adv. Dip. CBT, PG Cert. (Couples & Families), Cert. Ed., MBACP (Accred).*

Deb is 43, happily married with four children and has worked in community settings in adult education and therapy. Deb was a trainer and therapist for Relate and has worked with the police and prison services in educational and therapeutic roles as well as in Higher Education. Deb helped to develop the Renewal Therapy Service, is currently managing Hope Counselling and Training, and is working for the NHS as a High Intensity Therapist in IAPT in the Birmingham area of the UK.

Carl Jones' reflections

My motivation for choosing this training was based on an anxiety concerning the politics of psychotherapy and my perception of direction of statutory service and therapy provision. I believed my career to be potentially at risk by the so-called 'CBT revolution'. I noticed how 'CBT' was clearly what was required both within voluntary and statutory agencies when I was unsuccessful in securing a position in the NHS on four occasions but saw that those appointed possessed the 'magic' CBT qualification. I now concede that I supported an internal view that led me to avoid understanding or accepting REBT/CBT, believing it to be something of a demon – something I now accept was based in a fantasy. I view that my previous experience fuelled this and, within previous training(s), Person-centred therapy and philosophy appeared not to be valued, and was not seen as valid in comparison to other established approaches. The training at University of Warwick illuminated much to me, including raising my awareness of my process of defending the person-centred approach to the exclusion of all others, which was equally narrow and hypercritical.

Initially, the content of the course was challenging as I reflected upon my own level of competence as a therapist and just how person-centred am I. I welcomed the challenge, however uncomfortable the process was. In terms of the REBT/CBT input, and once I had lowered my person-centred armour, I began to reflect and compare from what Jeremy described as a position of a willing suspension of disbelief. From this and within supervision grew an appreciation and deeper acceptance for my practice as a psychotherapist, where I adapt and attune to clients/supervisees in an ethically grounded intent to be of use and help.

I found the style and presentation of the course particularly appealing as the mixture of extensive experience of the tutors, their confidence in delivery and engagement with the contrasting approaches of the person-centred approach and REBT/CBT, combined with the extensive course literature, made it inviting and engaging. It was clear to me both approaches are distinct and separate however many similarities are apparent. I received feedback from live video practice that my 'person-centred way of being' could also be viewed as Rational Emotive/Cognitive Behavioural in that empathic reflection was observed as working within an ABC framework and offering challenge to my client via inference chaining.

Although my core training was person-centred, it also held the view of integration with the rationale that no one modality holds 'the truth'. Consequently, REBT/CBT philosophy, theory and practice would appear supportive and beneficial to my own self-knowledge and practice, as I view self-awareness to be of paramount importance.

Theory/technique and philosophical understanding, I believe, supports my reflexive practice as a psychotherapist, including the ABCDE model, disputation, inference chaining, formulation and particular understanding of human behaviours and reactions, including anger, anxiety, phobias, depression, substance misuse and various medical diagnoses and emotional *disorders*.

Having graduated three years prior to the University of Warwick training, and with subsequent trainings under my belt, I was surprised at my reaction to being within a group/training context. I view some aspects, including the potential to be judged by others, as not '…good enough' (Winnicott, 1964), an activation of a transferential process based within my conditions of worth

(Tudor & Merry, 2002) of 'needing' to be liked and struggling with knowing new names and accepting difference.

The various aspects of the training placed emphasis on individual and group learning and I found some of this challenging within the time constraints. However, the focus of the course was clearly stated, delivered and did not disappoint. To experience strong and articulate argument and critical appraisal within the delivery of the training has subsequently encouraged my self-belief as a practitioner, giving me courage to articulate my beliefs and engage with others with differing views.

Learning is for me a lifelong commitment to myself and the field of psychotherapy. This training reignited my need to know and from a beginning place to look wider. I shall deepen my knowledge of REBT/CBT, person-centred psychotherapy and other knowledge in order to facilitate therapeutic change within relationships. Consequently, I am aware of my potential to be judgemental, no matter how seemingly justified or subtly out of awareness; I now strive to reflect upon my experiences and relationship with self and others to support acceptance and openness. Further to this, the award of Advanced Diploma in Cognitive Behavioural Methods for Person-centred Therapists did support me in securing a position within statutory mental health. Did I sell out? I view myself as an individual and I offer myself as a therapist. I hold the philosophy of the Person-centred approach as part of my way of being and believe there is value in all therapeutic approaches. I remain open in relationship, striving to offer reflexive, appropriate responses to each unique individual.

To sum up, I have found this training challenging and affirming. I have learned a new language for many things I knew and for some I did not. I welcome what has been offered and find myself in a place of acceptance from an informed position which is supportive of my philosophy, ethical stance and as a person in process.

Carl Jones MA (Person Centred Psychotherapy), PG Dip. Hum. Psychoth., Dip. Sup., Adv. Dip. CBT, UKCP Reg.

Carl is a UKCP-registered psychotherapist with 15 years' experience of working as a therapist. He has worked in therapeutic communities, as the service lead in a voluntary sector counselling service, as a specialist practitioner within statutory mental health and as a private psychotherapist. Carl has also provided supervision of practice for those working with children, adolescents, adults, students and practitioners.

Paul Fairchild's reflections

Although I originally trained in both humanistic and psychodynamic psychotherapy, I readily adopted the Person-centred approach for the simple reason that it resonated best with my own observations of human nature and elements of my personality: the core conditions of empathy, congruence and unconditional positive regard came rather more naturally to me than the analysis of transference and counter-transference. And having worked voluntarily for eleven years as a person-centred counsellor, I have not been disappointed with the outcome, having gained considerable evidence of the ability of such an approach to change lives. To this day I retain a strong sense of the immense privilege it is to be invited into the world of another person to witness their pain, anguish and, with time, the increased self-awareness that stimulates lasting change and a renewed sense of vision for the future. Nevertheless, I have become aware over the years that being essentially non-directive, person-centred therapy does not always lend itself to working in a time-limited capacity, being dependent on the client's own agenda, with its unpredictable ebb and flow. Furthermore, many clients over the years have welcomed, and indeed expected, greater intervention from me as a counsellor, specifically requesting a more practical approach to the resolution of their problems. I therefore embarked on the Advanced Diploma to enrich my practice and provide a different perspective on the therapeutic relationship.

I was initially surprised to discover that many concepts in CBT had natural counterparts in person-centred theory. For instance, while a preoccupation with the irrational beliefs of the client may be fundamental to CBT, the person-centred approach is far from averse to uncovering the core beliefs of the client, on which their self concept is founded. Indeed, an understanding of the conditions of worth under which they laboured and the sometimes irrational impact they may have on their self concept, is pivotal to understanding the client's emotional disturbance. Furthermore, although disputation in CBT terms may be rather too confrontational for the humanistic counsellor, challenging clients is no less integral to the person-centred approach, frequently serving as a catalyst for change. Perhaps most importantly, I discovered that few of the techniques that belong to CBT are inherently antagonistic to person-centred therapy and may even have direct parallels in the theoretical framework that underpins the approach. Instead, what differs between the two disciplines is their understanding and use of the relationship between client and counsellor: for the person-centred therapist wishing to embrace CBT methods, the most important issue is undoubtedly the extent to which the nature of the relationship may be affected.

Since completing the Advanced Diploma, the way in which I practise as a counsellor has not changed appreciably, but my conviction to work in a person-centred manner is now born of insight rather than ignorance of the alternatives. But although outwardly I remain true to my original convictions, the CBT concepts and techniques I have learned are active behind the scenes, illuminating my thinking and offering a different perspective on the journey on which each client has embarked. While identifying automatic negative thoughts and inference chaining may not impinge unduly on the counselling sessions I hold, their subliminal use helps inform my own understanding of my client's world and inspires lines of questioning that help expose aspects of their underlying process that may not otherwise have become apparent. It is this fresh source of insight that has become a valuable tool to my practice. Indeed, I have begun to view CBT concepts and techniques as an additional filter that might be applied sparingly to the lens through which I view the client's phenomenological world.

Nevertheless, for me, the most important legacy of the course was the realisation of just how powerful the synergy between fundamentally different approaches to counselling could be, if appropriately encouraged. All too often, established disciplines have become entrenched in positions that actively stifle dialogue. While counsellors of any disposition would recognise the need for relationships with clients that are based on mutual respect and acceptance, all too often we deny our colleagues the same respect, simply because their outlook and core beliefs may differ from our own. If we could only establish, between disciplines, the same relationship we strive to achieve in the counselling room, who knows what long-term benefits might emerge…

Paul Fairchild BSc (Hons), DPhil (Oxon), Dip. Couns., Adv. Dip. CBT, PG Dip., LATHE, FHEA.

Dr Paul Fairchild is a Lecturer in Medicine at the University of Oxford and a Fellow of Trinity College, Oxford. Since qualifying as a counsellor in 2000, he has worked in a voluntary capacity both in a primary health care setting and, more recently, in private practice.

Sarah Ashworth's reflections

From personal experience, I rated CBT quite strongly. The stoical philosophy underpinning the approach had, quite literally, saved my sanity.

Some difficult life experiences had led me to seek therapy two decades ago, and I was referred to an excellent person-centred therapist. As a result of our work together, I made significant changes in my life. Also, I finally felt comfortable being who I really was, as a result of her expression of genuine, challenging and empathic acceptance of me. However, I now realise that my tendency to put a negative spin on everything when life gets tough, had not been addressed. A few short years later after a painful divorce, loss of my business, birth of my daughter and an undiagnosed thyroid condition, I developed a serious mental illness. Medication didn't help and I'd already had counselling, so my psychiatrist referred me for CBT 'as a last resort'.

As the waiting list was long and my need for symptomatic relief was substantial, a CBT workbook was recommended. Over the following months, I painstakingly dug down and challenged my core beliefs, scheduled activities which lifted my mood and gave me a sense of mastery. I recovered and realised that it wasn't the adverse events which caused my misery, but how I reacted to and interpreted these events.

However, before I could finally accept the idea that *I* had been upsetting *myself*, I needed to have another human being understand, accept and not try to change my experience of having been upset by others, of having been rejected, of being no good, of being worthless. I needed to sob, shout, moan and whine and be as irrational as I bloody well liked, without someone suggesting that my personal philosophy was the root cause of my ills. I don't think CBT would have worked for me had I not had prior experience of good Person-centred therapy.

A decade later, I qualified as a Person-centred therapist after training at Warwick. While I was certain that the person-centred philosophy and way of being was absolutely necessary for clients to experience, I wasn't 100 per cent certain that the central conditions – no matter how exquisitely manifest by the therapist – were sufficient to effect permanent personality change in all cases; after all, this had been my experience! During subsequent years of practice, I found some clients got stuck in a repetitive ruminative cycle which didn't seem to be completely amenable to my way of being with them. I found myself introducing some of the practical elements of CBT which had been so helpful for me. But, it didn't feel right; I was wedded to the Person-centred approach and, on these occasions, I felt as guilty as if I had been having an extra-marital affair – despite the fact that the clients with whom I worked with in this way seemed to benefit.

When I heard Warwick was running an Advanced Diploma in Cognitive Behavioural Methods for person-centred counsellors, I was excited. I was surprised by the compatibility of the humanistic, existential philosophies underpinning both the Person-centred and CBT modalities. Previously, I'd thought that CBT had simply emerged from the dry, clinically objective and inflexible worlds of Skinner, Pavlov and Watson. I was delighted to be introduced to the ideas of Epictetus, Aurelius and, latterly, Ellis – who offered a rational but extraordinarily elegant philosophy to live life by. Moreover, I found the philosophies underpinning CBT and REBT to be as humanistic and optimistic as person-centred theory.

Somewhat depressingly, Sigmund Freud proposed that the efficacy of psychoanalysis was limited to transforming *'hysterical misery into common unhappiness'*. However, Person-centred and CBT/REBT theories offer far more light at the end of the therapeutic tunnel. While Carl Rogers believed in the innate ability of the individual to reach their full potential given the right conditions, Ellis also believed that all human beings have within them the capacity to overcome their irrationality and lead rational, fulfilling lives.

In terms of practical application, the Person-centred therapist works with here-and-now reality, while acknowledging that earlier conditions of worth will impact on the client's here-and-now experiencing. As the client experiences the acceptance, understanding and genuineness of the therapist, they are able to challenge the internalisation of these earlier conditions of worth, see themselves more realistically and be more fully themselves.

Similarly, the CBT/REBT therapist also focuses on here-and-now material while recognising that adverse formative experiences will have affected the development of unhelpful core beliefs or schema. Through challenging these often deeply held core beliefs through a variety of methods, the client can conceptualise themselves in a more helpful manner.

Traditionally, a warm relationship between REBT/CBT therapist and client was regarded as unnecessary; indeed, Ellis was heavily criticised for his irascible attitude towards 'Gloria'. However, it is now recognised that the relationship between client and therapist is one of the most important predictors in the success of the therapy, whatever the modality. Therefore, the central conditions of empathy, unconditional positive regard and therapist authenticity, which hallmark the Person-centred therapist's way of being, should also feature within the CBT/REBT therapist.

I learnt it was possible to *offer* CBT methods to clients from within a person-centred relationship as opposed to *delivering* CBT *to* a client in the more didactic way that is traditionally espoused. I could also continue to empathise and accept a client's frame of reference while skilfully weaving the principles and philosophy of REBT into the authentic way I challenged the client's interpretation of their world. Finally, I felt confident that the marriage of person-centred therapy with cognitive behavioural methods could lead to a more efficacious therapy than person-centred or CBT therapy as a single approach. Unfortunately, I wasn't able to benefit from this development when I was a client in need all those years ago. However, I can now offer current and future clients the best possible chance for living a self-actualising and rational life.

Sarah Ashworth BA (Hons), Dip. PC Couns., Adv. Dip. CBT, MBACP (Accred).

Sarah is currently employed as a Student Mental Health Co-ordinator at the University of Warwick and has worked as a therapist for a number of organisations and in private practice since 2002. Sarah also teaches on the Introduction to Counselling Courses at the University of Warwick.

Anne Thomson's reflections

I have discovered with joy and amazement that there beats within me a truly person-centred heart, and I enjoy nourishing it with a steady IV injection of philosophy, theory and practice. Nonetheless, I have always had a special liking for psychodynamic theory, which I find wonderfully intellectual and elegant. Ergo, I found myself on an REBT course feeling ignorant and a little resistant. However, since learning stuff is always appealing, I decided to focus on doing that.

For some reason I thought that CBT was an issue-focused therapy, and in my defence, the way in which CBT has been rolled out and applied within IAPT – short-term, computer programmes, and more significantly being practised by people who seemed to have limited counselling training and often medical backgrounds – there is a little evidence that I did not completely make that idea up. So I have been surprised by the pursuit of core beliefs and the goal of moving away from activating events to inferences and beliefs which I discovered on the REBT course.

I have found it interesting and helpful to apply it to myself, not because it suddenly revealed my core beliefs, but because it proposed a different strategy for breaking patterns of thoughts and behaviours that are associated with my core beliefs. I'm not prepared to accept that I am innately irrational, but I realise that I have my irrational moments and can become really unhappy because of my experiencing of the perceived motivations and assumed attitudes of others. This kind of reasoning is tenuous and thin on evidential support.

Central to the REBT approach is the concept and practice of disputation. It is used to highlight irrational and distorted beliefs that someone may hold about themselves and the world. I found myself shrinking from this because of the confrontational connotations I was putting on the word. I was relieved and intrigued to find that disputation wasn't about arguing or engaging in power struggles, but rather based on encouraging clients to reflect on what they believe and challenging their assumptions. Both irrationality and rationality are questioned so that both may be exposed. In this way the client begins to appreciate the nature of what is rational and what is irrational, and connect this to helpful and unhelpful ways of perceiving themselves; that irrationality creates feelings about the self that are generally negative and debilitating, whereas rational thinking offers perspective, and a realistic view of the self which generally promotes more positive and affirming feelings.

Within my person-centred therapeutic work I consider myself to be particularly challenging, which is experienced variously by myself and my clients. However, before doing the REBT course I would have been inclined to focus on being accepting of my clients, and empathic in ways which led me to share their experiencing without question. Confronted with global beliefs held by clients, I would find myself floundering and becoming rather overwhelmed by the scale and rigidity of their convictions. These days I find myself willing to challenge these global beliefs in the hope that by doing so their irrationality will be exposed to the client and the opportunity is presented to undermine the more specific beliefs which are disturbing the client in the 'here and now' of their lives. It seems that if a client comes to appreciate the irrationality of a global belief they hold about the world, they are more able to defuse it when it is manifested in their specific and particular life experience. This helps me to withdraw from the global and re-engage with this particular person in the present and in the specific. I find that being able to do this has enhanced my person-centred objectives considerably with certain clients.

I was listening to a close friend recently as she explained to me that she really believed she needed to lower her expectations of people so that she would not continue to be hurt by their apparent lack of kindness and caring. She held a standard of friendship which seemed to be at odds with the standard of others whom she sometimes experienced as harsh and even cruel. After a while I introduced the idea that perhaps it wasn't the behaviour that she found so hurtful, but the assumptions she was then making about herself and about others. She quickly acknowledged that it was what the behaviour meant to her that was so distressing and I wondered what it might be like if she shared how she experienced the behaviour with her friend. This encounter is an interesting example of how thinking from an REBT perspective helped me to help my friend in a very person-centred way.

I've believed for most of my adult life that it's not what happens to us that's important, but how we respond to the fact that misfortune is part of every life which determines the kind of people we become, and the extent to which we are basically content in our own skin. I find myself instinctively attracted to the idea that emotional disturbance is basically self-induced, and I like centring the responsibility for my own happiness firmly within myself. I will inevitably suffer 'the slings and arrows of outrageous fortune', but it is the meaning that I give to unhappy events which determines whether or not I am wounded by them.

Anne Thomson *BA (Hons), PGCE, MPhil., Cert. Couns., Dip. Couns. & Psychoth., Adv. Dip. CBT, NCS (Accred).*

Anne is a person-centred therapist with a private practice in Birmingham and is the regional therapist for the Police Firearms Officers' Association. She has experience in working with clients with severe psychological disorders under the auspices of the mental health charity MIND and Coventry's Mental Health Service. Until recently she taught Counselling Skills and Theory with Birmingham Adult Education Service and is a tutor on the Person-Centred Degree course in Counselling and Psychotherapy and co-tutor on the Advanced Diploma in Cognitive Behavioural Practice for Person-Centred Therapists at the University of Warwick. Anne is an accredited member of The National Counselling Association.

Catherine Date's reflections

I completed the course in December 2008 and undertaking this presented me with the opportunity to really reflect on how I work as a counsellor. I was both surprised and delighted to accept that I truly am person-centred through and through! I had the notion that, given a bit more insight and knowledge about the methodology of the CBTs, I would naturally embrace it and my practice would be significantly different as a consequence. By contrast, I actually became more confident and secure in my practising as a Person-centred therapist.

I hadn't realised the extent of the similarities between the two modalities before the course. While the concept of 'expert' is at the heart of the debate regarding differences between the two methodologies, there is arguably more similarity than difference between the Person-centred and the CBTs' approach to the definition of how the modalities differ in their understanding of role. It is misleading to claim that the CBT therapist places herself in the position of expert whereas the Person-centred therapist does not. Neither approach would agree that the therapist is an expert in the internal world of the client. As both have a secure foundation in phenomenology, both would concur that this would merely constitute poor therapy. The fundamental difference is one of attitude: the CBT therapist's attitude overtly prompts the client to reframe their thinking; the Person-centred therapist sits alongside the client in an attitude of empathic curiosity.

My involvement in a Self Directed Learning Group (SDLG) focusing on how therapists from both modalities work with challenging clients in order to promote change has had a lasting impact on my practice. The distinguishing factor between the Person-centred approach and the CBTs towards challenge seems to me to be about therapist intent, together with the elegant subtlety of delivery. Challenge within the Person-centred approach is something which happens if a counsellor is offering the therapeutic conditions. It is not something that I set out categorically to do, but rather through the moment-by-moment experiencing and reflecting of client activity. I have learnt that in the CBTs it comes from the theoretical framework, which is expressed through the therapist being congruent to the model. Thus the source of the challenge is from the theory rather than the therapist.

Working on this topic acted as further confirmation that I am inherently person-centred in my approach with clients and it is my natural way of being. This course has, however, empowered me in that I now better understand the principles upon which the CBTs' model of challenge rests. I also feel confident that I can employ these if and when the situation requires. I also now seem highly attuned to hearing irrational beliefs and, together with the specific learning and research I did for the SDLG topic, I feel much more empowered and confident about challenging clients. I recognised that challenging was a natural part of the way I worked, but I now have the resources to challenge differently should I feel it is in the best interests of the client and is congruent to my way of being.

I have been struck by the paradox of two truths in considering the powerful nature, coupled with the subtlety, of person-centred challenge. Once again I am charged with acknowledging how hard it is to be a person-centred therapist, being reliant on myself and the therapeutic conditions rather than a handy set of formulaic principles. This I have found to be quite thrilling, which makes me proud to call myself a Person-centred therapist.

Reflecting on the course as a whole, I found it personally very challenging. This was primarily to do with my busy-ness outside the course and the amount of topics covered within the 10-week period. It was stimulating in that it caused me to look at certain client issues in different ways, and frustrating in that I would have liked to have been able to spend a longer time exploring each topic. The introduction of case formulation has had a significant positive impact on my practice. Participating on the course promoted further reading and research; the supporting resources provided by the course tutors are abundant and have proved to be a useful resource to refer back to. For me, both as a person-centred practitioner and as a lecturer in counselling, the course has been most enlightening and gave me the opportunity to explore the rudiments of the CBTs in far greater depths than I had done previously. Like many ideologies and theories, the CBTs and Person-centred methodologies are united more by their similarities than disunited by their inherent differences.

Catherine Date Dip. Couns. & Psychoth., Adv. Dip. CBT, MBACP (Accred).

Catherine has been working as a counsellor in a variety of settings for the last twelve years. These include charitable, NHS and private sector settings. A particular focus of her counselling work has been with young adults. Currently, she has a small private practice and counsels in a sixth form college. She has a background in training and development, and for the past four years has been a lecturer within the Counselling Team at Warwickshire College, teaching on both Certificate and Diploma courses. As an independent practitioner she also offers supervision to placement counsellors in training at the Warwickshire-based charity Safeline, and she is currently studying for an Adv. Dip. in Supervision for Person-centred Counsellors.

Helen Walley's reflections

Cognitive behavioural therapy and person-centred therapy – were they not rivals? Why is my Rogerian, person-centred trainer leading a course like this? Where do I position myself in all the public debate about modality and working methods? Indeed, what do I feel about that? (Yes, feel!)

I had researched CBT during my training and of all the modalities found it prescriptive and dependent on my ability to deliver various prepared ways of questioning and assessing the thought processes of a client. That felt a bit scary. It was precisely because it brought out big, reactive feelings in me that I made the decision to face it head on and get some sense of what it was and what it wasn't in relation to my preferred way of working. The course offered me that opportunity.

I chose to be generous and respectful in my learning about CBT, considering carefully how I work as a person-centred counsellor, bringing to the counselling relationship my own particular mix of who I am, my values, and my own meaning of theories.

An early presentation of the philosophical and existential backgrounds of the two modalities helped me to see that though CBT does have some of its roots in behaviourism, it also has some in existential humanism, meaning that the uniqueness of the human experience is valued and there is a commitment to phenomenology. I found it illuminating to see the connections from a philosophical and phenomenological point of view and have gained insights from the connection between irrational beliefs and conditions of worth, external locus of evaluation and self concept, responsible hedonism and the actualising tendency. Epictetus, in saying 'Men are disturbed not by things but the views which they take of them', emphasises that we carry within ourselves disturbing emotions that may be fuelled by beliefs about ourselves and others. Rogers, when quoting Kierkegaard, said this:

> ...the deepest form of despair is to choose 'to be another than himself'. On the other
> hand, 'to will to be that self which one truly is, is indeed the opposite of despair' and this
> choice is the deepest responsibility of man. (Rogers, 1961)

By the end of the course I was aware of how profoundly informed I was of the
CBT approach. I also realised that I wouldn't draw any methods used in CBT
into my work as a person-centred therapist. What I have given more time to
researching and observing, since I did the course two years ago, is the complex
place of thinking, feeling and other types of self-experiencing that are part of
the client's, and my, frame of reference. I think I align myself most closely to
Greenberg when he says:

> An adequate theory must recognise two sources of experience, a conscious, deliber-
> ate, reflexive conceptual process (thinking) and an automatic, direct, schematic emo-
> tional process (feeling) and the constructive dialectical relationship between them.
> (Greenberg et al., 1993)

I was most struck on the course by the connection between pragmatic disputation, as used to challenge irrational beliefs in CBT, and challenge, as used in
Person-centred practice, which seems the most closely humanistic form of disputation. I know that I cannot challenge someone else's feelings. However, if a
thought process is disputed and the connection made with the feeling, then that
deeper, underlying feeling can be explored. This sort of challenge is not unusual in the person-centred approach. Whereas disputation in CBT can appear
more direct, in the Person-centred approach a challenge would be experienced
as more tentative, allowing the client to fully experience it and come closer to
their feelings, perhaps experiencing them for the first time.

Up until this time I had naïvely waded around in both my own feelings and my
clients' feelings, and not made any distinction between thought and feeling, or
understanding the complexity of their existence side by side in the client's frame
of reference. As a result of doing the course, I began to learn to tentatively ask my
clients such questions as 'As long as you think or believe this, how will you feel?'

Professionally, I feel and think that I am becoming a more robust therapist,
less afraid to challenge and more in touch with who I am. The deeper insight
into psychopathology and developing use of a formulation, also learnt on the
course, prepared me for the transition to working in a GP surgery.

I feel that it is important to have cognitive insight, information and understanding about what could be real for a given client. However, this is no substitute for being phenomenological, being present with and remaining empathic
with a client in their whole experiencing of themselves. Phenomenological
exploration is about holding everything about the client with equal value and
allowing myself to be as present with all of the client as I am able to be.

Doing the course convinced me that temperamentally, philosophically, emotionally, cognitively and spiritually I am most comfortable in my own skin as a

person-centred therapist. I think I know what Thorne meant when he said that 'knowledge and skills reside in the courage and the capacity to become more fully human' (Thorne, 2002: 21–22). That process continues....

Helen Whalley *BA (Hons), Adv. Dip. (Pastoral Studies), Dip. Couns. & Psychoth., Adv. Dip. CBT, PG Cert. Prof. Pract. (Counselling Supervision), MBACP (Accred,) UKRCP.*

Helen is a singer, listener, mentor, emotional thinker, mother, wife, Christian, Wirralian, and a person-centred therapist and supervisor who has practised as a therapist in a variety of agencies, including an English-speaking set-up in central Brussels with clients from a wide variety of cultures and backgrounds, a centre for health and healing in Birmingham, and an agency in Tamworth serving over five GP surgeries in the town. She has also worked in a GP surgery as their employed counsellor. Over the last three years she has run a private practice in Lichfield, which continues.

Some reflections on what Jeremy and Roger learned from working together

Jeremy's reflections on working with Roger

I consider this book to represent something of a milestone both personally and professionally as I believe that it reflects some very significant personal development that has occurred during the time I have spent working with Roger. I consider that my work with Roger has been a real journey, in which I have grown in my model by becoming significantly more immersed in his. I believe that I have developed a much more subtle, yet infinitely more complex understanding of the PCA and how this, as a practice, has a uniqueness rooted in 'the person' of the practitioner as opposed to being yet another application of a model. This is both a strength and a burden as it can so easily seem vague and dependent upon selection of the 'right candidate' as opposed to providing a clear training and study option by which skills can be easily rehearsed and learned. This is not to say that I reject my own training and what I see as a clear strength and benefit of the CBTs; rather, it is a powerful difference worthy of celebration. I would offer a note of caution to practitioners of the CBTs that, if you find yourself dismissing the PCA on the grounds that technique is not taught or part of the training, you have missed a critical point!

As Roger and I have worked together, students on our programme have often commented on our genuinely impromptu dialogues, commenting that they experience this as a very honest and genuine exchange between two practitioners immersed in their respective models but strongly motivated to accept and understand the difference between them. This is not to say that we don't enjoy ourselves and introduce the odd bit of fun in the form of obvious satirical send-up of one another!

Although not unique to my experiences in other aspects of my life and career, working with Roger has demonstrated to me just how important the relationships that we have with one another are. The saying that I understand to originate from John of Salisbury in his 1159 treatise, *The Metalogicon*, sums it up:

> We are like dwarfs sitting on the shoulders of giants. We see more, and things that are more distant, than they did, not because our sight is superior or because we are taller than they, but because they raise us up, and by their great stature add to ours.

I have an experience of Roger that has been repeatedly quoted as me describing him as 'authenticity on legs', and this is not an experience that has changed! At times overwhelming, but usually great fun and engaging, I have discovered that Roger embodies the PCA – this is truly 'part of his being'.

When I was first introduced to Roger and his colleagues on the course, I retained my 'missionary zeal' to convert everyone to the delights that had been my discovery and liberation through REBT. What I found was a warm, accepting, yet different perspective which was intriguing and ironically challenging. I guess I could have turned and fled back into the cosy warmth of my own perspective, and resorted to remain where I was and simply treat that which did not conform to my perspective as heresy. It is this, in part, that inspired me to work more closely with Roger and to write this book. Indeed, working with Roger has impacted upon my practice to a significant extent and I experience myself 'noticing' when clients are potentially dichotomising between what they often disguise as simple shades of difference but are, in reality, very significant schisms. I now regularly introduce the concept of increasing individual complexity as part of my therapeutic work, along with the use of 'and' instead of 'but' as a gentle way of disputing absolutist beliefs about the self, world and others. At times I can even hear Roger's voice repeating his mantra, 'Everything that comes before "but" is bullshit', which is such a humorous, useful and succinct insight that it could easily be constructed as a 'technique'. I trust, however, that my use of this represents a genuine understanding of Roger's intention and an acknowledgement of the therapeutic power of this.

Another strong feature that I believe has become more evident in myself is my sense that any model is simply that, a model, and therefore represents a hypothetical approximation to reality. As models develop support based on the acquisition of intimate technical knowledge, this necessarily includes a risk that people become 'followers', and the model develops an almost supernatural status of holy writ and dissent is viewed almost as evidence of either stupidity or madness. For me, this is always potentially dangerous, and consequently it seems that a modest modification of the Socratic principle that to follow the argument wherever it leads and readily question that which is considered to be given acts as a strong defence against it. As such, I consider myself to be an active heretic on the basis that while this might not necessarily lead me to ultimately accurate conclusions, it certainly assures me that I do not simply take for granted that which others have conjectured and attempted to prove to be the case. As for being heretical, I'll leave the last word to the English novelist and writer Graham Greene: 'Heresy is another word for freedom of thought.'

Roger's reflections on working with Jeremy

I guess the title of the book says it all. It has really felt like I have found a new 'brother'. Although both of us are very different as personalities, it has felt like we have some really strong shared values, as though we have been brought up in the same family. Of course, like most siblings there has been some rivalry between us and that has always been good natured with no animosity, though both of us have been capable of some piercing digs. For example, from me to Jeremy: 'Well if you worked at a proper university like Warwick instead of a former poly in Coventry, you'd know that understanding theory must come first!' Followed by Jeremy retorting: 'Ah well, an old man like you couldn't cope with the pace and energy of a young university.'

What has been most interesting, though, is to have experienced Jeremy's commitment to the same humanistic, existentialist principles and values that I do, along with his belief in the importance of the therapeutic relationship being the key to the best therapy. I have experienced him as really integrating qualities of exquisite irrationality alongside a solid acceptance of his own fallibility, clearly demonstrating the depth of his self-acceptance. While in many ways I see Jeremy as living in a way that is totally congruent with the CBT/REBT approach, its philosophy and practice, at the same time I see him as disputing the stereotype of the cool CBT technician through his innate warm and cultured ability to be relational.

For me, the notion of sitting on the shoulders of a giant does not sit well. Rather, I have had the sense of us learning to work together, which has for me felt like learning to walk alongside another giant and for neither of us to be in the shadow of the other. I've learned a great deal about being more accepting of my fallibility and have enjoyed becoming more adept at more naturally using inference chaining and disputation as part of my internal process, and even learned to share that with clients from time to time. I've also learned the value of the ABC etc. structure as a useful way of reflecting on my own issues, though I suspect that I will always be loath to use that with a client in the way that Jeremy does.

At the end, it feels like we have learned to be 'brothers in arms'. Both strongly reinforced in our individual beliefs about the ways we practise, and hugely respectful of each other's knowledge and expertise. We will both continue to challenge the need to dilute our approaches, the drive to move towards integration or pluralism. We are not saying our ways are best. We are saying they work for us and the clients we work with. I owe Jeremy a debt of gratitude for being a living example of the best of CBT and for being in a way that is totally congruent with the model. That has enabled me to get a deeper and fully respectful sense of the approach, which, paradoxically, has led to an even deeper strengthening of my belief in the Person-centred Approach as a way of being and to an even stronger belief that those six therapeutic conditions are both necessary and sufficient, for me and the work I do and the way I live my life.

A consideration of integration and 'pluralism'

Cooper and McLeod's (2010) suggestion that the presumption of the 'therapeutic monoculture', dominated by CBT, has arisen, and that this has marginalised the other modalities, actually represents a more fundamental issue of splitting and dividing within the world of counselling and psychotherapy and proposes a pluralistic approach to resolve the issue. In this model, they posit that, given individual differences, it seems logical that different methods will be helpful to different people at different times. Consequently, the average-top-marks-brand-comparison model of deciding the most effective mode of therapy is, frankly, meaningless.

As for Cooper and McLeod's position, we remain unclear as to whether this is, in effect, a position based on respect and trust, in which a practitioner can consider that an approach from a modality different from their own has potential benefit to offer, or a suggestion that a practitioner can integrate conflicting models into their own practice. The latter seems unachievable and is, by logical extension, a form of pragmatic non-integrative integration that is dependent upon therapists having a very precise (maybe unattainably precise) comprehension of their client's perspective. In their paper, it seems that Cooper and McLeod suggest that this is directed by 'the client's own goals [sic] for the therapeutic process' (2010: 13).

A more radical approach might be gained by a consideration of the need for a meta-therapeutic model that could, in due course, give rise to a more effective and realistic approximation to understanding human distress that does not fall into the trap of retaining all that has gone before, based on what appears to be an over-conscientious attention to being inclusive. At this stage, perhaps this is a case of watch this space...

A final word about similarity and dissonance?

To begin a final consideration of the similarities and dissonance between the CBTs and the PCA it may be of benefit to acknowledge that they are both deeply rooted within humanistic and existential philosophy. As a consequence, they are both phenomenological in their approach to individual emotional experience and particularly the nature of suffering.

From the PCA, the client's construction of reality is viewed as being based on an exquisite, yet fundamental, rationality in as much as people are able to direct their behaviour through a process of reason that is interlinked to a fundamental drive towards growth.

In contrast to the PCA, the CBTs, and particularly REBT, hypothesise that the client's construction of reality is based on irrationality and an erroneous assumption that can be disputed and challenged. As such, the CBTs theorise that the individual's construction of reality is dimensional (although this is, in practice, more usually graduated) between irrationality and rationality, where irrationality represents homeostasis.

A logical conclusion of this heritage and standpoint is that both CBTs and PCA consider the client to be the only expert in their own internal world. Ironically, both also implicitly assume that the client's experiencing of their internal world cannot be '*the* truth'. It is, perhaps, a confusion regarding the latter that leads some therapists from the PCA misguidedly to believe that the client is always right or that the client always knows best, which cannot logically be true.

As such, both the CBTs and PCA are interested in the phenomenology of the client. However, the CBTs are primarily interested in understanding the client and challenging their thinking about their phenomenology, whereas the PCA strives to communicate acceptance of the client's understanding of their own experience of their own phenomenology and to encourage clients to identify alternative choices.

Despite the language differences of each modality, the introjected values for PCA and the rigid irrational beliefs of the CBTs effectively represent an internal process as being the cause of emotional and behavioural distress. Also, each of these processes distort the concept of self and result in behaviours and processes which superficially appear to counteract this, and ultimately reinforce these self-defeating internal frames of reference.

In the PCA, the tendency to self-actualising is the drive towards becoming more fully functioning; a process of becoming more complicated in an increasingly complicated world. Connell (2004: 37–47) argues that a core difference between the two modalities is that the PCA concept of the 'actualising tendency is a more trusting view of human nature than the REBT view that human beings tend towards irrationality'. We argue that the REBT specifically, but also the CBTs in general, are in fact more similar in terms of actualisation. For the CBTs, where this is conceptualised it appears that it is considered to be a point of punctuation which requires ongoing work as opposed to an ongoing process. Consequently, it is possible to achieve a point at which the individual is actualised, or achieves self-acceptance.

As recorded in the preceding chapters, for the PCA, therapy requires the six necessary and sufficient conditions whereas for the CBTs these can be described as preferably necessary but certainly not sufficient. Thus, it is the client's experiencing of the PCA therapist's acceptance that enables the therapist to challenge client choices about thought, whereas in the CBTs it is the process of disputation of irrational thinking that is essential for this change. Clearly, therefore, a range of methods by which both therapist and client can develop effective means of doing so are considered essential to maximising therapeutic effect. For the CBTs, therefore, the techniques represent the active engagement in therapeutic process, whereas it is the experiencing of the conditions in PCA that represents the therapeutic process. At one level (and it is a somewhat 'traditional' criticism of the CBTs from within the PCA), is that the technique can become the therapy and, consequently, the process and client are ignored. It is also strongly argued that, within the PCA, the use of technique is avoided. However, it does seem worthwhile to ponder the question, 'When does a well-rehearsed or internalised conceptualisation of the model become a "technique"?'

It is at this stage that the PCA and CBTs differ most clearly. The conclusion is that the PCA posits that it is the unconditional acceptance of the client by the therapist which brings about the primary facilitation of change. In the CBTs it is the use of 'techniques' within a process of exposition regarding the interaction of characteristic thinking styles and content and challenging of the client's own conditional acceptance of themselves, others or the world that results in change. For the CBTs, the ultimate goal is the client achieving a realistic self-acceptance that represents the goal of therapy.

Given the centrality of the acceptance by the therapist within the PCA, it is of little surprise that the authenticity of the therapist is essential for therapy to take place within this approach. Contrary to this, while the CBTs require that the therapist is congruent with the model, it also requires a positive therapeutic relationship that is collaborative yet challenging.

Despite the very significant theoretical contributions of PCA regarding therapeutic process, for the CBTs therapeutic change is possible only if they apply significant effort and attention to changing how they think, feel and behave.

Within the PCA it is conceptualised that personality change occurs through the client's experiencing of the six *necessary and sufficient* conditions. Furthermore, Rogers detailed seven process stages of therapeutic growth that a good therapeutic relationship can promote. As noted, the CBTs assume that a therapeutic relationship must exist at some level in order for therapeutic work to take place. However, the extent to which this exists is considerably less defined or agreed. Within the CBTs, a core component is an educative role in which the therapist 'teaches' aspects of the philosophy and model to the client. Despite the negative connotations of the 'teacher–pupil' relationship, none of the CBTs conceptualises this element of the therapy to be a teacher–pupil relationship. Rather, it is conceptualised as a collaborative venture. Indeed, Josefowitzi and Myram (2005) note that the CBTs have even defined the 'collaborative relationship' in which the client is considered to be an equal to the therapist as opposed to the formation of a positive emotional bond or positive therapeutic alliance between them.

One of the most enduring differences between the PCA and CBTs is that of directionality. For the PCA, the authenticity of the therapist and the communication of acceptance within the therapeutic relationship are essential and therefore avoiding any therapist 'agenda' is prime. The maintenance of a non-directive attitude by the therapist enables the PCA practitioner to hold an intention to counsel and be therapeutic in their endeavours with the client while avoiding the lampooning stereotype of simply mirroring and repeating what the client says. Conversely, for the CBTs being directive is a necessary consequence of the model, in which it is only by active engagement with the model that the client is enabled to work towards change. Again, this does not amount to 'telling the client what to do and how to feel'. Rather, it is a coherent adoption and integration of the model. At a very fundamental level, the CBTs and PCA seem that they are markedly different in the demands and skills of the therapist... or are they? As for both of us, we remain of the opinion that it is neither coherent, practical nor ethical to 'do a bit of...' either approach.

Recommended reading

Connell, J. (2004) The differences and similarities of rational emotive behaviour therapy and person-centred counselling: A personal perspective. *The Rational Emotive Behaviour Therapist, 11*(1), 37–47.

Gilbert, P. & Leahy, R.L. (eds) (2007) *The Therapeutic Relationship in the Cognitive Behavioral Psychotherapies*. Hove: Routledge.

House, R. & Loewenthal, D. (eds) (2008) *Against and For CBT: Towards a Constructive Dialogue?* Ross-on-Wye: PCCS Books.

Josefowitzi, N. & Myram, D. (2005) Towards a person-centred cognitive behaviour therapy. *Counselling Psychology Quarterly, 18*(4), 329–336.

Shlien, J. (2003) *To Lead an Honourable Life: Invitations to Think about Client-centred Therapy and the Person-centred Approach*. Ross-on-Wye: PCCS Books.

Wills, F. and Sanders, D. (1997) *Cognitive Therapy: Transforming the Image*. London: Sage.

REFERENCES

Ackerman, S.J. & Hilsenroth, M.J. (2003) A review of therapist characteristics and techniques positively impacting the therapeutic alliance. *Clinical Psychology Review, 23*, 1–33.

BACP (2010) *Ethical Framework for Good Practice in Counselling and Psychotherapy* (revised edn). Lutterworth: BACP.

Baldwin, J.D. & Baldwin, J.I. (1998) *Behavior Principles in Everyday Life* (3rd edn). Englewood Cliffs, NJ: Prentice-Hall.

Baldwin, M. (1987) Interview with Carl Rogers on the use of self in therapy. In M. Baldwin & V. Satir (eds), *The Use of Self in Therapy* (pp. 7–16). New York: The Haworth Press.

Bandura, A. (1997) *Self-efficacy: The Exercise of Self-control*. New York: W.H. Freeman.

Barkham, M., Shapiro, D.A., Gillian, E.H., & Rees, A. (1999) Psychotherapy in two-plus-one sessions: Outcomes of a randomized controlled trial of cognitive-behavioral and psychodynamic–interpersonal therapy for subsyndromal depression. *Journal of Clinical & Consulting Psychology, 67*, 201–211.

Beck, A.T. (1967) *The Diagnosis and Management of Depression*. Philadelphia: University of Pennsylvania Press.

Beck, A.T. (1972) *Depression: Causes and Treatment*. Philadelphia: University of Pennsylvania Press.

Beck, A.T. (1975) *Cognitive Therapy and the Emotional Disorders*. New York: International Universities Press.

Beck, A.T. (1976) *Cognitive Therapy and the Emotional Disorders*. New York: International Universities Press; London: Penguin.

Beck, A.T., Rush, A.J., Shaw, B.F., & Emery, G. (1979) *Cognitive Therapy of Depression*. New York: Guilford Press.

Bellack, A.S. & Hersen, M. (1987) *Dictionary of Behaviour Therapy Techniques*. Oxford: Pergamon Press.

Biermann-Ratjen, E., Eckert, J., & Schwartz, H. (1997) *Gesprächspsychotherapie: Verändern durch Verstehen* (8th edn). Stuttgart: Kohlhammer.

Biglan, A. & Hayes, S.C. (1996) Should the behavioral sciences become more pragmatic? The case for functional contextualism in research on human behavior. *Applied and Preventive Psychology: Current Scientific Perspectives, 5*, 47–57.

Binder, U. & Binder, H.-J. (1994) *Klientenzentrierte Psychotherapie bei schweren psychischen Störungen: Neue Handlungs– und Therapiekonzepte zur Veränderung*. Frankfurt/M: Fachbuchhandlung für Psychologie.

Binder, U. & Binder, J. (1991) *Studien zu einer störungsspezifischen klientenzentrierten Psychotherapie: Schizophrene Ordnung – Psychosomatisches Erleben – Depressives Leiden*. Eschborn: Klotz.

Bodden, D.H.M., Dirksen, C.D., Bögels, S.M., Nauta, M.H., De Haan, E., Ringrose, J., Appelboom, C., Brinkman, A.G., & Appelboom-Geerts, K.C.M.M.J. (2008) Costs and cost-effectiveness of family CBT versus individual CBT in clinically anxious children. *Clinical Child Psychology & Psychiatry, 13*(4), 543–564.

Bordin, E.S. (1979) The generalisability of the psychoanalytic concept of the working alliance. *Psychotherapy: Theory, Research and Practice, 16,* 252–260.

Bozarth, J.D. (1993) Not necessarily necessary but always sufficient. In D. Brazier (ed.), *Beyond Carl R. Rogers: Towards a Psychotherapy for the 21st Century* (pp. 92–105). London: Constable.

Brazier, D. (1993) The necessary condition is love. In D. Brazier (ed.), *Beyond Carl Rogers.* London: Constable.

Bruch, M. & Bond, F.W. (eds) (1998) *Beyond Diagnosis: Case Formulation Approach in CBT.* Chichester: Wiley.

Bryant-Jefferies, R. (2003) *Time Limited Therapy in Primary Care: A Person-centred Dialogue.* Oxford: Radcliffe Medical Press.

Burns, D.D. (1980) *Feeling Good: The New Mood Therapy.* New York: Morrow and Co.

Casemore, R.B. (2002) It may be therapeutic but is it really counselling? *Health Professions Counselling and Psychotherapy Journal, 2*(1), 6–8.

Casemore, R. (2011) *Person-centred Counselling in a Nutshell* (2nd edn). London: Sage.

Cavanagha, K., Seccombe, N., & Lidbettera, N. (2011) The implementation of computerized cognitive behavioural therapies in a service user-led, third sector self help clinic. *Behavioural and Cognitive Psychotherapy, 39*(4), 427–442.

Chadwick, P.D.J., Williams, C., & Mackenzie, J. (2003) Impact of case formulation in cognitive behavioural therapy for psychosis. *Behaviour Research and Therapy, 41,* 671–680.

Connell, J. (2004) The differences and similarities of rational emotive behaviour therapy and person-centred counselling: A personal perspective. *The Rational Emotive Behaviour Therapist, 11*(1), 37–47.

Cooper, M. & McLeod, J. (2010) Pluralism: Towards a new paradigm for therapy. *Therapy Today, 21*(9), 10–14.

Cooper, M., O'Hara, M., Schmid, P.F., & Wyatt, G. (2007) *The Handbook of Person-centred Psychotherapy and Counselling.* Basingstoke: Palgrave.

Davenloo, H. (ed.) (1980) *Current Trends in Short-term Dynamic Therapy.* New York: Aronson.

Dryden, W. (1995a) *Rational-Emotive Behaviour Therapy: A Reader.* London: Sage.

Dryden. W. (1995b) The therapeutic alliance in rational-emotive behaviour therapy. In W. Dryden (ed.), *Rational-Emotive Behaviour Therapy: A Reader.* London: Sage.

Dryden, W. (2009) *Skills in Rational Emotive Behaviour Counselling & Psychotherapy.* London: Sage.

Dryden, W. & Mytton, J. (1999) *Four Approaches to Counselling and Psychotherapy.* London and New York: Routledge.

Eels, T. (2009) Contemporary themes in case formulation. In P. Sturmey (ed.), *Clinical Case Formulation: Varieties of Approaches* (pp. 293–315). Chichester: Wiley Blackwell.

Eels, T.D. (ed.) (2007) *Handbook of Psychotherapy Case Formulation.* New York: Guilford Press.

Elliott, R. (1984) A discovery-oriented approach to significant events in psychotherapy: Interpersonal process recall and comprehensive process analysis. In L.N. Rice & L.S. Greenberg (eds), *Patterns of Change* (pp. 249–286). New York: Guilford Press.

Elliott, R., James, E., Reimschuessel, C., Cislo, D., & Sack, N. (1985) Significant events and the analysis of immediate therapeutic impacts. *Psychotherapy, 22,* 620–630.

Elliott, R., Shapiro, D.A., Firth-Cozens, J., Stiles, W.B., Hardy, G.E., Llewelyn, S.P., & Margison, F.R. (1994) Comprehensive process analysis of insight events in cognitive-behavioral and psychodynamic-interpersonal psychotherapies. *Journal of Counseling Psychology, 41*(4), 449–463.

Ellis, A. (1948) A critique of the theoretical contributions of nondirective therapy. *Journal of Clinical Psychology, 4*, 248–255.

Ellis, A. (1950) An introduction to the principles of scientific psychoanalysis. *Genetic Psychology Monographs, 41*, 147–212.

Ellis, A. (1955) New approaches to psychotherapy techniques. *Journal of Clinical Psychology Monograph Supplement, 11*, 1–53.

Ellis, A. (1956) An operational reformulation of some basic principles of psychoanalysis. *Psychoanalytic Review, 43*, 163–180.

Ellis, A. (1957) Rational psychotherapy and individual psychology. *The Journal of Individual Psychology, 13*(1), 38–44.

Ellis, A. (1958) Rational psychotherapy. *The Journal of General Psychology, 59*, 35–49.

Ellis, A. (1959a) Rationalism and its therapeutic applications. *Annals of Psychotherapy, 1*, 55–64.

Ellis, A. (1959b) Requisite conditions for basic personality change. *Journal of Consulting Psychology, 23*, 538–540.

Ellis, A. (1962) *Reason and Emotion in Psychotherapy*. Secaucus, NJ: Lyle Stuart and Citadel Press.

Ellis, A. (1979) The biological basis of human irrationality: A reply to McBurnett and La Pointe. *Individual Psychology, 35*(1), 111–116.

Ellis, A. (2000) Rational emotive behavior therapy. In R.J. Corsini & D. Wedding (eds), *Current Psychotherapies* (6th edn). Itasca, IL: Peacock.

Ellis, A. (2001) *New Directions for Rational Emotive Behaviour Therapy: Overcoming Destructive Beliefs, Fellings, and Behaviours*. New York: Prometheus.

Ellis, A. (2002) *Overcoming Resistance: A Rational Emotive Behavior Therapy Integrated Approach* (2nd edn). New York: Springer.

Ellis, A. (2003) Early theories and practices of rational emotive behavior theory and how they have been augmented and revised during the last three decades. *Journal of Rational-Emotive & Cognitive-Behavior Therapy, 21*, 3–4.

Ellis, A. (2005) *The Myth of Self-Esteem*. New York: Prometheus.

Ellis, A. & Bernard, M.E. (1986) What is rational-emotive therapy? In A. Ellis & R.M. Grieger (eds), *Handbook of Rational-Emotive Therapy* (Vol. 2, pp. 3–30). New York: Springer.

Ellis, A. & Dryden, W. (1999) *The Practice of Rational Emotive Behaviour Therapy*. London: Free Association Books.

Ellis, A. & Harper, R.A. (1961) *A Guide to Rational Living*. Englewood Cliffs, NJ: Lawrence Erlbaum Associates.

Emmelkamp, P.M.G., Bowman, T.K., & Blaauw, E. (1994) Individualized versus standardized therapy: A comparative evaluation with obsessive-compulsive patients. *Clinical Psychology and Psychotherapy, 1*, 95–100.

Evans, R. (1978) *Carl Rogers: The Man and His Ideas*. New York: E.P. Dutton.

Evans-Jones, C. & Peters, E. (2009) The therapeutic relationship in CBT for psychosis: Client, therapist and therapy factors. *Behavioural and Cognitive Psychotherapy, 37*, 527–540.

Eysenck, H.J. & Rachman, S. (1965) *The Causes and Cures of Neurosis*. London: Routledge and Kegan Paul.

Fehringer, C. (2002) *Because of the Noise of Your Actions, I Cannot Hear What You Say: On the Art of Balancing Distance and Involvement in a Significant Therapeutic Relationship. Person-Centred and Experiential Psychotherapies.* Ross-on-Wye: PCCS Books.

Finke, J. (1994) *Empathie und Interaktion: Methodik und Praxis der Gesprächspsychotherapie.* Stuttgart: Thieme.

Frenzel, P., Keil, W.W., Schmid, P.F., & Stölzl, N. (eds) (2001) *Klienten-Personzentrierte Psychotherapie. Kontexte, Konzepte, Konkretisierungen.* Vienna: Facultas Universitätsverlag.

Fullerton, D.T., Cavner, J.J., & McLaughlin-Reidel, T. (1978) Results of a token economy. *Archives of General Psychiatry, 35,* 1451–1453.

Gendlin, E.T. (1996) *Focusing-oriented Psychotherapy: A Manual of the Experiential Method.* New York: Guilford Press.

Gilbert, P. (1992) *Depression: The Evolution of Powerlessness.* Hove: Lawrence Erlbaum Associates.

Gilbert P. (2007) Evolving minds and compassion in the therapeutic relationship. In P. Gilbert & R.L. Leahy (eds), *The Therapeutic Relationship in the Cognitive Behavioral Psychotherapies.* Hove: Routledge.

Gilbert, P. & Leahy, R.L. (eds) (2005) *Compassion: Conceptualisations, Research and Use in Psychotherapy.* London: Routledge.

Gilbert, P. & Leahy, R.L. (eds) (2007) Introduction and overview: Basic issues in the therapeutic relationship. In P. Gilbert & R.L. Leahy (eds), *The Therapeutic Relationship in the Cognitive Behavioural Psychotherapies.* Hove: Routledge.

Goldiamond, I. (1974) Toward a constructional approach to social problems: Ethical and constitutional issues raised by applied behavior analysis. *Behaviorism, 2*(1), 1–84.

Goldstein, K. (1939) *The Organism.* New York: American Book Co.

Greenberg, L.S. (2007) Emotion in the therapeutic relationship. In P. Gilbert & R.L. Leahy (eds), *The Therapeutic Relationship in the Cognitive Behavioural Psychotherapies.* Hove: Routledge.

Greenberg, L.S., Rice, L.N., & Elliott, R. (1993) *Facilitating Emotional Change: The Moment-by-Moment Process.* New York: Guilford Press.

Greenberg, L.S., Watson, J., & Lietaer, G. (1997) *Experiential Psychotherapy: Different Interventions.* New York: Guilford Press.

Hardy, G.E., Cahill, J., & Barkham, M. (2007) Models of the therapeutic relationship and prediction of outcome: A research perspective. In P. Gilbert & R.L. Leahy (eds), *The Therapeutic Relationship in the Cognitive Behavioural Psychotherapies* (pp. 24–42). London: Routledge.

Harper, D. & Moss, D. (2003) A different kind of chemistry? Reformulating 'formulation'. *Clinical Psychology, 25,* 6–10.

Harris, B. (1979) Whatever happened to little Albert? *American Psychologist, 34*(15), 1–160.

Hayes, S.C. (1993) Analytic goals and the varieties of scientific contextualism. In S.C. Hayes, L.J. Hayes, H.W. Reese, & T.R. Sarbin (eds), *Varieties of Scientific Contextualism.* Reno, NV: Context Press.

Heath, P.L. (1967) Nothing. In *The Encyclopedia of Philosophy* (Vol. 5). New York: Macmillan & Free Press.

Heidegger, M. (1962) *Being and Time.* Translated by J. Macquarrie & E. Robinson. Oxford: Blackwell.

Hjelle, L.A. & Ziegler, D.J. (1992) *Personality Theories: Basic Assumptions, Research, and Applications* (3rd edn). New York: McGraw-Hill.

House, R. & Loewenthal, D. (eds) (2008) *Against and For CBT: Towards a Constructive Dialogue?* Ross-on-Wye: PCCS Books.

Husserl, E. (1912) *Phenomenology and the Foundations of the Sciences: Third Book: Ideas Pertaining to a Pure Phenomenology and to a Phenomenological Philosophy.* Translated by T.E. Klein & W. Pohl (1980). The Hague: Martinus Nijhoff.

Jacobson, N.S., Schmaling, K.B., Holtzworth-Munroe, A., Katt, J.L., Wood, L.F., & Follette, V.M. (1989) Research-structured vs. clinically flexible versions of social learning-based marital therapy. *Behaviour Research and Therapy, 27,* 173–180.

Johnston, D. & Dallos, R. (2006) *Formulation in Psychology and Psychotherapy.* Hove: Routledge.

Josefowitzi, N. & Myram, D. (2005) Towards a person-centred cognitive behaviour therapy. *Counselling Psychology Quarterly, 18*(4), 329–336.

Kahneman, D. & Tversky, A. (1979) Prospect theory: An analysis of decisions under risk. *Econometrica, 47,* 313–327.

Kierkegaard, S. (1844) *Philosophical Fragments.* Translated by H. Hong & E.H. Hong (1985). Princeton, NJ: Princeton University Press.

Kinderman, P. & Lobban, F. (2000) Evolving formulations: Sharing complex information with clients. *Behavioural & Cognitive Psychotherapy, 28*(3), 307–310.

Kirschenbaum, H. (2007) *The Life and Work of Carl Rogers.* Ross-on-Wye: PCCS Books.

Kirschenbaum, H. & Henderson, L. (1990) *Carl Rogers Dialogues.* London: Constable.

Klein, D.N., Schwartz, J.E., Santiago, N.J., Vivian, D., Vocisano, C., Costonguay, L.G., Arnow, B.A., Blalock, J.A., Markowitz, J.C., Rothbaum, B.O., & McCullough, J.P. (2003) Therapeutic alliance in depression treatment: Controlling for prior change and patient characteristics. *Journal of Consulting and Clinical Psychology, 71,* 997–1006.

Kluckhohn, C. & Murray, H.A. (eds) (1948) *Personality in Nature, Society and Culture.* New York: Knopf.

Kuyken, W., Fothergill, C.D., Musa, M., & Chadwick, P.D.J. (2005) The reliability and quality of cognitive case formulation: Fool's gold? *Behaviour Research & Therapy, 43,* 1187–1201.

Léduc, A., Dumais, A., & Evans, I.M. (1990) Social behaviorism, rehabilitation, and ethics: Applications for people with severe disabilities. In G. Eifert & I. Evans (eds), *Unifying Behavior Therapy: Contributions of Paradigmatic Behaviorism.* New York: Springer.

Mackay, H.C., Barkham, M., Stiles, W.B., & Goldfried, M.R. (2002) Patterns of client emotion in helpful sessions of cognitive-behavioral and psychodynamic-interpersonal therapy. *Journal of Counseling Psychology, 49*(3), 376–380.

Malan, D. (1979) *Individual Psychotherapy and the Science of Psychodynamics.* London: Butterworth.

Martin, D.G. (1972) *Learning-Based Client-Centered Therapy.* Monterey, CA: Brooks/Cole.

Martin, D.J., Garske, J.P., & Davis, M.K. (2000) Relation of the therapeutic relationship with outcome and other variables: A meta-analytic review. *Journal of Consulting and Clinical Psychology, 68,* 438–450.

Maslow, A. (1954) *Motivation and Personality.* New York: Harper.

Mearns, D. and Thorne, B. (2007) *Person-centred Counselling in Action* (3rd edn). London: Sage.

Meichenbaum, D. (1977) *Cognitive Behavior Modification: An Integrative Approach.* New York: Plenum Press.

Meichenbaum, D. (1985) *Stress Inoculation Training.* New York: Pergamon Press.

Miles, T.R. (1966) *Eliminating the Unconscious: A Behaviourist View of Psycho-analysis.* New York: Pergamon Press.

Milner, J. & O'Byrne, P. (2004) *Assessment in Counselling: Theory Process and Decision Making.* Basingstoke: Palgrave.

Moore, R.H. (1983) Inference as A in RET. *British Journal of Cognitive Psychotherapy, 1*(2), 17–23.

Mowrer, O.H. (1951) Two-factor learning theory: Summary and comment. *Psychological Review, 58*(5), 350–354.

Murray, E.J. & Foote, F. (1979) The origins of fear of snakes. *Behaviour Research & Therapy, 17*, 489–493.

Neenan, M. & Dryden, W. (1996) The intricacies of inference chaining. *Journal of Rational-Emotive & Cognitive-Behavior Therapy, 14*(4), 231–243.

Neenan, M. & Dryden, W. (2011a) *Cognitive Therapy in a Nutshell* (revised edn). London: Sage.

Neenan, M. & Dryden, W. (2011b) *Rational Emotive Behaviour Therapy in a Nutshell* (revised edn). London: Sage.

Nietzsche, F. (1973) *Beyond Good and Evil*. Translated by T. Hollingdale. London: Penguin.

Nye, R. (1996) *Three Psychologies: Perspectives from Freud, Skinner and Rogers*. New York: Brooks/Cole.

O'Hara, M. (1998) Person-centered and experiential therapy in an age of cultural transition. *Person, 1*, 5–14.

Osatuke, K., Glick, M.J., Stiles, W.B., Greenberg, L.S., Shapiro, D.A., & Barkham, M. (2005) Temporal patterns of improvement in client-centred therapy and cognitive-behaviour therapy. *Counselling Psychology Quarterly, 18*(2), 95–108.

Owens, R.G. & Ashcroft, J.B. (1982) Functional analysis in applied psychology. *British Journal of Clinical Psychology, 21*, 181–189.

Padesky, G.A. & Beck, A.T. (2003) Science and philosophy: Comparison of cognitive therapy and rational emotive behavior therapy. *Journal of Cognitive Psychotherapy: An International Quarterly, 17*, 211–229.

Parjares, F. & Miller, M.D. (1994) Role of self-efficacy beliefs and general math ability in mathematical problem-solving: A path analysis. *Journal of Educational Psychology, 86*, 193–203.

Pavlov, I.P. (1927) *Conditioned Reflexes*. New York: Dover.

Perls, F.S. (1976) *The Gestalt Approach and Eyewitness to Therapy*. New York: Bantam.

Persons, J. (1989) *Cognitive Therapy in Practice: A Case Formulation Approach*. London: Norton.

Phillips, J. (2005) Idiographic formulations, symbols, narratives, context and meaning. *Psychopathology, 38*, 180–184.

Pierson, H. & Hayes, S.C. (2007) Using acceptance and commitment therapy to empower the therapeutic relationship. In P. Gilbert & R.L. Leahy (eds), *The Therapeutic Relationship in the Cognitive Behavioural Psychotherapies*. London: Routledge.

Polster, E. & Polster, M. (1973) *Gestalt Therapy Integrated*. New York: Vintage Books.

Prouty, G. (1990) Pre-therapy: A theoretical evolution in the person centred/experiential psychotherapy of schizophrenia and retardation. In G. Lietaer, J. Rombauts, & R. Van Ballen (eds), *Client Centred and Experiential Psychotherapy in the Nineties* (pp. 645–658). Leuven: Leuven University Press.

Prouty, G. (1994) *Theoretical Evolutions in Person Centred/Experiential Therapy: Applications to Schizophrenic and Retarded Psychoses*. Westport, CT: Praeger.

Rachman, S. (1977) The conditioning theory of fear-acquisition: A critical examination. *Behaviour Research & Therapy, 15*, 375–387.

Rachman, S. (1981) The primacy of affect: Some theoretical implications. *Behaviour Research & Therapy, 19*, 279–290.

Rachman, S. (1990) The determinants and treatment of simple phobias. *Advances in Behaviour Research & Therapy, 12*, 1–30.

Robertson, D. (2010) *The Philosophy of Cognitive Behavioural Therapy (CBT): Stoic Philosophy as Rational and Cognitive Psychotherapy*. London: Karnac.

Robinson, P.J. & Wood, K. (1984) The Threat Index: An additive approach. *Journal of Death & Dying*, *15*(2), 139–144.

Rogers, C.R. (1942) *Counselling and Psychotherapy*. Boston, MA: Houghton Mifflin,

Rogers, C.R. (1951) *Client-Centred Therapy: Its Current Practice, Implications and Theory*. London: Constable; Boston, MA: Houghton Mifflin.

Rogers, C.R. (1956) The necessary and sufficient conditions of therapeutic personality change. *Journal of Consulting and Clinical Psychology*, *60*(6), 827–832.

Rogers, C.R. (1957) The necessary and sufficient conditions of therapeutic personality change. *The Journal of Consulting Psychology*, *21*, 95–103.

Rogers, C.R. (1959) A theory of therapy, personality and interpersonal relationships, as developed in the client-centred framework. In S. Koch (ed.), *Psychology, A Study of a Science: Vol. 3: Formulations of the Person and the Social Context* (pp. 184–256). New York: McGraw-Hill.

Rogers, C.R. (1961) *On Becoming a Person: A Therapist's View of Psychotherapy*. London: Constable.

Rogers, C.R. (1977) *Carl Rogers on Personal Power: Inner Strength and Its Revolutionary Impact*. New York: Delacorte Press.

Rogers, C.R. (1980) *A Way of Being*. New York: Houghton Mifflin.

Rush, A.J., Beck, A.T., Kovacs, M., & Hollon, S.D. (1977) Comparative efficacy of cognitive therapy and pharmacotherapy in the treatment of depressed outpatients. *Cognitive Therapy & Research*, *1*, 17–37.

Sachse, R. (1992) *Zielorientierte Gesprächspsychotherapie: Eine grundlegende Neukonzeption*. Göttingen: Hogrefe.

Sachse, R. (1999) *Lehrbuch der Gesprächspsychotherapie*. Göttingen: Hogrefe.

Safran, J.D. & Segal, Z.V. (1990) *Interpersonal Process in Cognitive Therapy*. New York: Basic Books.

Sanders, P. (ed.) (2004) *The Tribes of the Person-centred Approach: An Introduction to the Schools of Therapy Related to the Person-centred Approach*. Ross on Wye: PCCS Books.

Sartre, J.-P. (1946) *Existentialism and Humanism*. Edited by P. Mairet (1974). London: Methuen.

Sartre, J.-P. (1992) *Being and Nothingness*. Translated by H. Barnes. London: Routledge.

Schmid, P.F. (1991) Souveränität und Engagement: Zu einem personzentrierten Verständnis von 'Person'. In C.R. Rogers & P.F. Schmid, *Person-Zentriert: Grundlagen von Theorie und Praxis* (4th edn, pp. 15–164). Mainz: Grünewald.

Schmid, P.F. (1994) *Personzentrierte Gruppenpsychotherapie: Ein Handbuch. Vol. I: Solidarität und Autonomie*. Cologne: Edition Humanistische Psychologie.

Schmid, P.F. (1998a) 'Face to face': The art of encounter. In B. Thorne & E. Lambers (eds), *Person-Centred Therapy: A European Perspective* (pp. 74–90). London: Sage.

Schmid, P.F. (1998b) 'On becoming a person-centred approach': A person-centred understanding of the person. In B. Thorne & E. Lambers (eds), *Person-Centred Therapy: A European Perspective* (pp. 38–52). London: Sage.

Schmid, P.F. (1999) Personzentrierte Psychotherapie. In G. Sonneck & T. Slunecko (eds), *Einführung in die Psychotherapie* (pp. 168–211). Stuttgart: UTB für Wissenschaft – Facultas.

Schmid, P.F. (2002) *Person Centred Psychotherapy*. Available online at: www.pfs-online.at/papers/paper-pct.htm (accessed April 2011).

Schön, D.A. (1971) *Beyond the Stable State*. London: Temple Smith.

Schulte, D. (1997) Behavioural analysis: Does it matter? *Behavioural and Cognitive Psychotherapy*, *25*, 231–249.

Schulte, D., Kunzel, I.L., Pepping, G., & Schulte-Bahrenberg, T. (1992) Tailor-made versus standardized therapy of phobic patients. *Advances in Behaviour Research and Therapy*, *14*, 67–92.

Seligman M. (1970) On the generality of the laws of learning. *Psychological Review*, *77*, 406–418.

Seligman M. (1971) Phobias and preparedness. *Behavior Therapy*, *2*, 307–320.

Shlien, J. (2003) *To Lead an Honourable Life: Invitations to Think about Client-centred Therapy and the Person-centred Approach*. Ross-on-Wye: PCCS Books.

Skinner, B.F. (1938) *The Behavior of Organisms: An Experimental Analysis*. New York: Appleton-Century.

Skinner, B.F. (1971) *Beyond Freedom and Dignity*. Middlesex: Pelican.

Stiles, W.B., Barkham, M., Mellor-Clark, J., & Connell, J. (2008) Effectiveness of cognitive-behavioural, person-centred, and psychodynamic therapies in UK primary-care routine practice: Replication in a larger sample. *Psychological Medicine*, *38*, 677–688.

Stiles, W.B., Morrison, L.A., Haw, S.K., Harper, H., Shapiro, D.A., & Firth-Cozens, J. (1991) Longitudinal study of assimilation in exploratory psychotherapy. *Psychotherapy*, *28*, 195–206.

Stiles, W.B., Startup, M., Hardy, G.E., Barkharn, M., & Reynolds, S. (1996) Therapist session intentions in cognitive-behavioral and psychodynamic-interpersonal psychotherapy. *Journal of Counseling Psychology*, *43*(4), 402–414.

Strong, S.R. (1968) Counselling: An interpersonal process. *Journal of Counselling Psychology*, *15*, 215–224.

Sturmey, P. (1996) *Functional Analysis in Clinical Psychology*. Chichester: Wiley.

Sturmey, P. (ed.) (2009) *Clinical Case Formulation: Varieties of Approaches*. Chichester: Wiley.

Swildens, H. (1988) *Procesgerichte Gesprekstherapie: Inleiding tot een Gedifferentieerde Toepassing Van De Cliëntgerichte Beginselen Bij De Behandeling Van Psychische Stoornissen*. Leuven/Amersfoort: Acco/de Horstink.

Tausch, R. & Tausch, A-M. (1960) *Gesprächspsychotherapie: Einfühlsame, hilfreiche Gruppen – und Einzelgespräche in Psychotherapie und alltäglichem Leben* (9th edn). Göttingen: Hogrefe.

Thorndike, E.L. (1905) *The Elements of Psychology*. New York: A.G. Seiler.

Thorne, B. (1998) *Person-centred Counselling and Christian Spirituality: The Secular and the Holy*. London: Whurr.

Thorne, B. (2002) *The Mystical Power of Person-centred Therapy: Hope beyond Despair*. London: Whurr.

Trower, P., Jones, J., Dryden, W., & Casey, A. (2011) *Cognitive-behavioural Counselling in Action* (2nd edn). London: Sage.

Tudor, K. (2008) Person-centred therapy, a cognitive behavioural therapy. In R. House and D. Loewenthal (eds), *Against and For CBT: Towards a Constructive Dialogue?* (pp. 118–136). Ross-on-Wye: PCCS Books.

Tudor, K. (2010) Being in process, being in context: A person-centred perspective on happiness. In D. Loewenthal & R. House (eds), *Critically Engaging CBT*. Maidenhead: Open University Press/McGraw-Hill Education.

Tudor, K. & Merry, T. (2002) *Dictionary of Person-centred Psychology*. London: Whurr.

Tudway, J.A. (2007) Clinical psychology. In H. Cooligan (ed.), *Applied Psychology* (2nd edn). Abingdon: Hodder Education.

Turkat, I.D. (1990) *The Personality Disorders: A Psychological Approach to Clinical Management*. New York: Plenum.

Valentine, C.W. (1930) The innate bases of fear. *Journal of Genetic Psychology*, *37*, 394–419.

Voncken, M.J. & Bogels, S.M. (2006) Changing interpretation and judgmental bias in social phobia: A pilot study of a short, highly structured cognitive treatment. *Journal of Cognitive Psychotherapy: An International Quarterly*, *20*(1), 59–73.

Walen, S.R., DiGiuseppe, R., & Dryden, W. (1992) *A Practitioner's Guide to Rational-Emotive Therapy* (2nd edn). Oxford: Oxford University Press.

Wason, P.C. (1966) Reasoning. In B.M. Foss (ed.), *New Horizons in Psychology*. Harmondsworth: Penguin.

Watson, J.B. & Rayner, R. (1920) Conditioned emotional reactions. *Journal of Experimental Psychology, 3*, 1–14.

Wills, F. and Sanders, D. (1997) *Cognitive Therapy: Transforming the Image*. London: Sage.

Wilkins, P. (2010) *Person-centred Therapy: 100 Key Points*. London and New York: Routledge.

Williams, C., Martinez, R., Dafters, R., Ronald, L., & Garland, A. (2011) Training the wider workforce in cognitive behavioural self-help: The SPIRIT (Structured Psychosocial InteRventions in Teams) training course. *Behavioural and Cognitive Psychotherapy, 39*(2), 139–149.

Winnicott, D.W. (1964) *The Child, the Family, and the Outside World*. London: Penguin.

Wolpe, J. (1981) The dichotomy between classically conditioned and cognitively learned anxiety. *Journal of Behaviour Therapy & Experimental Psychiatry, 12*, 35–42.

Wolpe, J. & Rachman, S. (1960) Psychoanalytic evidence: A critique based on Freud's case of Little Hans. *Journal of Nervous & Mental Disease, 130*, 77–88.

Yankura, J. & Dryden, W. (1994) *Albert Ellis: Key Figures in Counselling and Psychotherapy*. London: Sage.

Young, J.E. (1990) *Cognitive Therapy for Personality Disorders: A Schema-Focused Approach*. Sarasota, FL: Professional Resource Press.

Ziegler, D.J. (1999) The construct of personality in rational emotive behavior therapy (REBT) theory. *Journal of Rational-Emotive & Cognitive-Behavior Therapy, 17*, 19–32.

Ziegler, D.J. (2000) Basic assumptions concerning human nature underlying rational emotive behavior therapy (REBT) personality theory. *Journal of Rational-Emotive & Cognitive-Behavior Therapy, 18*, 67–85.

Ziegler, D.J. (2002) Freud, Rogers, and Ellis: A comparative theoretical analysis. *Journal of Rational-Emotive & Cognitive-Behavior Therapy, 20*(2), 76–91.

Ziegler, D.J. (2003) The concept of psychological health in rational emotive behavior therapy. *Journal of Rational-Emotive & Cognitive-Behavior Therapy, 21*(1), 21–36.

Zuroff, D.C. & Blatt, S.J. (2006) The therapeutic relationship in the brief treatment of depression: Contributions to clinical improvement and enhanced capacities. *Journal of Consulting and Clinical Psychology, 74*, 130–140.

INDEX

Page numbers in *italics* refer to figures.